New Aeon Tantra

Some Other Titles from Falcon Press

Gregory Peters
Yogini Magic: Sorcery, Enchantment & Witchcraft of the Divine Feminine

Christopher S. Hyatt, Ph.D.
Undoing Yourself with Energized Meditation and Other Devices
Secrets of Western Tantra: The Sexuality of the Middle Path

Christopher S. Hyatt, Ph.D. with contributions by Wm. S. Burroughs, Timothy Leary, Robert Anton Wilson et al.
Rebels & Devils: The Psychology of Liberation

S. Jason Black and Christopher S. Hyatt, Ph.D.
Pacts with the Devil: A Chronicle of Sex, Blasphemy & Liberation
Urban Voodoo: A Beginner's Guide to Afro-Caribbean Magic

Antero Alli
Angel Tech: A Modern Shaman's Guide to Reality Selection
Experiential Astrology: From the Map to the Territory

Peter J. Carroll
The Chaos Magick Audios
PsyberMagick

Phil Hine
Condensed Chaos: An Introduction to Chaos Magic
Prime Chaos: Adventures in Chaos Magic

Joseph Lisiewski, Ph.D.
Kabbalistic Handbook for the Practicing Magician
Ceremonial Magic & the Power of Evocation

Israel Regardie
The Complete Golden Dawn System of Magic
The Golden Dawn Audios

Denny Sargent
Naga Magick: The Wisdom of the Serpent Lords
Tantra for All: The Path of Nath Tantrika

Steven Heller
Monsters & Magical Sticks: There's No Such Thing As Hypnosis?

For up-to-the-minute information on prices and availability, please visit our website at
originalfalcon.com

New Aeon Tantra

Secrets of Typhonian Magick & Western Tantra

by
Gregory Peters

Introduced by
Michael Staley

THE *Original* FALCON PRESS
TEMPE, ARIZONA, U.S.A.

Copyright © 2024 C.E. by Gregory Peters

All rights reserved. No part of this book, in part or in whole, may be reproduced, transmitted, or utilized, in any form or by any means, electronic or mechanical, including photocopying, recording, or by any information storage and retrieval system, without permission in writing from the publisher, except for brief quotations in critical articles, books and reviews.

International Standard Book Number: 978-1-61869-150-7
ISBN: 978-1-61869-151-4 (mobi)
ISBN: 978-1-61869-152-1 (ePub)
Library of Congress Catalog Card Number: 2024938657

First Print Edition 2024
First eBook Edition 2024

Cover by Kat Lunoe

All material quoted from Aleister Crowley and the cards of the *Thoth Tarot* are copyright © 1996–2012 Ordo Templi Orientis (O.T.O.)

Ordo Templi Orientis International Headquarters
JAF Box 7666
New York, NY 10116-4632 USA

The paper used in this publication meets the minimum requirements of the American National Standard for Permanence of Paper for Printed Library Materials Z39.48-1984

Address all inquiries to:
The Original Falcon Press
1753 East Broadway Road #101-277
Tempe, AZ 85282 U.S.A.

(or)
PO Box 3540
Silver Springs NV 89429 U.S.A.

website: originalfalcon.com
email: info@originalfalcon.com

Dedicated to the memory of the three great initiators of my life:

Soror Meral
who started me on the Path

Frater Aossik
who showed me the Way

and

Choegyal Namkhai Norbu
who introduced me to the nature of Mind

Whoever gazes upon that Radiant Blackness
falls eternally in love.
— *Ramprasad Sen*

Knowledge of the Self, O Goddess, is the only means to final liberation. He who knows it is truly liberated in this world.
— *Mahanirvana Tantra*

That which produces bliss should be used in worship since it ravishes the heart.
– *Tantraloka*

From waking levels Her Play unfolds.
— *Outer Gateways, S'lba 53 6*

This shall regenerate the world, the little world my sister, my heart & my tongue, unto whom I send this kiss.
— *Liber AL vel Legis, I:53*

The revival of tantric elements in *The Book of the Law* may be evidence of a positive move on the part of Aiwaz to forge a link between Western and Oriental systems of magick.
— *The Magical Revival*

Contents

PREFACE & ACKNOWLEDGEMENTS 13
INTRODUCTION: THE SPIDER'S WEB by Michael Staley 19
BEGINNINGS 45
Chapter 1 PRELIMINARY INSTRUCTIONS 55
    Yoga 56
    Surya Namascar: The Sun Salutation 61
    Lunar Adorations 63
    The Song of the Syrens 64
    Dietary Considerations 71
    Thelemic Refuge 72
    The Mala 74
    Who Are You? 78
Chapter 2 CULT OF THE INFINITE 81
    The Slopes of Abiegnus 83
    Beyond the Infinite 87
    The Radiant Eternity 90
    The Heart of the Master 94
Chapter 3 BABALON 97
Chapter 4 THE HOLY BOOKS 109
Chapter 5 THE TRUE WILL 113
Chapter 6 TANTRIK VOWS 121
Chapter 7 SOUND & VISION 133
    Mantra 135
    Yantra 141
    Mandala 144
    The Tattvas 148

Chapter 8 PRELIMINARY RITUALS & MEDITATIONS 153
- The Rite of Dedication 153
- The Lantern of Thebes 156
- The Vajra Tower 160
- The Midnight Sun 164
- The Victorious City 168
- The Pool of Reflection 174

Chapter 9 THE DIAMOND SAPPHIRE GEM OF RADIANT LIGHT 177
- Preparation 181
- Opening 191
- Refuge and Dedication 194
- Formulation of the Light 200
- The Diamond Sapphire Gem of Radiant Light 203
- Final Dedication and Closing 206
- Additional Notes on Performance 210

Chapter 10 ADVANCED RITUALS & MEDITATIONS 217
- The Armor of the Great Goddess 223
- The Arrow of Arjuna 228
- Awakening the Interior Stars 230
- The Adamantine Star of Horus 243
- The Sevenfold Palace of the Goddess 245
- The Boat of Millions of Years 251

Chapter 11 CAKES OF LIGHT & THE GRAIL OF WINE 255
- The Cakes of Light 255
- The Grail of Wine 257

Chapter 12 TANTRIK SADHANAS 265
- The Great Seal of the Goddess 265
- The Heart of the Master 279
- The Sadhana of Lalita-Babalon 287
- The Sixteen Jeweled Palace 301
- The Starry Yantra 306
- The Feast of the Stars 311

Chapter 13 THE FIVE-FOLD WORSHIP OF THE GODDESS 319
    Notes on Practice 323
Chapter 14 THE MANTRA OF REVEALING 333
    An Examination of the *Mantra of Revealing* 334
    The Call of the Children of the Stars 335
Chapter 15 THE HIDDEN GOD 337
    The Practice 342
Chapter 16 SUPPORTING PRACTICES 345
    The Lunar Adorations 345
    Establishing the Place 349
Chapter 17 THAT WHICH REMAINS 359
    The Little Song "Do as You Please" 362
HISTORICAL INFLUENCES & FURTHER READING 365
    Essential Reading List 366
GLOSSARY 373
ABOUT THE AUTHOR 385

Figures

Figure 1 Stele of Ankh-ef-en-Khonsu (The Stele of Revealing) 11
Figure 2 'The Magus' Card of the Thoth Tarot 55
Figure 3 Thelemic Armor 73
Figure 4 'The Chariot' Card of the Thoth Tarot 97
Figure 5 The Sri Yantra 141
Figure 6 Vajra 149
Figure 7 The Tattvas 150
Figure 8 Lantern of Thebes 158
Figure 9 The Vajra Tower 160
Figure 10 Harpocrates Giving The Sign of Silence 164
Figure 11 The Sign of Typhon-Apophis 169
Figure 12 The Sign of Baphomet 171
Figure 13 Diamond Vajra 173
Figure 14 Diamond Sapphire Altar 181
Figure 15 Red Three-Angled Heart 183
Figure 16 Yoni Mudra (Mudra of Union) 184
Figure 17 Kali Yantra 184
Figure 18 The Sign of Osiris Risen 186
Figure 19 Nuit 220
Figure 20 'The Hanged Man' Card of the Thoth Tarot 222
Figure 21 'The Star' Card of the Thoth Tarot 222
Figure 22 Vajra Mudra 227
Figure 23 The 'Art' Card of the Thoth Tarot 239
Figure 24 Set-Beast 244
Figure 25 The Sixteen Jeweled Palace 304
Figure 26 Sanskrit 'A' 340
Figure 27 Tibetan 'A' 341
Figure 28 Kanji 'A' 341
Figure 29 Egyptian 'A' 342
Figure 30 'The Moon' Card of the Thoth Tarot 346
Figure 31 Gregory Peters 385

Figure 1
Stele of Ankh-ef-en-Khonsu
(The Stele of Revealing)
(Egyptian Museum of Cairo)

PREFACE & ACKNOWLEDGEMENTS

*I give respect and gratitude to all of my teachers,
past, present and future!*

This book spans several decades of work. An earlier version, published as *The Magickal Union of East & West*, covered many of the rituals and instructions centered around the *Diamond Sapphire Gem of Radiant Light*. This new edition has been greatly revised and expanded with new material.

Through these practices, you will learn to explore the regions of consciousness that were otherwise asleep—to "rise up & awake" into the embrace of the Holy Guardian Angel, and to build communities around these practices. When working with these rituals, you will connect with the primordial current of Initiation that has come down through the ages, always adapting and anticipating the flow of the lifewave as expressed in consciousness, and reflecting outwardly in the dynamic play of experience as the Typhonian, or Stellar Gnosis.

The work has come a long way, and has been in continual use by individuals and groups around the world that have been drawn to explore and break the conventional boundaries of the illusory self. What started as an occasional working group—an experiment—grew into a small, but persistent, international group of occultists that continues to make its presence known in unexpected and sometimes mysterious ways. Over the years there have been several offshoots started by people who have been inspired by the work, and created their own unique interpretations. Throughout it all, a core group of people have continued to work with the rituals and practices, practices which bring you to the knowledge of the True Will.

Unlike many systems which become institutionalized over time, this path is not set in stone, and continues to defy being pinned down to any authority—resisting ossification and orthodoxy. Each individual that dives into it, ends up going deep into their own mysteries, unlocking their individual creativity which expresses itself in countless ways. The work itself took on a significant shift in 2011. This was the year when, over the course of about 11 days, new rituals and instruction were received and prepared during highly-focused, intense periods of solitary ritual and communion. What developed in those days was an entirely new system that expanded upon the original work. The new material opened up the non-dual tantra of *The Book of the Law*, and commenced a new cycle of tantrik magick and exploration.

§ § §

Aleister Crowley (1875–1947) was a highly influential occultist, poet, writer, mountain climber, overall explorer of consciousness, and breaker of social taboos. He is best known as the founder of *Thelema*, a spiritual philosophy that emphasizes the individual's pursuit of their True Will as the guiding principle of life.

Crowley's life and work were marked by a deep interest in the occult, mysticism and esoteric traditions from around the world. He studied various mystical systems, including ceremonial magic, astrology, tarot and Eastern philosophies. His extensive knowledge and experiences led him to develop his own spiritual path: Thelema.

Thelema is centered around the dictum *"Do what thou wilt shall be the whole of the Law,"* emphasizing personal freedom, self-expression, and the discovery of your true purpose and destiny. Crowley saw each individual as a unique expression of the divine, and encouraged them to embrace their individuality, and follow their inner calling.

One of the key texts of Thelema is *The Book of the Law,* which Crowley claimed to have received through a revelatory experience in 1904. This book laid out the core principles and practices of Thelema, and became the foundational text of the philosophy. Crowley went on to publish numerous works exploring various aspects of Thelema, including rituals, meditations and philosophical treatises. Much more will be said about Crowley, and Thelema throughout this book, ultimately showing that the current with which Crowley had established contact was a development of a far older heritage known as the *Typhonian Tradition.*

Crowley's provocative lifestyle and controversial reputation contributed to his notoriety during his lifetime. However, his ideas and teachings have had a lasting impact on the occult and esoteric communities. His work continues to inspire spiritual seekers, artists and individuals interested in the exploration of consciousness, personal growth, and the mystical dimensions of existence.

Taking up the thread that Crowley had begun, Kenneth Grant (1924–2011) went on to further develop and deepen Thelema, and show its connections and origins in a much older current—the *Typhonian Tradition.* A British occultist, author and ceremonial magician, Kenneth Grant became widely known to many as the magical heir and torchbearer of Crowley's esoteric teachings.

Grant's interest in the occult was sparked in his early years when he corresponded with Crowley, and eventually became his student and personal secretary. After Crowley's death in 1947, Grant further developed and propagated Crowley's teachings, while evolving them and opening them to the vast depths of the Typhonian Tradition.

Throughout his life, Grant authored numerous books, and his nine-volume series of the *Typhonian Trilogies* is hands-down one of the most significant magical and philosophical works of the Western occult tradition, let alone its importance to Thelema. Grant's writings often blended Western occultism with Eastern mysticism, Hindu and Buddhist tantra, and explored the trans-dimensional and non-dual core of Thelema.

Grant's work emphasized the role of cosmic forces, extraterrestrial entities, and the exploration of the subconscious in magical practices. Grant's work showed that the universe is inhabited by powerful alien intelligences, with which magicians can consciously establish contact to gain esoteric knowledge and power.

Grant's interpretations of Crowley's teachings—which evolved our understanding of Thelema and its many roots—continue to influence modern occultists and magicians interested in exploring the cutting-edge boundaries of esoteric knowledge and practice.

§ § §

After over a decade of working with this tantrik material, privately and in small groups, this book now releases the material to the public. In many circles, both in Western occult communities, as well as Buddhist and Hindu tantrik schools, it has become apparent that the long-standing cultures of secrecy are no longer serving the traditions they were originally meant to protect. In this regard, the comments by the 14th Dalai Lama are relevant who, in speaking of the 17th century Luktang Temple of Tibet (Temple of Serpents) remarked that, *"The time of secrecy is over and is not relevant in Western society. Unless these practices become better known they will become completely lost.*"[1] Similarly, these practices thrive in new environments and the collective insights gained from the experience of people actually working with the material.

Throughout history, esoteric traditions have been veiled in secrecy, accessible only to select initiates. But human consciousness is undergoing a transformative shift, characterized by an increasing desire for transparency and interconnectedness. The information age has connected the world like never before, enabling individuals to seek knowledge, and explore diverse perspectives at their fingertips. As people question traditional institutions, the relevance of secrecy in esoteric traditions appears outdated and incongruent with the impulse to preserve these systems.

By openly sharing these spiritual technologies, we contribute to the collective pool of knowledge, encouraging unity and interconnectedness. This shared consciousness can lead to better understanding and cooperation.

And secrecy can inadvertently lead to misinterpretations and misuse of esoteric knowledge by those few who possess it. When information is accessible and openly discussed, reputable sources can ensure the teachings are presented accurately, reducing the potential for misunderstandings.

§ § §

I want to express my gratitude to several individuals and groups who have played a significant role in the creation of this work.

First and foremost, I extend a special thank you to Charlotte Moore, who has been dedicated to this project from the very start, and continues to lead an international collective of practitioners.

---

[1] hyperallergic.com/252891/tibets-secret-temple-the-long-hidden-tantric-murals-of-lukhang-palace

I also want to thank Monika Mayer-Kielmann, Suzanne Davenport, and all the members of Ordo Sunyata Vajra.

Deep appreciation goes to my friend and colleague Michael Staley, with whom I have collaborated over the decades in the Typhonian Order. Michael also wrote the illuminating *Introduction* to this book.

I am indebted to the late Donald Michael Kraig (Shambhala Nath) who initiated me into *The Arcane Magical Order of the Knights of Shambhala* (AMOOKOS) and the Adinatha *sampradaya* (tradition) of tantrika. He also supported an earlier edition of this book.

Gratitude also goes to "Mad" Mike Magee (Lokanath Maharaj), who has been tirelessly providing translations of Hindu Tantras, and ensures that none of us let our egos get out of hand.

Deep thanks also to John Power (Vilasanath), who I have worked with for many years in Uttara Kaula *sampradaya* of tantra.

I want to thank my friend Phil Hine for his unwavering willingness to share his vast experience in both tantra and occultism.

My gratitude for all the *sadhakas*, wild yogis and magicians of the Adinatha, Uttara Kaula, Typhonian Order, Ordo Sunyata Vajra, and A∴A∴, as well as all the individual tantrikas and renegade sorcerers doing their Will, who have found some value in this work.

Thanks to my publisher, The Original Falcon Press and Nicholas Tharcher, for their commitment to keeping daring and rebellious material in print.

Finally, thanks and gratitude to Natasha for her endless enthusiasm and support while I worked on this project, the completion of which always seemed to be "just around the corner."

Aom. Ha!

— Gregory Peters
Carcassonne, Bombay & California, 2023 CE

INTRODUCTION: THE SPIDER'S WEB
by Michael Staley

Tantra is often thought of as an esoteric tradition of India, though there are also tantras of Chinese and Tibetan origin, for instance. The term is two-fold: firstly, as a Hindu or Buddhist mystical or magical text; and secondly, as indicating adherence to and practise of the doctrines or principles of the Tantras, often involving techniques such as *mantra*, visualisation, meditation, yoga and ritual. Tantra is thought to have developed from the middle of the first millennium CE in both Hinduism and Buddhism. However, given that Hinduism emerged more than four thousand years ago, it would be surprising if Tantra were not at least of a similar age, and probably earlier, given that it would likely have developed from antecedents.

It was an Englishman, Sir John Woodroffe, who published many Tantras with English commentaries whilst serving as an advocate in British India. His interest was apparently sparked by a court case that he was hearing, when suddenly he was unable to focus on the facts of the case. Mentioning this to an assistant, he was informed that a *"tantrik sadhu"* had been hired to recite a *mantra* outside the courthouse, to cloud the judge's mind in favour of the defendant. The *sadhu* was chased away, and Woodroffe's mind quickly cleared. As a result, Woodroffe and his wife developed a lifelong interest in Tantra and Hinduism, translating some of the tantric texts themselves. Over a number of years, they published a formidable body of work, ranging from *Introduction to the Tantra Śāstra* in 1913 to *Principles of Tantra*. Between these two are a great many substantial and diverse works, including *Śakti and Śākta*, *The Serpent Power*, *Hymn to Kali (Karpuradi-Stotra)*, *The Garland of Letters*, and *The World as Power*. *Śakti and Śākta* is an arrangement of lectures and addresses on a range of subjects. *The Garland of Letters* is a study of *śabda* (sound). *The Serpent Power* is a consideration of the background to *Kundalini*.

Some of this work was published under the name "Arthur Avalon"; this was not simply a personal pseudonym, as Woodroffe explained in the Preface to the first edition of *Śakti and Śākta*:

> "The present work deals with its subject only in a very general and, as far as the matter permits, popular way. I refer those who wish to pursue it further to the other works on Tantra Śāstra which are published under the name 'Arthur Avalon' to denote that they have been written with the direct co-operation of others and in particular with the assistance of one of my friends who will not permit me to mention his name."

In the same Preface, Woodroffe speaks of the *Śākta Tantra* thus:

> "The Śākta Tantra is a Sadhana Śāstra of Monistic (Advaitavāda) Vedānta. It is to me a profound and powerful system, and its doctrine of Śakti or Divine Power is one of the greatest evolved, through spiritual intuition, by the human mind which, according to its teaching, is a manifestation of the Divine Consciousness Itself (Śiva)."

This is expanded upon in the Foreword to *The Garland of Letters*, written by T.M.P. Mahadevan and dated March 18, 1955:

> "The philosophy of Śāktism is a kind of non-dualism (advaita), similar to that of Kashmir Śaivism. In both the systems, the highest Reality is styled Śiva-Śakti. Śiva and Śakti are not different; they are one. Śiva is consciousness as

stasis (cit); Śakti is consciousness as dynamic (cidrūpiṇi). Śiva is pure awareness, which is the ground of all existence. Through his Parā Śakti, he effects the manifestation of the universe. He is the sole and whole cause of the world. Only, he becomes the cause, not in his aspect as stasis, but through his dynamic aspect which is spoken of as his feminine part. The main difference between Kashmir Śaivism and Śaktism is that while the former lays relatively greater stress on the Śiva-aspect, the latter emphasizes more the Śakti. Between the Śaiva and Śākta philosophy on the one hand, and Advaita-Vedānta on the other, there is close kinship. Advaita too teaches that the ultimate Reality is non-dual, and that it is of the nature of pure consciousness. But for it, the world-process is not real. The world, according to Advaita, is māyika, illusory appearance. The theory of world appearance is here called vivarta-vāda. The corresponding doctrine of the Śaiva and Śākta schools is known as ābhāsa-vāda. According to this view, the universe consists of appearances which are all real in the sense that they are aspects of the ultimate Reality.[2]"

We can infer from the passage by Padoux that the term *tantra* can be applied to any pursuit of what might be considered as a "spiritual culture." It is not a specific, laid-down set of practices to be pursued; it is more diverse than that. Neither is it something specific to the East; indeed, there are many students and practitioners in the West. Over the course of the last century or two, there have been attempts to bring Eastern methods and teachings to the West, such

---

[2] Sir John Woodroffe, *The Garland of Letters* (Ganesh & Company, Madras, 1989), pp. iii–iv.

as, for instance, the series edited and published by the German academic Max Muller as *Sacred Books of the East*. In 1875, Helena Petrovna Blavatsky founded the Theosophical Society with the intention of bringing Eastern concepts to the attention of Westerners.

In the early 20th Century, Aleister Crowley had a similar aim to that of the Theosophists, and developed practices which incorporated Yogic methods. For instance, one of his basic set of instructions was *Liber E vel Exertorium*, which incorporated techniques such as *asana, pranayama* and *dharana*. His paper, *Liber HHH*, sets out three guided visualisations, the third of which draws upon the imagery of *Kundalini Yoga* to set up a current of light cycling between the cavity of the brain and the base of the spine. Another paper, *Liber Astarte*, is essentially an exercise in *Bhakti Yoga*. Crowley took a strong interest in other traditions and religions, incorporating them into what for want of a better word is his "system," and recommended that his students likewise develop a solid basis so that when illumination came, it struck on solid ground and fertile soil.

Crowley started out with the Hermetic Order of the Golden Dawn who themselves incorporated Eastern techniques into their instructions, such as meditation of the *Tattva* cards. The object of the Order was not so much to impart a rigid body of instruction as to encourage their initiates to find their own voice. They were expected, for instance, to create their own Tarot cards, to create their own set of flashing colours; out of this, each developed his or her own Magical Universe. This gave Crowley a very solid basis for further development, and he usually observed in his diaries the anniversary of his first initiation into the Golden Dawn. As late as 1946, for instance, for Monday 18 November he recorded: "48th Anniversary of my First Initiation!"

In April 1904, in Cairo, Egypt, Crowley received *The Book of the Law* over three days—a brief, enigmatic text the depths of which he never really fathomed. Crowley wrote a brief verse-by-verse commentary to accompany an account of the text and the circumstances of its reception, published in *The Equinox* Volume One Number 7 in 1913. He wrote a larger commentary whilst at the Abbey of Thelema in Cefalu, Sicily, in the early 1920s, and continued revising the commentary in later years, as can be seen from the typescript of it archived in the Gerald Yorke Collection as OS K2.

§§§

Thelema is a Greek word meaning *Will*. However, although it can be used to indicate the will of the individual, more often it denotes the Will of God, the divine Will, or carrying out a task on behalf of someone else. This is reflected in the precept *"Every man and every woman is a star."* Stars are parts of a greater whole, and have orbits which reflect and express this. Similarly, as individuals, our True Will reflects our place on the greater whole. There is a parallel here with the tantric tradition of *Svecchācāra*, 'Own way'. In *Shakti and Shakta* Woodroffe has this to say:

> "Lastly, the doctrine that the illuminate knower of Brahman (Brahmajñani) is above both good (Dharma) and evil (Adharma) should be noted. Such an one is a Svechacari whose way is Svechacara or "do as you will." Similar doctrine and practices in Europe are there called Antinomianism. The doctrine is not peculiar to the Tantras. It is to be found in the Upanishads, and is in fact a very commonly held doctrine in India. Here again, as so stated and as understood outside India, it has the appearance of being worse than it really is. If Monistic views are accepted, then theoretically we must admit that Brahman is beyond good and evil, for these are terms of relativity applicable to beings in this world only. Good has no

meaning except in relation to evil and vice versa. Brahman is beyond all dualities, and a Jñani who has become Brahman (Jivan-mukta) is also logically so. It is, however, equally obvious that if a man has complete Brahman-consciousness he will not, otherwise than unconsciously, do an act which if done consciously would be wrong. He is ex hypothesi beyond lust, gluttony and all other passions. A theoretical statement of fact that a Brahmajñani is beyond good and evil is not a statement that he may will to do, and is permitted to do, evil. Statements as regards the position of a Jivanmukta are mere praise or Stuti. In Svecchacara there is theoretical freedom, but it is not consciously availed of to do what is known to be wrong without fall and pollution. Svecchacarini is a name of the Devi, for She does what She pleases since She is the Lord of all. But of others the Shaktisangama Tantra (Part IV) says—

Yadyapyasti trikalajñastrailokyakarshana-kshamah Tatha'pi laukikacaram manasapi na langhayet.

('Though a man be a knower of the Three Times, past, present and future, and though he be a Controller of the three worlds, even then he should not transgress the rules of conduct for men in the world, were it only in his mind.')"[3]

Crowley expected people to reach their own understanding of *The Book of the Law*. His *Tunis Comment* of 1923 reflects this, declaring: *"All questions of the Law are to be decided only by appeal to my writings, each for himself."* Thereby, of course, he was still setting bounds since this remark suggests that understanding of the Law should not be sought outside his writings.

---

[3] Woodroffe, *Śakti and Śākta* (Ganesh & Co., Madras, 1975), pp. 397–398.

On the basis of references within *The Book of the Law* to a successor who would understand more, Crowley anticipated keenly the arrival of this person, and for a while thought this would be his Magical Son, Charles Stansfeld Jones. Growing dissension between the two men persuaded Crowley that this was not the case, but no one else came along to assume that mantle. However, Crowley had very rich magical and mystical experiences, such as the Abuldiz Working of 1911, and in particular, the Amalantrah Working of 1918. Unfortunately for him, his pressing need for money at the time of the Amalantrah Working meant that he interpreted the visions as oracles for his financial affairs, and some years later he admitted that he had missed the significance of the Working.

Although Crowley died in poverty and obscurity, his work was diverse and profound, an excellent example of someone taking influences from a multitude of sources, and transforming those influences through his mystical and magical experiences to distil an inherent body of work that has, in its turn, been an influence on many others. His work is a veritable spider's web.

Despite Crowley's making occasional allusions to Tantra, he doesn't seem to have taken much of an interest in it, which might seem curious given that Woodroffe published his work in the 1910s and the 1920s. In the early 1940s Crowley was writing the letters which were collected together for a book, the working title of which was *Aleister Explains Everything*, published after his death as *Magick Without Tears*. In the second of three chapters dealing with 'The Three Schools of Magick', he had a positive view:

> "We may complete the whole tradition of the Indian peninsula very simply. To the Vedas, the Upanishads, and the Tripitaka of the Buddhists, we have only to add the Tantras of what are called the Vamacharya Schools. Paradoxical as it

may sound the Tantrics are in reality the most advanced of the Hindus. Their theory is, in its philosophical ultimatum, a primitive stage of the White tradition, for the essence of the Tantric cults is that by the performance of certain rites of Magick, one does not only escape disaster, but obtains positive benediction. The Tantric is not obsessed by the will-to-die. It is a difficult business, no doubt, to get any fun out of existence; but at least it is not impossible."[4]

Elsewhere in the same book, Crowley related how in his earlier years

"I also studied all varieties of Asiatic Philosophy, especially with regard to the practical question of spiritual development, the Sufi doctrines, the Upanishads, the Sankhya, Veda, and Vedanta, the Bhagavad-Gita and Purana, the Dhammapada, and many other classics, together with numerous writings on the Tantra and Yoga of such men as Patanjali, Vivekananda, etc. etc. Not a few of these teachings are as yet wholly unknown to scholars. I made the scope of my studies as comprehensive as possible, omitting no school of thought however unimportant or repugnant."[5]

In 1944, Crowley was contacted by David Curwen who had made a study of tantra, and who lent him an unpublished Comment on a Tantric text, the *Anandalahari*. Curwen was an occultist with a particular interest in alchemy. In the 1930s, his researches had led him to the Latent Light Culture, an organisation then based in Tinnevelly, Tamil Nadu, India. The Latent Light Culture was the

---

[4] Crowley, *Magick Without Tears* (ed. Regardie), Llewellyn Publications, St. Paul, USA, 1973), pp. 74–75.
[5] Ibid, pp. 231–232.

outer arm of an inner order, The Holy Order of Krishna. Under their aegis, he embarked on a correspondence course with a tantric guru, Pareswara Bhikshu, who had already written a number of books such as *A Series of Eleven Lessons in Karma Yoga* (1928) and *A Series of Lessons in Bhakti Yoga* (1930), both published by the Yogi Publication Society, Chicago, USA. Within these books there are references to Aleister Crowley, and it is clear from these remarks that Bhikshu was familiar with Crowley's work. At some stage of the course, Curwen received from Bhikshu a copy of an unpublished Comment on the *Anandalahari*. Sometime after this, dissension appears to have set in between Curwen and his guru, as a result of which the guru severed contact in 1939, but leaving Curwen with the Comment.

There are several references to Crowley in the Comment. In a comment on verse XIX of the *Anandalahari*, the author remarked:

"Makara has another meaning from the mediaeval interpretation of wine, women, flesh and fish; to the Tamils the makara is a fluid derived from women, obviously something that prevents senescence or ageing. For ages the Siddhas have been stating that the excretions from women—called cow in the Vedas—are of great value. Mention is also made in the Upanishads, such as the Kalagni Rudra, on this subject. In some of the yamalas the use of the tongue, physical contact, and even mesmeric passes have been spoken of to get at the genital secretions—we use the words that Aleister Crowley uses but, alas, he has failed—from the women."

At this point in the typescript, Crowley inserted an annotation: *"I don't know to which passage he refers; he has not seen my MS on the subject. But—no failure!"*

Some weeks after being loaned the Comment, Crowley loaned it to Gerald Yorke for his opinion, remarking:

> "I am sending you under separate cover registered a private MS. which has been lent to me. I have found it of considerable interest so far as I have gone with it. I must ask you to let me have it back as soon as you are through with it as I must return it to the sender."[6]

Yorke replied quickly, but unfortunately his letter is not available. However, Crowley responded to Yorke equally quickly, appreciative of his remarks:

> "I am interested and a little surprised at the extent of your knowledge of all these subjects. You must have put in a great deal of hard work."[7]

Crowley also made the Comment available to his colleague and eventual successor, Karl Germer, as Germer later remarked in a letter of 15th June 1948 to Gerald Yorke:

> "Have you met Curwen personally? I know nothing of him, except that A.C. sent me a document from him years ago."[8]

In a letter of January 1946, Crowley wrote to Curwen citing Kenneth Grant and suggesting that he contact Grant:

> "By the way it might interest you to meet some of the very young generation. I should perhaps have mentioned the man in my previous letter, but I was overworked and nervous. The

---

[6] Crowley to Yorke, 16th October 1945. See Henrik Bogdan, *Brother Curwen, Brother Crowley* (The Teitan Press, York Beach, USA, 2010), p. xxix.
[7] Crowley to Yorke, 20th October 1945. Ibid, p. xxx.
[8] Germer to Yorke, 15th June 1948. See *The Incoming of the Aeon of Maat* (Starfire Publishing, London, 2020), p. 380.

name is G. Kenneth Grant. I believe he works for a bookseller in the city and it should therefore be easy for you to arrange to lunch together. He is a very strange, though decidedly interesting man, and I should very much value your opinion of him. Do you think in particular that he can ever develop into a responsible leader? He was down here for some weeks with me, but under rather trying conditions for him and I feel that I may have treated him too severely."*

Curwen subsequently wrote to Grant toward the end of January, 1946. Following a telephone conversation, the two men met a few days later, in early February. Grant had long been interested in Eastern Mysticism, remarking *"My main interest was (and still is) in Oriental Mysticism"*[10], and had for some time become increasingly absorbed in Tantra. Curwen lent him the typescript of the Comment on the *Anandalahari*, which Grant studied over the next few days, making detailed notes. Soon after, Grant wrote to Crowley on 6 March, remarking:

"I have been in touch with a certain Mr. Curwen who seems to have quite a lot of knowledge of matters magical. He got in touch with me through your giving him my name & address, & I am currently glad you mentioned me to him. I am at present busily engaged in studying that aspect of Yoga that most intrigues me—the Tantras."

Receiving no reply, Grant wrote again to Crowley on 17 March:

"I wonder whether you would explain to me matters relative to Tantra Yoga & the Philosopher's Stone.

---

[9] Crowley to Curwen, 22nd January 1946. See Grant, *Remembering Aleister Crowley*, p. 51.
[10] Grant, *Remembering Aleister Crowley*, p. v.

> *I think I am very near to understanding the secret of the IX°, yet the practical aspects of the matter evade me as yet. I believe the 'Star Sapphire' enshrines the secret but I would like authoritative confirmation on this point.*
>
> *The Dikshas Bhairavi & Gomaya (relative to Tantric Yoga) are also rather confused in my mind, although I have discovered a lot from the Hatha Yoga Pradipika on this point, as well as from parts of your own work. Also, much more of Liber AL is now clearer to me."*

Grant wrote in *Remembering Aleister Crowley* (p. 47) that a few days after this he received from Crowley the Word of the Equinox, and in a postscript, Crowley referred to the matters raised by Grant in his earlier letters:

> *"Curwen knows 100 times as much as I do about Tantra. But I do not advise it.*
>
> *Re IX°. Be wary. If you do get the secret you have to be sworn in, or get into trouble with the Secret Chiefs. And that costs well over £100!"*

In the course of a subsequent letter to Kenneth Grant, Crowley expanded on his views of both Curwen and Tantra:

> *"You ask me about Curwen: I do not know exactly what you want to know. The essence of him is that he is a completely disappointed man, and has a tendency to cavil. As I indicated in my last, I do not think Tantra is at all advisable. A very intelligent and internationally eminent member of the Order who knows him says epigrammatically that there is something batrachian about him. His first word was 'reptilian', and then he altered it, but there is no doubt of the extent of his knowledge of his subject. It may be some residual bourgeois instinct in me, but I find the Tantra somehow unclean.*

> *What is even more important, especially for a young man, is that their aspirations are so contemptible, and they allow their minds to be completely preoccupied by subjects which I can only describe as excremental.*"[11]

The tenor of Crowley's remarks on Tantra reminded me of two passages highlighted by Grant in *The Magical Revival*. The first is by Jean Marquès-Rivière, who in his book *Tantrik Yoga* wrote:

> "*In order to complete this survey we must mention that the Tantriks admit the existence among them of certain Magicians, the Vâmâchârins, who know of the existence of the kundalini and the subtile centres but who deliberately either turn the divine energy from its right path and use it to obtain relative immortality, or for certain human satisfactions, or they stop at certain chakras in order to obtain extraordinary powers and win applause and profit. Certain Tantrik sexual practices proceed from the falsified application of the divine laws.*"

In a footnote to the last sentence, Marquès-Rivière added, somewhat darkly:

> "*I was able to know personally the absolutely depraved and abnormal sexual appetite of these false yogis. The method used is called the Prayoga, through which it is possible to visualize and animate certain female entities who are called Succubes.*"[12]

---

[11] Crowley to Grant, 3rd April 1946. Private collection.
[12] Jean Marquès-Rivière, *Tantrik Yoga* (Rider & Co., London, n.d. [1940]), p. 68.

The other passage is by Woodroffe from the Introduction to *The Serpent Power*. After mentioning a couple of authors who connected Tantra with the ruinous consequences of "phallic sorcery," he continued:

> *"Is this so? It is possible that perverse or misguided concentration on sexual and connected centres may have the effect alluded to. And it may be that the Commentator Lakṣmīdhara alludes to this when he speaks of Uttara-Kaulas who arouse Kuṇḍalinī in the Mūlādhāra to satisfy their desire for world-enjoyment and do not attempt to lead Her upwards to the Highest Centre which is the object of Yoga seeking super-worldly bliss. Of such, a Sanskrit verse runs 'they are the true prostitutes.' I have, however, never heard Indians refer to this matter, probably because it does not belong to Yoga in its ordinary sense, as also by reason of the antecedent discipline required of those who would undertake this Yoga, the nature of their practice, and the aim they have in view, such a possibility does not come under consideration. The Indian who practises this or any other kind of spiritual Yoga ordinarily does so not on account of a curious interest in occultism or with a desire to gain 'astral' or similar experiences."*

And, in a footnote to the final sentence, Woodroffe added:

> *"Those who practise magic of the kind mentioned work only in the lowest centre, have recourse to the Prayoga, which leads to Nāyikā-Siddhi, whereby commerce is had with female spirits and the like."*[13]

---

[13] Sir John Woodroffe, *The Serpent Power* (Ganesh & Co., Madras; Eighth Edition, 1972), pp. 14–15.

In the Glossary to his book, Marquès-Rivière defines *Prayoga* as *"a kind of sexual yoga."* In fact, *Prayoga* is a broad term, referring to *sadhana* (esoteric ritual) or the execution of a specific event—concentration, visualisation, ritual etc.—depending on the context in which it is applied.

The Comment to the *Anandalahari* was subsequently referenced by Grant throughout the *Typhonian Trilogies*. This was not, of course, the extent of Grant's interest in Tantra. His library contained most of the volumes published by Woodroffe, of whom he thought very highly. The most significant of these to him was *Hymn to Kali (Karpuradi-Stotra)*. It was in 1954 that Grant first came across it, as he related in a letter of 11 July 1954 to his friend Duff Mellis, then living in India:

> *"Anyhow, two days after my meeting with the Swami I chanced upon a certain book I had been wanting (but wanting only to complete a collection of books I had by the author who wrote it, and not in any desperate sense of inner urgency).[14] The book gives an almost complete (and, I venture to think, a complete) ritual of Dakshina Kalika which so strongly appealed to me that I immediately decided to adopt the Vidya-rajni of that Devata and forthwith began worshipping Her in my heart in various ways and by Japa of Her Mantra. Then, in one of your letters, you mentioned something about Japa which I needed just at that moment to confirm my inner decision to adopt DakshinaKalika as my Chosen Ideal. The Ritual is Vira in pattern but may be adapted to either the Pasu or Vira Paths, i.e. with Japa and*

---

[14] This is a reference to *Hymn to Kali (Karpuradi-Stotra)* by Arthur Avalon. Kenneth Grant's library includes a heavily-annotated copy of the Second Edition, published by Ganesh & Co., Madras, 1953.

with Japa and Shakti united (or so I understand the text). As you know my main difficulty on the Path at present is the reconciliation of the sexual current with the Spiritual Goal, and I can only direct this current, not sublimate it; therefore I feel pulled to this Sadhana as being the only one I can reasonably adopt if I am not to cripple my nature."

Kenneth Grant is another example of someone who took influences from a variety of sources, and fashioned therefrom his own Magical Universe. In 1939, when only 14 or 15, Grant came across a copy of Crowley's *Magick in Theory and Practice,* and was enthralled. He set about studying as much of Crowley's work as he could find, and made several attempts to contact Crowley, finally succeeding in 1944, and in December that year, meeting Crowley at the Bell Inn, Aston Clinton. Subsequently, Grant lived for several months in 1945 at 'Netherwood' as Crowley's Secretary, receiving magical tuition in exchange for his secretarial services. At this time, Grant was developing an interest in Tantra, and—as has been related in more detail above—Crowley put Curwen in touch with him. Curwen loaned him the unpublished Comment on the *Anandalahari,* and this made a strong impact on Grant; several of the volumes of the *Typhonian Trilogies* contain accounts of aspects of the Comment, and some passages are quoted directly. So far as Indian Tantra is concerned, Grant's first detailed description of this was set out in a chapter of *Cults of the Shadow.*

Like Crowley, Grant read widely; like Crowley, he took from diverse sources, transmuting them through his magical and mystical experience to distil an inherent body of work. Like Crowley, he thought that people should discover what *The Book of the Law* meant *to them.* He wrote thus to a student, Fraser Scott, on 23 May 1952:

"The Book of the Law (being a Class 'A' Publication, and therefore one of the 'Holy Books') has a different message for each of us. This means that at different levels of the World-Experience, different facets of the Book mean very different things simultaneously. No single verse (one might say, no single word) can be resolved by a single Qabalistic interpretation. What the book means to you now (i.e. at this particular stage of your internal development) at the various levels of Consciousness, is determined by the nature of your Magical Progress and bhava generally. I am going to send you (under separate cover and probably tomorrow) Therion's Comment on the Book beginning with Chapter One, which—when same has been returned—will be followed by the other two Chapters. Therein you will see quite a different interpretation of the verse, but I want you to realize right from the start that no one interpretation is valid for every individual. Read carefully what is said on page 47 of the copy I sent you:

'All questions of the Law are to be decided only by appeal to my writings, each for himself.'

So please bear in mind that what I send you in this direction is but one interpretation of the Book, and therefore partial as any other. But it may give you further inspiration to go ahead with your private exegesis and help you to establish a true and firm link with the Current that only concentrated study and meditation thereupon may give."

In July 1950, Grant heard a radio programme on the BBC Home Service. Entitled 'The Sage of Arunachala', it was about the life and work of Ramana Maharshi, who had died in April that year. Grant was intrigued by the radio programme, and this sparked a growing awareness of and immersion in *Advaita*. This peaked in the summer of 1952 when he had an epiphany into the supreme importance of *Advaita*, as described in a letter to Paul Brunton:

> *"Perhaps it is only fair to give you a rough (a very rough) idea of the nature of my deep interest in all matters connected with Sri Ramana Maharshi, and from what source my devotion springs. For about twelve years (I am now 28) I have been intensely interested in Occultism in all its forms, and I have concentrated more particularly in the study of Oriental metaphysics and philosophy. During this extended and very absorbing study of the subject I naturally had the usual ups and downs associated with the subject, and finally discovered a thread which I followed throughout the mazes and labyrinths of the occult jungle. Then, suddenly—and with no apparent warning—I was, through a friend,[15] acquainted with the Life of Bhagavan Sri Ramana through the book Self Realization by Sri Narasimhaswami. And then my edifice of power and poetry toppled about me and I knew that I had been feeding the insatiable cravings of the ego throughout these long years of devotion to a subject which became at once puerile, purposeless, and even dangerous. So I wrote to the Ashram for all the available publications on and by Sri Ramana, and, through some great good luck, was able to get in contact with two of the Devotees who had actually lived in the Ashram with Bhagavan—Mouni Sadhu and, later, Mr. Arthur Osborne.*
>
> *It was through reading the book Maha Yoga by a writer calling himself 'Who' that I first understood and grasped the*

---

[15] Likely Gerald Yorke, with whom Grant worked closely at this time, and who had an extensive library.

profound significance of Advaita Vedanta, of Buddhism (which I had always misunderstood) and of practically everything that had proved in the past an intellectual or emotional stumbling block. I mean that although I had studied the subject deeply from various angles, I had never before seen the entire field with such singular lucidity and depth—had never fathomed the subject at all deeply enough to realize that one must give up all the things that interest the ego and devote oneself to the task of 'unlearning' all that is unnecessary to the great Quest of Atmavichara.[16] *Naturally I have difficulties in re-adjusting my outlook and ruthlessly cutting out my past ideas on the subject of Magic, to which too close and detailed a direction of attention and concentration has created certain vasanas within me which are proving painfully difficult to dislodge, let alone totally eradicate. I have always considered the Sangsara as an illusory manifestation and so I had no difficulty in accepting the main tenets of the Advaitavada as outlined so wonderfully in Maha Yoga; but unfortunately I used the greatest stumbling block to attainment—i.e. sex—as a positive sadhana in itself, and thus I seem to have done wrong. However, if I may be permitted the liberty, I would like to go into the matter with you and—again if I may—ask your advice on several matters, because I understand you are deeply learned not only in the theory but also in the practice of the Secret Wisdom Traditions of East and West. Please, therefore, write to me and gladden my heart by saying it is possible for us to meet and talk these things over. I had, of*

---

[16] *Atma Vichara*, lit. self-enquiry, is the constant attention to the inner awareness of "I" or "I am." It was recommended by Ramana Maharshi as the most efficient and direct way of discovering the unreality of "I" or "I am."

course, heard your name and read some of your books many, many years before Mouni Sadhu drew your name to my attention, but I read your books at a very early stage in my development—when I was all too keen on magic rather than on the metaphysics of Consciousness and Reality—so I could not at that time appreciate the remarks you made about Bhagavan in A Search in Secret India.[17] *Now, of course, I absorb everything that is written about Him with a zeal and a passion you will, I think, easily understand."*[18]

Advaita is a broad field, and Grant soon immersed himself in the work of other Sages too, such as Anandamayi Ma, Pagal Haranath, Ramakrishna, and Atmananda (Krishna Menon). During this time, he lost interest in Western occultism. However, these interests resurged throughout 1954, but deepened by his insight.

Advaita is a Sanskrit term meaning 'not divided.' There is a useful analogy, whereby existence may be likened to a play in which all the roles are played by the one actor, Brahman; however, he's become so immersed in each role that he has forgotten that he is the one actor playing all the roles. There have been various Sages of *Advaita* over the last hundred years or so, such as Ramana Maharshi, Anandamayi Ma, Atmananda (Krishna Menon), and Haranath. Though the core of undifferentiated consciousness is common, the techniques leading to the core are diverse. Ramana Maharshi, for instance, taught the technique of *Atma Vichara,* or 'enquiry into awareness' epitomised as 'Who am I', seeking to locate the sense of "I". Haranath taught the repetition of Name. In reality,

---

[17] Paul Brunton was the pen-name of Raphael Hurst (1898–1981). *A Search in Secret India* was first published in the UK in 1934 by Rider & Co.
[18] Grant to Brunton, 27 October 1952. Private collection.

the aspirant is best served trying a variety of techniques and developing his or her own techniques from them.

Some think that *Advaita* regards "objective reality" as being merely an illusion, of lesser worth than "undivided reality." In fact, the maxim *"Samsara is in Nirvana, and Nirvana is in Samsara"* addresses this point. In *The Matrix and Diamond World Mandalas of Shingon Buddhism* by Adrian Snodgrass, there is a passage which is relevant here:

> *"The distinguishing characteristic of the Esoteric Doctrine is radical non-dualism (advaita, 'not two'). The exoteric schools of Buddhism perceive that the dharmas of the phenomenal world are in continual flux, changing from one instant to the next, and deduce from this that they are Void (sunyata, koku), lacking in self-nature, and in some sense illusory or unreal. Esoteric Buddhism accepts that the dharmas are transitory and fleeting, but totally rejects the view that they are in any way unreal. Even though the things of the sensible world are ephemeral and every-changing, they are real, just as they are. The physical world and its Voidness are two aspects of a single Reality; there is no Void without phenomenal forms and no phenomenal forms without their Voidness. Forms and the Void are indissolubly merged, and they are both equally real. Unenlightened men, however, see only one aspect of this Reality, whereas the Awakened Buddhas see both aspects in their instantaneous union."*

To live in what is considered to be "the real world," we have developed logic and rationality, thinking that these are principles of truth derived from observation when, in fact, they are pragmatic—what is needed to get by. The world of logic and rationality is a bubble within which we are insulated from the irrationality of the universe. It is this awareness which lies at the core of *Advaita*, as of *Thelema*, and we weave our practices from what is to hand, synthesising in this way a unique approach to Reality.

Salvador Dali's paranoiac-critical method is referenced several times throughout Kenneth Grant's *Typhonian Trilogies*, and essentially concerns the perception of apparently irrational links between objects. Dali set out the essence of the paranoiac-critical method in his essay *Conquest of the Irrational*, published by Julian Levy, New York, 1935. At the outset of the essay, Dali quotes a remark by André Breton from a lecture given at Brussels in June 1934:

> *"Dali has endowed surrealism with an instrument of primary importance, in particular the paranoiac-critical method, which has immediately shown itself capable of being applied equally to painting, poetry, the cinema, to the construction of typical surrealist objects, to fashion, to sculpture, to the history of art and even, if necessary, to all manner of exegesis."*

Dali was not content simply to take advantage of irrational links when they were perceived, but to develop methods of stimulating such links in order to utilise them in his paintings and drawings.

Rationality is essentially a construct that we have developed, enabling us to function in an irrational universe. To that end, we have evolved concepts such as Time, Space, morals, etc. as pragmatic necessities, working theories, rather than discoveries of Truth. An example of these links that are seemingly irrational is *gematria*. In a few Classical languages (e.g., Hebrew and Greek), each letter corresponds to a number, and there is deemed to be a relationship between words that share the same enumeration. Crowley's *Sepher Sephiroth* is a compendium of Hebrew words grouped in terms of enumeration.

As occultists, we have our own experiences of links that are apparently irrational, and to illustrate this I shall recount some of my own.

In the late 1980s I worked with Crowley's *Reguli* for the best part of a year. In the last month or so of the Working, I noticed that physical violence was occurring in my immediate vicinity, and I sensed a connection with my Working. Things came to a climax when flames erupted from under the bonnet of a car which had stopped at traffic lights a few yards away from me. When I saw what was happening, I felt immediately a strong sensation in my solar plexus, and knew beyond doubt that this phenomenon was connected with my Working; it was a sensation which I have not forgotten and which is still clear.

In 1991, I undertook a Working based on Crowley's *Liber Samekh* which utilises the accumulation of practice—once a day for the first moon, twice a day for the following two moons, thrice a day for the next three moons, four times per day for the next four moons, and then continual practice for the eleventh, culminating moon. In this way, there is the development of a cumulative intensity. A few months into the practice, I woke one morning to brilliant sunshine. In my living room, on the window sill, there was a cactus which I had had for many years. Now it was basking in the sun. As I gazed at it, there was a sensation of overlay, of perichoresis; the cactus seemed to be immersed in a clear, fast-running stream, and was now the centre, the essence of consciousness. It was a powerful epiphany, and still vivid whenever I recall it.

In 2019 I was with a group of friends when a black obsidian globe was discovered. Looking at it, I was reminded that for many years I had hankered after a black obsidian globe for scrying purposes. A few months later, in May 2020, I came to the living room one morning to find a black obsidian globe on my desk. My wife had come across the globe in an old box of possessions; she had assumed that the globe was mine. I felt sure that it wasn't; that due to my hankering after such an object for so long, I would have remembered procuring such a thing. At the time, I was several months into a Lunar Working, built around observance of the passage of the lunation into the stations of the zodiac. Gradually, the globe was integrated into the Working, and became the focus. There was always a sense of familiarity with the globe, and one day I suddenly realised that the globe was connected with, and a continuation of, the cactus/essence of consciousness experience recounted above. This realisation was a shock; irrational though it was, the identity was clearly felt. Since then, I have developed a Working around the black obsidian globe—a Working which is not static, but dynamic in the sense that it continues to mutate.

The image of a Spider's Web brings to mind the French term *bricolage,* defined as construction or creation from a diverse range of things. It is the use of whatever is at hand, weaving the diverse elements together, and synthesising from them something new. The term is often associated with the French anthropologist Claude Levi-Strauss who in his book *The Savage Mind* (1962) used *bricolage* to describe the characteristic patterns of mythological thought, recombining that which is at hand to create something new.

We are all *bricoleurs,* taking from a variety of influences, and catalyzing then through our own magical and mystical experience to synthesise an inherent body of work that will, in its turn, be one of a number of influences from which others will synthesise their inherent body of work.

Weaving the web, we live our lives through many dimensions. An example is artwork, and the English artist Cecil Collins had some pertinent thoughts on this in Notes to the catalogue to an exhibition in early 1965:

> *"I am not very interested in what is called 'pure painting', or objects d'art. I am concerned with art as poetic consciousness, or as metaphysical experience. A picture lives on many different levels at once, it is an interpenetration of planes of reality, it cannot be analysed or anatomised into single levels because one level can only be understood in the light of others. The reality or interior life of the picture can only be realised as a total experience, and this totality, for me, is poetic consciousness."*

And, later in the same Notes:

> *"Beneath the tyranny and captivity of the mediocre culture of our own technological civilisation, there still flows the living river of human consciousness, within which is concentrated in continuity, the life of the kingdoms of life, animals, plants, stars, the earth and the sea, and the life of our ancestors, the flowing generations of men and women, as they flower in their brief and tragic beauty. And the artist is the vehicle of the continuity of that life, and its guardian, and his instrument is the myth, and the archetypal image."*

The considerations throughout this Introduction are an echo of the definition of Tantra already quoted by André Padoux:

> *"The Sanskrit word tantra is from the verbal root TAN, which means 'to extend,' 'to spread,' hence 'to spin out,' 'weave,' 'display,' 'put forth,' and 'compose.'"*

Contemplating this definition, and bearing in mind the considerations above, we can see that, far from Tantra being an Eastern way of working, it is simply an approach to what might be termed esotericism, and is thus universal. This is the approach taken by Gregory Peters.

BEGINNINGS

"Let the immortal depths of the soul be opened, and open all thy eyes at once to the Above, for if the mortal draw near to the fire he shall have light from God. Thou shouldst speed to the light and to the rays of the Father. And when thou beholdest the most holy fire, flashing formless with dancing radiance through the depths of all the worlds, then listen to the voice of fire. Believe thyself to be out of body and so thou art; for divine things are not accessible to mortals who fix their minds on body; it is for those who strip themselves naked, who speed aloft to the height."
— Chaldean Oracles

"Aiwass, 'the minister of Hoor-paar-kraat', therefore equates with the 'solar-phallic-hermetic Lucifer; The Devil, Satan or Hadit of our particular unit of the Starry Universe. This serpent, Satan, is not the enemy of Man, but He who made Gods of our race, knowing Good and Evil; He bade 'Know Thyself!' and taught Initiation.'"
— Kenneth Grant, *Aleister Crowley & the Hidden God*

I n ancient Greece, across the portico of the Temple of the Pythian Apollo in Delphi, was the injunction *gnothi seauton*: "know thyself." Humankind has an unquenchable thirst for knowledge, as is seen in the manifold religions, mythologies, philosophies, cults and superstitions from antiquity to the present. The gnostic journey is unique; it is a path of unity and wholeness, as self-discovery leads to the ultimate realization of the divine.

Eastern schools have long traditions of teaching practices that assist the student in achieving the realization of oneness, or wholeness, with reality. In the West, the ancient mystery schools carried on this tradition, and continue to this day in their heirs and reconstructions. The somewhat modern schools of Jungian psychology carry on the work in another form that may prepare the aspirant for the currents of light—or pure consciousness—that will be released to flow unrestricted in the integrated, whole Self.

Samadhi is a term used in Eastern mysticism to denote a condition of union or wholeness that is beyond the illusion and constraints of temporal time and consciousness—in other words, *samadhi* refers to the direct experience of non-dual consciousness. It is one of the traditional eight limbs of yoga as described by Patanjali, and is the direct result of certain practices of meditation and yoga. This term finds its cognate in the Western idea of *gnosis,* the direct experience of reality in non-dual awakening. In the yogic and Hindu traditions, *samadhi* refers to a state of profound meditative absorption and union with the divine. There are different types or levels of *samadhi*, each with its unique characteristics and depth of experience:

- *Savikalpa Samadhi*: Also known as "*samadhi* with mental modifications" or "*samadhi* with seed," this is an initial stage of *samadhi* where the practitioner experiences a deep, meditative absorption while still maintaining some level of awareness of the external world, and the distinction between the self and the object of meditation.

- *Nirvikalpa Samadhi*: In this state of "*samadhi* without mental modifications" or "*samadhi* without seed," the practitioner enters a state of complete absorption, where all mental activities and modifications cease. The distinction between the self and the object of meditation dissolves, leading to a state of pure consciousness and transcendence of duality.
- *Sahaja Samadhi*: This is considered the highest form of *samadhi*, often referred to as "natural" or "effortless" *samadhi*. In this state, the practitioner experiences a continuous state of union and divine consciousness, even while engaged in everyday activities. It is said to be a state of spontaneous and integrated enlightenment.

To these are added additional categories:

- *Asamprajnata Samadhi*: Also known as "non-dual *samadhi*" or "formless *samadhi*," this state goes beyond the realm of conceptual understanding and perception. It transcends all mental constructs, and even the sense of individual self. It is a state of pure awareness, devoid of any content or object.
- *Samprajnata Samadhi*: This type of *samadhi* involves a meditative state with specific cognitive processes or "seeds" of knowledge. It is characterized by the presence of thoughts, images and a certain level of mental activity, yet the practitioner remains absorbed in the object of meditation.

Yoga, meditation and magic are not the only avenues to such realization, but they are time-tested techniques which have proven their ability to help the mind "wake up" to Self-Realization. The spontaneous experience and integration of *Sahaja Samadhi* may open up unexpectedly during "flow states"—including the ecstatic, consciousness-expanding experience of orgasm. Aleister Crowley noted that the formula of Babalon is *"constant copulation or Samadhi on everything" (The Vision and the Voice)*. This is reminiscent of occult artist-magician Austin Osman Spare's realization that *"All things fornicate all the time."* Sex magick, and to a much deeper extent certain tantrik practices, are directly associated with these transformative states of consciousness. Working with "bliss" (*ananda*) is a keynote of tantric ritual work, be it through actual physical workings with a consort, or through meditative visualization practices that harness highly erotic imagery in a ritualistic context.

Through a regular discipline of practice and self-investigation, it is possible to achieve firsthand experience of *samadhi* and the resulting gnostic breakthrough. The benefits of this experience are profound. With stabilization and recurring immersion in the Infinite Light (or LVX) of the Gnostics, the Great Work itself may be accomplished—to become liberated while living.

The best method for such work is to have a guide who has already walked some distance on the path. In some cases, it may not be possible or practical to connect with a school or teacher due to distance, time or other factors. This should in no way keep an aspirant from practicing. The earnest spiritual seeker will find the school that best fits their developmental stage and requirements. As it has always been, *when the student is ready, the teacher will appear.* In the meantime, it is important to begin a regular practice in preparation for when the inner teacher establishes contact. The real guide is the inner guru, the awakened consciousness. Any external teachers are reflections of this true inner awareness, and true teachers emphasize this reliance on Self, and turn the student back again and again onto their true, Awakened Self.

§ § §

Although the practices in this book were designed and written with the philosophy of *Thelema* as the underlying basis, it is important to understand that they are not tied to one particular philosophical or religious point of view. They are designed solely to enable diligent and earnest students to achieve real change in their lives, to experience different levels of consciousness firsthand, and to achieve *gnosis*—self-knowledge—which is to experience the presence of the divine directly. However, it may be useful to review the particulars of the spiritual philosophy underlying the author's experience and training.

> *"The word of the Law is Thelema.*
> *Who calls us Thelemites will do no wrong, if he look but close into the word. For there are therein Three Grades, the Hermit, and the Lover, and the man of Earth. Do what thou wilt shall be the whole of the Law."*
> — *Liber AL vel Legis, I:39–40*

Thelema, a Greek word meaning "will," is a spiritual philosophy most often associated with the magician, mystic, yogi, poet, adventurer and prolific writer Aleister Crowley (1875–1947). In 1904, while in Cairo, Egypt, Crowley earthed the current of *Thelema* in a short book received by direct voice dictation, *Liber AL vel Legis (The Book of the Law)*. The book was received over the course of three days on April 8th, 9th and 10th, from what Crowley deemed a "praeterhuman"[19] intelligence identifying itself as Aiwass, "the minister of Hoor-paar-kraat," the Egyptian god of silence. The book was thus literally a reception of the Voice of Silence, an expression of primordial stellar wisdom that lies nameless in infinity. Its three short chapters contain a wealth of spiritual and practical philosophy. Interpretable on many levels simultaneously, the book's message deepens and opens with the understanding and initiation of the individual.

§§§

Although this is not a requirement, you may discover that it would be helpful to have some background in Raja Yoga and meditation, as well as the foundational techniques of ceremonial magick. This book is not intended to cover such basics, as instruction is easily found. Many books present these fundamental techniques. A good starting place for yoga is Patanjali's *Eight Limbs of Yoga*, available in many editions. *Raja Yoga* by Swami Vivekananda is a good commentary and introduction to Patanjali's aphorisms, and also includes good primers on *bhakti*, *karma* and *jnana* yoga. *Eight Lectures on Yoga* by Aleister Crowley is also an excellent introduction to the fundamentals of yoga, stripped of the unessential jargon and cultural trappings that often cloud writings on yoga. A solid introduction to the fundamental techniques of Western ceremonial magick is *Modern Magick* by Donald Michael Kraig. More advanced students would do well to work with Crowley's *Magick in Theory and Practice (Magick: Book 4)*, the *magnum opus* of Western ceremonial magick. For doctoral and specialist levels of training, the work of Kenneth Grant is recommended, in particular for the

---

[19] "Beyond human" or "more than human."

tantrik and nondual insights into the deeper aspects of this Work and their expression of creative occultism. See the Appendix for additional suggestions. Working with the material in these books would provide a good background in the elements of meditation, breath work, visualization, ritual and energy work.[20]

Those without such fundamental training should seek it out; however, the lack thereof is certainly not a barrier to progress, and the methods in this book will assist in developing concentration, relaxation, visualization and similar skills of which the benefits are manifold. In particular, the central rite of the *Diamond Sapphire Gem of Radiant Light* is easily practiced and adapted to a variety of environments and levels of skill, and should be open and accessible to anyone who feels called to partake of its beneficial effects. The supplementary practices will add to this experience, and bring an increased depth to workings and to your competency, eventually opening the way for the true guru within to establish contact.

One meaning of *tantra* is "to weave." In one sense, this is the weaving of multiple types of practices into one integrated system: *mantra, pranayama* (breath control), yoga *asana*, and ritual actions into one coherent and transformative practice. In another sense, this "weaving" refers to the "consciousness of the continuity of existence" *(AL, I:26)*[21], which is the reward of such practice. Life and death, for the *tantrika* (practitioner of tantra), are experienced as phases of one reality; i.e., different phases of the life cycle. In many ways, the reception of *The Book of the Law* was the first movement

---

[20] See also my book *Yogini Magic: The Sorcery, Enchantment & Witchcraft of the Divine Feminine* (The Original Falcon Press, 2022) for a discussion on meditation, as well as a specialized form of tantrik magic.

[21] For compactness, most references to *Liber AL vel Legis (The Book of the Law)* in this book will be of this form, or simply *Liber Legis*.

of tantra's adaptation to the West, and throughout this book we examine and put into practice the ideas of tantra in the context of a Western esoteric paradigm.[22]

Through practices that utilize the body—integrating all of the senses—consciousness is brought to the forefront of awareness. The ever-present moment, the light of presence that is outside of time, becomes the center of awareness. Eastern tantrik traditions of Hinduism and Buddhism are composed of techniques that have been used for hundreds of years to encompass a complete approach to liberation and Gnostic illumination through full use of the mind and body. These techniques do not require moving to India and studying for years under a guru. Rather, you can bring them into your daily life *right now.*

Tantrik practitioners do not attempt to escape this life, or ignore the physical reality of this world. They do not perform empty rites, or recite mindless platitudes in the hope of some great reward in an afterlife. Rather, the tantrika lives in the world, in the present, their eyes and minds open and observant of the world in all of its beauty and all of its ugliness; they perceive the living power of the universe that flows through and composes all of manifestation, and embrace this living and way of being, rejoicing in the endless play of the material world, all the while aware and connecting to that radiant Eternity that is the true foundation of the world.

Practitioners of *New Aeon Tantra* find true equipoise in their daily lives. They live from the center, and their light radiates out, resulting in balanced health, ease of mind and emotions, and confidence in their daily affairs. At center, they live life according to their

---

[22] In this book, *tantra* (lower case) usually refers to a set of practices, whereas *Tantra* (capitalized) refers to the texts or holy books associated with the philosophy.

dharma ("Way"), embracing the world, yet unattached; living in society, yet not bound by it; no longer confined by the illusion of separation. This is the path of True Will, a center of Love and Life.

For the tantrika, the body is a holy instrument, even as all of manifestation is filled with light and is divine. All of the bodily senses are used to assist the work; life itself becomes the laboratory of the tantrika, as the senses are the gateway to the world, and the world is the gateway to the Truth underlying all of manifestation.

The path of tantra is a practical one of will *(iccha)*, knowledge *(jnana)*, and action *(kriya)*. These aspects are represented by the three *Shaktis* (female powers), conceived of as taking up residence in the human body. Approaching the goddesses ritualistically stimulates the corresponding energies, develops these qualities in consciousness, and evokes countless other energies into the body. In this way we experience the Goddess as both transcending the universe, and as imminent within every aspect of existence. Within the symbolism of Thelema, this Goddess presents herself as the star-goddess Nuit—transcendence embodied; and Babalon, the Scarlet Woman who is the visceral, immanent and powerful Queen of the Universe. For the tantrik, nothing need be considered "impure", and every aspect of experience can be used to attain the ultimate bliss of realization. *"That which produces bliss should be used in worship, since it ravishes the soul" (Tantraloka).*

The practices of *New Aeon Tantra* will assist you in developing and purifying your natural talents and inherent abilities, where you will live life according to Will, with consciousness stabilized in the primordial awareness of eternity.

Chapter 1
PRELIMINARY INSTRUCTIONS

Within the esoteric colleges of the Western mysteries, the ceremonial magician utilizes a number of magical accoutrements: robes, crowns, rings, diagrams and more. The Eastern mysteries are just as elaborate, with countless implements of a sacred nature that assist the *sadhaka* (practitioner) in their rites. One need only take a look at Atu I: The Magus card of the *Thoth Tarot* to see an altar of implements; similarly, the lists of ritual items in the tantrik *sadhanas* (magical rituals) are extensive.

Figure 2
'The Magus' Card of the Thoth Tarot
(© Ordo Templi Orientis)

For the practices of *New Aeon Tantra*, you are free to utilize any of these devices as you see fit. The primary tool is *yourself*—and specifically, *Awareness*.

First, prepare yourself. Not only is your body the laboratory of your workings, but more so it is the Temple of the Divine. Treat it with the respect such a holy place deserves. Maintain good hygiene, exercise appropriately, and eat properly for your own equilibrium. For ritual preparation, a cleansing bath is a good preliminary that will help to prepare both the mind and body. Some basic stretches help reinforce the body-mind connection and get the energetic levels of the body activated and working in harmony. Hatha yoga is an excellent means of maintaining flexibility and health.

Yoga

"Yoga means Union."
— Aleister Crowley, *Eight Lectures on Yoga*

One of the most important explorations that Aleister Crowley gave to us is the distillation of Yogic techniques into the West. Across most of his writings on magick and mysticism, the thread of Yoga is a solid foundation from which all other work commences. The basic outline of yogic practices given in Crowley's instruction for members of his magical organization, the A∴A∴, is *Liber E*. These are further elaborated upon in Crowley's *Book 4 Part I*, as well as his smaller work, *Eight Lectures on Yoga*. In discussing the teachings of the "Great Men" of the past, Crowley writes in *Book 4*:

> *"It is by freeing the mind from external influences, whether casual or emotional, that it obtains power to see somewhat of the truth of things."*

Even more succinctly, in *Eight Lectures on Yoga,* Crowley informs us of the *"whole of the technique of Yoga":*

"Sit Still. Stop thinking. Shut up. Get out!"

Crowley's adaptation of yoga strips out cultural trappings and superstition to reveal a systematic set of physical and mental exercises which will aid the magician in concentration, control of force, and increased vitality and health.

The *Yoga Sutras,* attributed to Patanjali, first outlined the path of *ashtanga* (eight-limbed yoga) as a set of guidelines on how to live, with attention to diet, self-discipline, and ethical and moral considerations. The aphorisms are deeply embedded in *Samkhya,* a classical Indian philosophical system that seeks to explain the nature of reality and human experience. Through a dualistic model, *Samkhya* posits two main aspects of ultimate reality: *purusha* (pure consciousness) and *prakriti* (matter/energy). *Prakriti* is made up of three *gunas* (qualities): *sattva* (purity), *rajas* (activity), and *tamas* (inertia) which combine in various ways to create the universe.

The human being is seen as a combination of *purusha* and *prakriti,* with *purusha* being the true self or consciousness, and *prakriti* being the physical body and mind. The aim of *Samkhya* is to attain liberation *(moksha),* which is achieved by separating *purusha* from *prakriti* through knowledge and discrimination.

Crowley took the aphorisms, stripped them of any overt *Samkhya* underpinnings and focused on the practical exercises themselves. In the process, he fully incorporated them into his Thelemic model, bracketing on a framework of the Qabalistic *Tree of Life* and its associations, along with the moral implications of the True Will.

The first limb is *yama,* a set of five ethical standards to be followed: *ahimsa* (non-violence), *satya* (speaking the truth), *asteya* (non-stealing), *brahmacharya* (sexual continence), and *aparigraha* (non-attachment). Crowley redefined *yama* to reflect the changes in consciousness and responsibility which humanity has progressed to, by saying *"Do what thou wilt shall be the whole of the Law. That is Yama."*

The second limb is *niyama*, traditionally interpreted as five observances of self-discipline and witnessing of the sacred in your life. These are *saucha* (cleanliness), *samtosa* (contentment), *tapas* (spiritual austerities), *svadhyaya* (introspection), and *Isvara pranidhana* (surrender to God). In *Eight Lectures on Yoga*, Crowley interprets this limb generally as *"virtue,"* expanding them from five to seven virtues which correspond to the seven sacred planets of the ancients. Saturn represents the virtue of discipline and endurance, as well as embracing the Trance of Sorrow. Jupiter represents the *"vital, creative, genial element of the cosmos"* as the selflessness of universal love, and the Trance of Joy. Mars stands for the virtue of energy, the ability to conquer obstacles on the path—in particular physical obstacles—as well as courage and passion. The Sun is ascribed the virtue of harmony, the *"centralization of the faculties, their control, their motivation."* To Venus is given the *"ecstatic acceptance of all possible experience and the transcendental assumption of all particular experience into the one experience."* Mercury represents the virtue of adaptability and indifference, the adroitness and flexibility that is requisite in both the mind and body of the *yogin* to master the path. Finally, the Moon is the purity of aspiration, as well as the many *siddhis* (magick powers) which will arise. Crowley also adds planetary associations for Uranus and Neptune. The *niyama* for Uranus is *"the discovery of the True Will,"* further stating that this *niyama "is the most important of the tasks of the Yogi because, until he has achieved it, he can have no idea who he is or where he is going."* For Neptune, he attributes spiritual intuition, the *"imaginative faculty, the shadowing forth of the nature of the illimitable light,"* as well as a strong dose of humour. For Pluto, however, we are told that he is *"the utmost sentinel of all; of him it is not wise to speak,"* after which he explains that this is because *"nothing at all is known about him."* Kenneth Grant, in his *Typhonian Trilogies*, has written extensively on the significance of Pluto. Of particular note in this context, Pluto is said to guard *"the underworld (subconsciousness), the region that contains the key to the magical revival promised in the present Aeon."* (*The Magical Revival*). Though the connection to the subconscious, the Scorpionic sexual aspect is indicated as the inner *lingam*—the serpent fire or *kundalini*—and its use as a vehicle of consciousness expansion. The *niyama* of Pluto could very well be the conscious control of this magical force.

The third and fourth limbs of *ashtanga* are *asana* (the various postures necessary for meditation), and *pranayama* (the control of breath). Whereas traditional yoga utilizes several sets of *asanas* for practice and mastery, Crowley recommended selecting one position and mastering it. *"The real object of Asana is control of the muscular system, conscious and unconscious, so that no messages from the body can reach the mind."* Crowley points out the many health benefits of *asana*, including:

> *"The conquest of Asana makes for endurance. If you keep in constant practice, you ought to find that about ten minutes in the posture will rest you as much as a good night's sleep."*

Crowley defined *pranayama* as *"control of force,"* again cutting through profuse amounts of mystic obfuscation in the traditional literature by describing the process thus:

> *"This simply means that you get a stop watch, and choose a cycle of breathing out and breathing in. Both operations*

should be made as complete as possible. The muscular system must be taxed to its utmost to assist the expansion and contraction of the lungs."

He also describes the classic results of *pranayama* practice: perspiration, automatic rigidity, *buchari-siddhi* (jumping about like a frog), and levitation.

The fifth and sixth limbs are *pratyahara* (the withdrawal of senses), and *dharana* (concentration). The former is described in *Eight Lectures* as *"introspection, but it also means a certain type of psychological experience,"* citing the direct experience of feeling that you do not have a nose, as an example. Going into much more detail in *Book 4,* he describes the process of simply watching the mind think. With *dharana,* we move into concentration proper. Here *Liber E* gives several practices for training the mind to concentrate one-pointedly, such as visualizing the elemental *tattvas* for a minute or more, and eventually working up to more complex images. Other practices given in *Eight Lectures* for concentration include *Liber Astarte, Liber III vel Jugorum,* and the practice *"useful when walking in a christian city"* of saying *Apo Pantaos Kakodaimonos!* ("Away from here, all evil spirits!"), with an *"outward and downward sweep of the arm,"* anytime one passes a person in *"religious garb."*

Dhyana and *Samadhi,* the seventh and eighth limbs of yoga, are traditionally associated with "meditation" proper, and ecstasy, respectively. One necessarily leads to the other, with *samadhi* as the crown of the system. In essence, the development of single-pointed concentration, along with active introspection and awareness, lead to ecstatic bliss—of *samadhi.*

Surya Namascar: The Sun Salutation

A core practice from *hatha yoga* is *Surya Namascar*—the Sun Salutation. This practice may be used as a preliminary to all of your work. In addition to the general benefits of yoga listed previously, it has the additional benefit of attuning your consciousness to the sun. You may find that if you perform *Surya Namascar* at the two twilights of the day (sunrise and sunset), you will begin to have an increased consciousness of the sun and its central position in our lives. An increase of overall energy and emotional balance is the natural result of nurturing this connection.

Repeat the entire sequence at least three times. For the first round, go slowly to warm up; on the second round go a little faster; and finally, with the third round, perform the sequence in a flowing movement. The objective is to limber up the body and get it energized, not to do some kind of fast calisthenics and start sweating.

1. At sunrise, stand facing east (the rising sun). At sunset, face west (the setting sun).

2. Stand straight with your feet together. Imagine a brilliant white sphere above your head with a white light streaming into it from above. Place your palms together, touching your chest. Sense the energy pouring into you, filling you with vitality and awakening every cell of your body.

3. Now breathe in deeply while you raise your arms above your head and bend backward from the waist.

4. Bend forward from your hips, as you breathe out slowly. (Knees should be slightly bent; you do not want any strain on your lower back.) Hands are flat on the floor beside your feet. At this point, your head should be near your shins.

5. Breathe in and stretch your right leg behind you so your foot is at a right angle to your leg and resting on its toes. The left leg is vertical to the floor and your head is back.

6. While you breathe, place your left foot back to match the right foot. The body is now in a straight line, supported only by your toes and hands, which are in a vertical line.

7. Still holding your breath, lower your body and rest your toes, knees, chest, palms and forehead on the floor. Stomach and pelvis are off the floor, with hands by your shoulders, elbows bent, and arms by your sides.

8. Breathing out, lie flat on the ground. Feel the energy coursing through your body.

9. Breathe in as you raise your head, and then the upper part of your torso. Pelvis is flat on the ground and the head is back.

10. Hold your breath, and bring your feet flat onto the floor and raise your hips to form an inverted V shape.

11. Still holding your breath, bring the right foot forward so it is vertical, and the left leg is back (the reverse of #5).

12. Breathe out as you bring the left leg up and place your feet together between your hands. Straighten your legs (with knees slightly bent) and place your head on your shins.

13. Breathe in as you straighten up from the hips. Bring your arms up, and stretch them backward as you bend back from the waist. Hold your breath as you look backward.

14. Breathe out as you straighten your body. Now raise your arms over your head and back again as you bend your elbows to place your hands together at your chest. See a radiant sphere of

golden solar energy in your heart center, its rays penetrating and warming your entire body.[23]

Lunar Adorations

Even as we attune to the solar currents with the Sun Salutations, a yogic union is achieved through the mental concentration of reciting the *gayatri* (song or hymn) *mantra* when the moon is seen in the sky:

> **Om bhur bhuvah svah**
> **tat savitur vareṇyaṃ**
> **bhargo devasya dhimahi**
> **dhiyo yo nah pracodayat**

> *"Om, we meditate on the effulgent glory of the divine light.*
> *May it inspire our understanding."*

Alternatively, the many forms of the Goddess in India each have their own *gayatri*, which also may be used. Here are some examples:

Tripurasundari:
> **Om Tripurasundari vidmahe**
> **kameshvari dhimahi**
> **tanno klinne pracodayat**

> *"Om, let us contemplate Tripurasundari,*
> *let us think of Kameshvari,*
> *may that wetness direct."*

---

[23] For visual instruction, see newaeontantra.com/2014/09/07/sun-salutation-illustrated

Kali:
> **Om mahakalyai ca vidmahe**
> **smasana vasinyai ca dhimahi**
> **tanno kali pracodayat**
>
> *"Om, let us contemplate the Great Goddess*
> *who takes away darkness,*
> *let us think of She who resides in the cremation grounds,*
> *may she grant increase."*

If you have a chosen and preferred form of the Goddess (*Ishtadevi*), it is best to use the *gayatri* associated with Her, or compose your own verse in celebration of Her. Use what inspires you! Greek epics, the Holy Books of Thelema, Egyptian Pyramid texts, and so on are just a few sources to explore.

The Song of the Syrens

The Full Moon is a deeply inspiring and magically powerful time. Throughout the ages, the moon in this phase has been associated with nocturnal rites, dream imagery, and occult powers. It is considered a potent time for spiritual practices, magical workings, and rituals. Lunar deities or goddesses, such as Selene and Artemis, are often associated with the Full Moon, connecting it to feminine qualities, intuition and the cycles of nature.

During the Full Moon, psychic sensitivity is increased, making it easier to connect with higher consciousness and receive spiritual insights. This is a time of transformation and release, encouraging the magician to let go of negativity, old patterns, and emotional baggage for personal growth and renewal.

Many occult practitioners use the Full Moon for divination, gaining deeper insights into their spiritual path through tarot readings, scrying and other forms of divination. Ritual celebrations are common, involving meditation, chanting, spellwork and offerings to lunar deities.

The Full Moon is also rich in esoteric symbolism, representing completion, illumination and the integration of opposing forces. It signifies wholeness and the harmonization of dualities in traditions like astrology and alchemy.

Lunar magic is a significant aspect of Full Moon practices, with practitioners harnessing its energy for various intentions, such as healing, abundance and protection.

In tantrik workings, the Full Moon increases the potency of *mantras*; and *japa* (mantric recitation) has its power multiplied during this time.

At such times, the *Song of the Syrens* has a lyrical potency that resonates with this work. As will become apparent throughout this book, the *Song of the Syrens* plays a key role that unlocks some of the core realizations of New Aeon Tantra.

> **Mu pa telai, O chi balae**
> **Tu wa melai Wa pa malae: —**
> **A, a, a Ut! Ut! Ut!**
> **Tu fu tulu! Ge; fu latrai,**
> **Tu fu Tulu Le fu malai**
> **Pa, Sa, Ga. Kut! — Hut! — Nut.**
> **Qwi Mu telai AI OAI**
> **Ya Pa melai; Rel moai**
> **u, u, u. Ti — Ti — Ti!**
> **Se gu melai; Wa la pelai**
> **Pe fu telai, Tu fu latai**
> **Fu tu lu. Wi, Ni, Bi.**

Translation of Song

I

Silence! the moon ceaseth (her motion),
That also was sweet
In the air, in the air, in the air!
Who Will shall attain!
Who Will shall attain
By the Moon, and by Myself, and by the Angel of the Lord!

II

Now Silence ceaseth
And the moon waxeth sweet;
(It is the hour of) Initiation, Initiation, Initiation.
The kiss of Isis is honeyed;
My own Will is ended,
For Will hath attained.

III

Behold the lion-child swimmeth (in the heaven)
And the moon reeleth: —
(It is) Thou! (It is) Thou! (It is) Thou!
Triumph; the Will stealeth away (like a thief),
The Strong Will that staggered
Before Ra Hoor Khuit! — Hadit! — Nuit!

IV

To the God OAI Be praise
In the end and the beginning!
And may none fall
Who Will attain
The Sword, the Balances, the Crown!

This "song" was identified as the Bathyllic language of the Sappho-Calypso Angel by Crowley in *Liber 418*. From the text, *"And it is the song of the syrens. And whoever heareth it is lost."* What are we to make of this? Other than the note in the text, Crowley had nothing further to say about the Bathyllic language, the Sappho-Calypso Angel, or the Song. We are then left to our own intuitions and direct experience to come to an understanding of this enigmatic mystery. It may be useful to explore some of the terms as they appear in historical accounts.

In Greek mythology, the Syrens were dangerous and seductive creatures, usually depicted as female figures with the head of a woman and the body of a bird. They were said to inhabit an island surrounded by rocky cliffs and treacherous waters, somewhere in the Mediterranean Sea, although the exact location varies in different accounts.

The Syrens possessed enchanting and irresistible singing voices that could mesmerize sailors passing by their island. Their songs were so beautiful and alluring that sailors would be drawn toward the island, lured by the promise of their captivating music. But the Syrens had malicious intentions; once the sailors approached, the ships would be wrecked on the treacherous rocks, leading the sailors to their death.

In Homer's epic poem *The Odyssey*, Odysseus encountered the Syrens during his long journey back to Ithaca after the Trojan War. To protect his crew from falling victim to the Syrens' allure, Odysseus had his men plug their ears with beeswax so they couldn't hear the song. Curious about the enchanting music, Odysseus had himself tied to the mast of the ship to resist their lure while safely passing by the Syrens' island.

The mythology of the Syrens has been referenced and depicted in various works of literature, art and music throughout history, emphasizing their symbolic significance as temptations and dangers that humans must navigate on their journey of Self-Realization.

What are we to make of the mysterious Sappho-Calypso angel and the Bathyllic language? Calypso was a nymph of the mythical island of Ogygia. In *The Odyssey*, Calypso is described as a beautiful and immortal goddess-like figure, the daughter of the Titan, Atlas. She is a seductive and enchanting figure whose name literally means *"she who conceals."* When Odysseus becomes shipwrecked on her island after facing numerous trials on his way back home from the Trojan War, Calypso rescues him and offers him immortality if he becomes her lover and stays with her forever.

Calypso keeps Odysseus as her captive lover for seven years, during which time he becomes conflicted between his desire for immortality and the longing to return to his wife, Penelope, Eventually, the god Hermes is sent by Zeus to Ogygia, delivering Zeus's command for Calypso to release Odysseus and allow him to continue his journey home. Although reluctant, Calypso obeys the command, and Odysseus departs the island on a makeshift raft. With Calypso we see themes of hidden sexuality, the life force or *kundalini* that is wrapped seven times at the base of the spine. The sexual force, at first unbound, comes under the regency of the intellect (Hermes) and the higher consciousness (Zeus).

Sappho was a Greek poet who lived on the island of Lesbos around the 6th century BCE. She is considered one of the greatest lyric poets of antiquity, and is often referred to as the "Tenth Muse." Unfortunately, much of her poetry has been lost over time, but she was highly admired in her day and continues to be a significant figure in the history of literature.

Sappho's poetry focused on themes of love, desire and personal emotions. She composed her verses in the form of short lyric poems, often in the Aeolic dialect of Ancient Greek. Her works were primarily intended to be sung or accompanied by music, as she was also known as a skilled musician and the founder of a school of poetry.

One of the unique aspects of Sappho's poetry is her representation of love and relationships between women. While she did write about heterosexual relationships, some of her most famous surviving poems express love and desire for other women. Her intimate and passionate expressions towards female friends and companions have led some scholars to believe that she may have had romantic relationships with women. The term "lesbian" derives from the name of the island, Lesbos, where Sappho lived.

The *Song of the Syrens*, then, brings in all of this symbolism to a vehicle of self-realization and transcendence, by means of the sexual nature. The ego, or false self, is transcended, rendering the split-mind consciousness clear so the pristine clarity of the Self shines through as pure Awareness. In this sense, the "hearer" is "lost," and the illusory self is immersed in the radiance of the eternal Self.

The *Song* represents multiple layers of experience. It can be a powerful tool for self-realization and transcendence in and by itself, without any further ritual framework. The traditional mythology of the Syrens represent the allure of worldly desires and temptations that can captivate the ego. In this context, the ego symbolizes the identity formed by external influences, social conditioning, and attachments to material pleasures, which often obscure the true nature of the individual.

In one sense, the Syrens' song can be seen as a metaphor for the distractions and illusions that keep individuals trapped in a fragmented state of consciousness, preventing them from experiencing the fullness of their true selves. The lure of the Song represents the seductive nature of worldly pursuits that keep individuals entangled in a cycle of desires and attachments, leading to a state of inner turmoil and confusion.

For the tantrika, living according to her Will *(Svecchacara)*, and seeking self-realization and transcendence, the *Song of the Syrens* becomes an opportunity for transformation. By recognizing the illusory nature of the ego and its attachments, the individual can begin the journey toward dissolving the ego and unifying the split-mind consciousness. This process of transcending the ego allows the radiant clarity of the true Self to shine through, symbolizing the pure awareness that exists beyond the realm of material desires and transient identifications.

The concept of being "lost" in the *Song of the Syrens* implies a surrendering of the illusory self. In this surrender, you become immersed in the experience of the eternal Self, which is beyond the limited constructs of time and space. By letting go of the ego and its attachments, you gain access to a higher state of consciousness characterized by spiritual clarity and wisdom. What is lost is the false ego and the illusion of separation. This creates space, allowing pure, pristine, radiant Awareness to shine through.

In essence, the *Song of the Syrens* serves as a transformative catalyst that enables you to rise above the illusion of the ego and its limited perceptions. Through this process of self-realization and transcendence, you gain access to the eternal Self— pure awareness, unbounded and free from the constraints of the material world.

The theme of self-realization and transcendence is, of course, not limited to the *Song of the Syrens*. Similar motifs can be found in various spiritual and philosophical traditions, where the relinquishing of the false self and the recognition of the eternal Self are considered essential steps on the path to enlightenment, awakening or liberation. However, with this one simple paean, we have the lyrical nectar to unlock higher states of bliss. The recitation is an opportunity for deep introspection, to recognize the illusions that bind you, and embrace the radiant clarity of the eternal Self. It emphasizes the transformative power of surrendering the ego, and the profound liberation that comes with the realization of your true nature as pure awareness and consciousness.

Practical Instruction

When the Song is sung, no visualizations or thoughts are required. Rather, this is a moment of spontaneous Awareness. Simply breathe normally, in a relaxed way, while reciting the Song without distraction. Allow the vibrations to flow through your body, thrilling consciousness, and coordinating the aspects of body, speech and mind. No past, no present, no future. Be in the present moment—in the eternal Now.

Dietary Considerations

Unlike many other systems, there are no specific dietary restrictions for the practice of *New Aeon Tantra*; rather, the approach is practical. A diet heavy in meat tends to be more grounding and earthier, while a vegetarian diet tends to be lighter, and may help the opening of the psychic faculties. Everybody is different though, and these are only the most basic of general guidelines.

Find a balance that works best for your body type, and tune it as necessary, depending on the practical aspects of consciousness you are trying to develop and emphasize. You may find that a vegetarian diet works best the majority of the time, but occasional meat is required to maintain grounding and not get lost in psychic realms. However, it may be just as likely that too little meat renders you incapable of concentration, and you find yourself lost in realms akin to daydreaming. Pay attention to how diet affects your consciousness, and tune it accordingly. Treat your body as an instrument that requires regular maintenance and tuning to fulfill its purpose.

In any case, moderation seems to be a good guide: drink enough water, and ensure that the foods you choose are high in nutrients. Stay away from processed foods that are high in calories and fat, but extremely low on *prana* (life force); and do not overindulge in any food, sweets or alcohol, if for no other reason than to discover that meditation is quite difficult when your stomach is working on digesting prime rib. Your body is the result of millions of years of evolution, a work of art with a wisdom built into its very cells. Pay attention to what it tells you. Ultimately, your inner guidance is the only true direction here.

Whenever you eat, it is good to be mindful. Every act, including giving our bodies nutrition, should be done with consciousness and awareness. One simple practice is to take a moment to raise your awareness to the divine, and then bless your food. As you take a deep breath in, see a brilliant sphere of white light above your head. Silently acknowledge the divine, and give thanks. Next, hold your hands out over your meal, breathe out in one long, relaxing breath, and visualize streams of white light flowing into your food. Now enjoy your meal, and know that it is condensed light.

Thelemic Refuge

The *Thelemic Refuge* is a simple ritual that may be used to produce a *kavacha* (magical armor). It is preliminary to almost every practice of *New Aeon Tantra*, as well as a protective and empowering practice that may be done on its own throughout the day. It is also a good practice to perform at the two twilights, either before or after *Surya Namascar*.

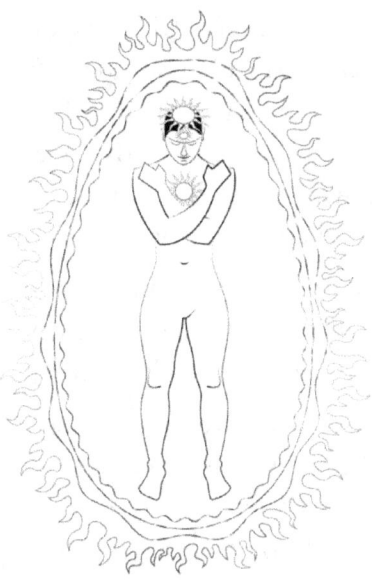

Figure 3
Thelemic Armor
(Kat Lunoe)

In the traditional *Tantras* (holy books) of India, each deity has its own *kavacha* that the practitioner assumes during worship for protection, empowerment and attunement to the predominant energies of the deity. In the rites of *New Aeon Tantra,* there is one general *kavacha,* which utilizes the energies of the Thelemic pantheon of Nuit, Hadit and Ra-Hoor-Khuit. Assumption of magical armor is a form of Banishing Ritual. As with a traditional pentagram rite, *Thelemic Refuge* involves both an invocation of the divine as well as a protective, radiant shield of light that will surround your sphere of sensation.

On another level, this practice is similar to the Buddhist act of taking refuge in the *Three Jewels of the Buddha, Dharma and Sangha*. In our practice, we take refuge in the cosmic goddess of

Infinite Space and Infinite Stars (the One or All or Naught), the individual point event or singularity, and the Eternal Child of these. As such, Thelemic Refuge is truly redirecting the consciousness to the Self as the point of union between the One and the All, the finite and infinite, the human and the divine. Our refuge is in our Self, and the Truth contained therein. The process is simple:

1. Stand upright, or sit comfortably with your spine erect. Take three cleansing breaths by inhaling slowly, and then relax all your muscles while you exhale slowly and without tension.

2. Next, cross your arms over your chest, right over left. Hold yourself in this position, with head bowed, and repeat these words from chapter III, verse 17, of *Liber AL vel Legis*: *"Nu is your refuge, as Hadit your light; and I am the strength, force, vigour of your arms."*

3. See yourself surrounded by radiant, golden light, flowing and pulsating around your sphere of sensation in an egg-shaped chrysalis of flaming light. As your inner perception adjusts, you may become aware of a very thin layer of electric blue light underlying the golden fire. You may also be aware of a current of energy flowing up and down your spine, and an awakening in centers in your heart, forehead and above the crown of the head.

With the visualization of the armor of the Star Goddess and her retinue in place, you may now go on to further work, or remain in contemplation and deeper meditative practices.

The Mala

The majority of these practices benefit from the use of a *mala* (a rosary of 111 beads). These are easily found at Tibetan Buddhist centers; you may even prefer to construct your own.

Why 111 beads? Traditionally the *mala* is constructed of 108 beads, with the addition of three beads that represent the levels of consciousness. In the *Tantras* it is said that the number of breaths per day is 21,600, split evenly between the currents of the sun and the moon. Multiplying 108 by 100 equals 10,800. Multiplying 2 by 10,800 equals 21,600. The three additional beads may also be thought of as the Three Jewels of Thelema: Nuit, Hadit and Ra-Hoor-Khuit. Occultly, the number 111 refers to the sun as well as to the full extension of the Hebrew letter *aleph*. This letter is associated in the *Sepher Yetzirah* with the "Scintillating Intelligence," which is *"the essence of that curtain which is placed close in order of the disposition, and this is a special dignity to stand before the Face of the Cause of Causes."*[24]

Before use, the *mala* should be endowed with life; or in Western usage, purified, consecrated and dedicated to the Great Work. This may be accomplished in any number of ways; a simple example of *mala* preparation is given here. Feel free to use this, modify it to your own tastes, or write your own.

The *mala* will be a regular tool in your work with *New Aeon Tantra*. Its initial preparation should be done to establish an energetic connection to the work, and seal it into this important tool. You may wish to repeat this preparation regularly as part of your daily practice.

Preparation of the Mala

To prepare a new *mala*, you will need some fresh water; incense of an uplifting, solar nature; a single candle; and Abramelin oil.

---

[24] W.W. Westcott, *Sepher Yetzirah: The Book of Formation and the 32 Paths of Wisdom* (Kessinger Publishing, 1992), a reprint of the 1887 translation.

When ready, go to a location where you can be assured of privacy for at least twenty minutes. Performing this rite outside in nature, with the warm rays of the sun shining down upon you, is a wonderful approach; seated in your own personal temple or room works just as well.

Begin with the *Surya Namascar: The Sun Salutation*. Then take *Thelemic Refuge*. Next, holding the *mala* with both hands, sprinkle some of the water onto it while saying, *"For pure will, unassuaged of purpose, delivered from the lust of result, is every way perfect."*[25] Pause for a moment to see streams of purifying astral water flow over the beads, caressing and cleansing them.

Now pass the beads over the incense smoke, allowing the tendrils of perfumed smoke to intertwine across the beads, while saying, *"I am uplifted in thine heart; and the kisses of the stars rain hard upon thy body."*[26] See the beads glowing with radiance as they are consecrated to the service of the Great Work.

Now take some of the Abramelin oil into your right hand, and rub it into the beads while breathing in a slow, rhythmic fashion. Hold the *mala* in both hands above the candle, allowing the flame to warm both your hands and the beads as the oil heats gently in the flame, while saying, *"This shall regenerate the world, the little world my sister, my heart & tongue, unto whom I send this kiss."*[27]

Hold the *mala* in the left hand. Hold the right hand before it with the palm facing the *mala*, as though it were going to emit a current of energy into the beads. In this position, recite the *mantras*:

A ka dua
Tuf ur biu

---

[25] *Liber AL vel Legis*, I:44.
[26] Ibid., II:62.
[27] Ibid., I:53.

Bi a'a chefu
Dudu ner af an nuteru

several times to radiate a current of energy in your body, while at the same time focusing your consciousness.

When ready, take the central *meru* bead (aka the *guru* bead) of the *mala* in between the right thumb and the first and middle fingers. Focus on the bead, and feel the radiant energy of the divine flowing through you. Whisper **A ka dua** to the bead. Allow the energy to flow through your breath, and the vibration of your voice into the bead, filling it with radiance. Now move to the bead immediately to the right of the guru bead, and repeat the process with the words **Tuf ur biu.** Continue to the next bead with **Bi a'a chefu**. Continue to the next bead, and whisper **Dudu ner af,** and then to the fifth bead with **an nuteru**. Move to the next bead, and continue this process, reciting the *mantras* again in the same sequence. This continues repeatedly while moving in a clockwise direction across the *mala* until you have chanted over every bead.

When complete, take the *mala* gently in both hands and bring it to your lips, kissing it softly. You may then place it around your neck, with the guru bead facing up at the nape of the neck. When not in use, the *mala* may be kept wrapped in silk, or placed on your altar, or worn under the clothing around your neck. Alternatively, you may carry the *mala* wrapped around your wrist.

Your *mala* is a sacred instrument. Do not let anyone else handle it after you have prepared it. (The exception may be a guru who will bless the *mala* for you.) The beads will absorb the radiance of your workings, and over time become a powerfully charged talisman of light. Treat it as though the Goddess Herself were in the beads.

Who Are You?

We confront this question head on. This is the ultimate subject of self-inquiry that must be answered for *yourself*. You will likely spend many years in search of the answer to this one simple question. Once discovered, The Answer will then guide you as a Lamp shining in the Darkness. In the meantime, you need to have a way to refer to yourself outside of your daily existence.

A deeper aspect to this question comes from the practice of meditation, specifically the practice advocated by Sri Ramana Maharshi (1879–1950), a renowned Indian sage and spiritual teacher known for his teachings on self-inquiry and the practice of *Nan Yar* ("Who am I?"). His teachings revolved around the path of *Advaita Vedanta*, emphasizing the direct realization of your true nature as the ultimate goal of spiritual practice.

The core practice associated with Maharshi is the self-inquiry method known as "Who am I?" or *Atma Vichara*. This practice involves turning your attention inward, and continuously questioning the nature of the self. By asking yourself, "Who am I?" or "To whom does this thought arise?" you seek to uncover the underlying essence of your being, and directly experience the true Self beyond the mind and body.

Maharshi taught that the ego—the sense of a separate self—is an illusion created by the mind. Through self-inquiry, he encourages you to dive deeply into your own consciousness, transcending the identification with thoughts, emotions and external phenomena. The aim of this practice is to discover the true nature of the self, which he described as pure awareness or consciousness.

According to Maharshi, the true Self is ever-present, unchanging and devoid of personal attributes or limitations. By consistently questioning the source of the "I"-thought, and directing your attention inward, you gradually dissolve the ego and abide in the realization of the pure, infinite consciousness that underlies all experience.

§ § §

As a type of self-inquiry, the act of selecting a magical name is a powerful adjunct which helps to ground the practice. Your magical name should reflect those aspects of yourself that you wish to highlight. Consider what you aspire to; what are your highest ideals, your ultimate vision of yourself? Synthesize these aspirations into a simple phrase or word. Some people like to use a name from history—a historical figure or subject from myth that inspires or stimulates the imagination. To find the right name, go deeply into meditation and self-analysis to find what really drives you right now, at this stage in your development.

The name will be your secret, a representation of your aspiration. As you progress, the name may change, so do not be overly concerned with finding the perfect name at the onset. This is a process of discovery; along the way you will learn many things about yourself, and you will continue to grow as your practice deepens.

When you begin your practices, silently assume the name you have chosen. For the duration of your rituals, you *are* your aspiration. Forget about any shortcomings, and instead focus on what is pure and in direct touch with the Divine. As your practice continues to deepen, you will experience the living truth of your name, as that which is ideal and eternal becomes more in alignment with the transient, until, eventually, there is no difference. When this occurs, you will truly know the answer to the question, **"Who am I?"**

Chapter 2
CULT[28] OF THE INFINITE

"In all systems of religion is to be found a system of Initiation, which may be defined as the process by which a man comes to learn that unknown Crown."
— *Liber LXI, v. 2*

"For the colours are many, but the light is one."
— *Liber Cordis Cincti Serpente, I:3*

Consciousness is a continuum, a unity that transcends all attempts at language. In Thelema, this can be visualized in the form of the Star Goddess *Nuit* (Figure 19), the *"consciousness of the continuity of existence" (AL, I:26)*.

The process of initiation is the direct experience of the continuum with increasing levels of clarity. Like peeling away the layers of an onion, the fabric of illusion that is weaved continuously by

---

[28] Modern bias makes it necessary to say a few things about the word "cult." While these days there are many negative associations with the word, we use it here in the older and correct form of connoting a group of particular practices or beliefs directed toward a particular deity. The Roman cult of Mithras, for example, was devoted to the Persian god of light, and had its own group of rituals and practices that were unique to that particular system. Early Christianity was rightly termed a cult by the Romans. In our own case, a *cult* of the *infinite* denotes a specific set of practices devoted toward Self-Attainment and spiritual illumination. In this sense, Nuit, the Goddess of Infinite Space and of Infinite Stars, may be thought of as our patron deity.

nature is refined and clarified, so the true nature may shine through brilliantly.

At the individual level, the Great Work may be defined as the process whereby you are brought to the realization of your divine nature. This is a gnostic experience—the direct experience of reality—outside the confines of the false ego's illusory sense of separation in time and space. This direct perception of truth is a universal experience, unconfined by affiliation to any particular religion, philosophy, or culture. Rather, it marks the unifying characteristic of all spiritual philosophies and religions. Gnosis is free.

On a cosmic scale, the Great Work may be thought of as an evolutionary movement—the Aeons. Consisting of approximately two thousand years, the Great Ages of Humanity are marked by characteristic archetypes: the Mother, the Father, the Child. It is with this concept of aeons that the evolutionary life force clothes itself in the symbolism of its age, with corresponding rites, mythologies, beliefs and effects on the psychospiritual constitution of living beings. The last great age was known as the Aeon of Osiris, and was characterized by monotheistic and paternalistic religions such as Christianity, Islam and Judaism. In March of 1904, Crowley announced that we had entered the Aeon of Horus, with *The Book of the Law* being received shortly thereafter.

While the aeons help to represent aspects of an evolutionary current that affects all of humanity, it is not necessarily automatic for everyone to connect with the prevailing energies; similarly, it is not accurate to say that one aeon supersedes or replaces another. Rather, the dawn of an aeon signifies what may be, for some, an increased potential that *may* be tapped into. Especially at the early stages of such an event, it is up to each individual to consciously step into the stream of the New Aeon. As a synthesis and universal key of the many traditions and philosophies that came before it, Thelema finds a universal applicability and expression as the summit of the initiatory current at this point in linear time.

The Slopes of Abiegnus

At the heart of *The Book of the Law* and Thelema is the core philosophy expressed as **Do what thou wilt shall be the whole of the Law.** Despite superficial interpretations, this is not a license to do whatever one pleases without care for the consequences. Rather, the *Law of Thelema* is an injunction of the natural order of the cosmos to do your *True Will*—the very core and purpose of being, the *dharma* of your existence—and nothing else. **Find your True Will** and **Do it**, and do nothing else. At this level, Thelema is celebrated as the Cult of the Individual, with freedom as the triumphant banner being displayed. It might be argued that what one pleases is exactly this Will, for in the truest sense we are already doing our Will despite ourselves. Looking a little deeper, however, you can see that we are continually confused as to our true nature. Even our simple wants and whims are conditioned by family, culture, psychological complexes, health, the media, the weather, and so on. These unconscious *kleshas* (obstacles) obscure our True Will. Traditionally the *kleshas* fall into five categories:

1. Avidya (Ignorance): Avidya represents the fundamental misunderstanding of the true nature of reality. It is the ignorance of your divine nature, and the interconnection of all things. *Avidya* leads you to perceive yourself as separate from the divine, or as an isolated entity which results in suffering and the perpetuation of the cycle of birth and death *(samsara)*.

2. Asmita (Egoism): *Asmita* refers to the identification with the ego or the false sense of self. It is the tendency to define yourself based on external factors such as possessions, accomplishments or social status. This identification with the ego creates a sense of separation from others, and fosters attachment, pride and a constant need for validation.

3. Raga (Attachment): *Raga* is the attachment to, or craving for pleasurable experiences and sensory gratification. It is the desire for things to be a certain way or for experiences to bring lasting satisfaction. Attachment leads to clinging, grasping and the fear of losing what you value, thereby causing suffering and preventing spiritual growth.

4. Dvesha (Aversion): *Dvesha* is the aversion to, or repulsion from unpleasant experiences or situations. It is the tendency to avoid discomfort, pain or situations that challenge your sense of security or well-being. It arises from the fear of suffering, and the desire to protect yourself from perceived threats, but it ultimately reinforces the cycle of suffering by creating resistance and conflict.

5. Abhinivesha (Fear of Death): *Abhinivesha* is the fear of death or the instinctual drive for self-preservation. It is the deep-seated fear of annihilation or the unknown that arises from the attachment to the physical body and the ego's identification with it. This fear underlies many other fears and attachments, driving much of human behavior and perpetuating the cycle of suffering.

§ § §

It requires deep self-knowledge to come to a clear understanding of who we are and what our role is, and to *consciously* embody the True Will and live it to the full. It is through the practices of meditation, yoga and magick that we may work to make the unconscious conscious, and by shedding light on these otherwise hidden influences we can learn to transform them, releasing their energy blocks and achieving the spontaneous freedom of the True Will.

This True Will might be likened to a great cosmic storehouse of all the potential energy in the universe, ready at our disposal, should we only open it up with the key. Sri Ramana Maharshi, the great Advaitist saint, expressed this quest as *Who am I?* It is in Silence that the answer is found.

> "Then saith the prophet and slave of the beauteous one: Who am I, and what shall be the sign? So, she answered him, bending down, a lambent flame of blue, all-touching, all penetrant, her lovely hands upon the black earth, & her lithe body arched for love, and her soft feet not hurting the little flowers: Thou knowest! And the sign shall be my ecstasy, the consciousness of the continuity of existence, the omnipresence of my body." (AL, I:26)

The corollary to Thelema is *agape*, a Greek word meaning "love." **Love is the law, love under will.** This love is the universal *bhakti* of the mystics, that all-embracing unity of the universe, the plenum or Void of all creation. In *The Book of the Law*, this principle is expressed by the Egyptian star goddess Nuit, the Goddess of Infinite Space and Infinite Stars. In *agape*, we find the cult of the infinite, the creative womb matrix of reality. *Agape* is seen as identical to Thelema, two expressions offering different angles into the whole, neither existing without the other in a dynamic play of individual and unity, one and all, self and Self, two and naught. The striving for individual freedom is indeed the flow of universal radiant energy. The cult of the individual is seen to be identical with the cult of the infinite. Each is real on its own plane—and the two, in fact, are identical when seen from the core.

Thelema is the quintessence of a current, the Stellar Gnosis, that has been around since before the dawn of time. Influences of the Stellar Gnosis are found throughout history; its first appearance was associated with legends of Lemuria and the sunken city of Atlantis. The Predynastic ages of Ancient Egypt, and the later Draconian cults of the Dark Dynasties, saw a resurgence of the Stellar tradition that carried over into Western traditions of Hermeticism, the Qabalah, and Gnostic Christianity. In the East, the great "non-dual" philosophies of the *Prajna-Paramita* traditions of Buddhism, Tao and Vedantist philosophy, to name a few, have carried on these teachings in veiled form.

In particular, the pristine clarity of Mahayana Buddhism—flowering into China's Taoism, and emerging as Ch'an Buddhism and the Tibetan development of Dzogchen—share a deep heritage with Thelema. Similarly, the tantrik, Saivite, Advaitist and Vedanta currents of the Indian subcontinent are continuations of this ancient heritage. It is from understanding these earlier traditions that Thelema opens up its hidden beauty and deeper, esoteric levels of interpretation. The Thelemic tradition finds its heart in deep streams far beyond the abyss of reason.

§ § §

Thelema transcends Crowley. In 1532, Francois Rabelais described an "Abbey of Thelema" in his book *Gargantua and Pantagruel,* with the injunction of the Law of *Fay ce que vouldras* ("Do what you will") written above the entrance to the door. And Saint Augustine of Hippo wrote of the Law under the guise of *Dilige et quod vis fac* ("Love, and do what you will"). The Adinath sect of *vamamarga* (left-hand path) tantrikas, an Indian lineage of *yogin* that dates back to about 900 CE, expresses the Law as *svecchacara* ("Live according to your own will"). And in his final teaching, the historical Buddha Gautama directed his disciples to, *"Be to yourselves your own light. Be to yourselves your own refuge. Do not go looking for any other light or refuge."* Thelema has now evolved into the message of *Liber AL vel Legis,* and the One Law of *Do what thou wilt.* Eventually something will come along to replace Thelema. The gnosis is not static, nor is it locked into a particular model from history; rather, it is a dynamic, evolving, ever-growing process—a spiraling growth back toward infinity.

Beyond the Infinite

> *"But your holy place shall be untouched throughout the centuries: though with fire and sword it be burnt down & shattered, yet an invisible house there standeth, and shall stand until the fall of the Great Equinox when Hrumachis shall arise and the doublewanded one assume my throne and place. Another prophet shall arise, and bring fresh fever from the skies; another woman shall awake the lust & worship of the Snake; another soul of God and beast shall mingle in the globed priest; another sacrifice shall stain the tomb; another king shall reign; and blessing no longer be poured To the Hawk-headed mystical Lord!"*
>
> — *Liber AL vel Legis,* III:34

For the present, the bulk of humanity is under the influence of the Hawk-Headed Lord of Silence & Strength, represented by the falcon-headed deity Horus in Egyptian iconography. This is not some external deity to be worshipped, but a symbol of the immediate and direct awakening to the living current of instruction and all attainment, the **Hidden God** enshrined in the secret **Heart of the Master,** at the *adytum* (Greek: "innermost sanctuary") of your **Inmost Self**. Identified as the Aeon of the Crowned and Conquering Child, this age presents humanity with a task to consciously step forward into the New Aeon of dawning consciousness, a lucid, clear awareness that transcends all concepts of time and space.

> *"Then the priest answered & said unto the Queen of Space, kissing her lovely brows, and the dew of her light bathing his whole body in a sweet-smelling perfume of sweat: O Nuit, continuous one of Heaven, let it be ever thus; that men speak not of Thee as One but as None; and let them speak not of thee at all, since thou art continuous!" (AL, I:27)*

At the heart of Thelema is the idea of *sunyata*—emptiness, or the Void. This is represented in the imagery of Nuit, the Goddess of Infinite Space and Infinite Stars. *Sunyata* is a label for something that is beyond words, because anything that is expressed in words is an expression of the split mind—it's not nihilism, and it's not eternalism. Hui Neng, the sixth patriarch of Ch'an Buddhism, writes of the Void in the *Platform Sutra* as of the nature of everything, luminous and clear, "containing all *dharmas*":

> *"Learned Audience, when you hear me talk about the Emptiness, do not at once fall into the idea of vacuity [...] the illimitable Emptiness of the universe is capable of holding myriads of things of various shape and form, such as the sun, the moon, stars, mountains, rivers, men, dharmas pertaining to goodness or badness, deva planes, hells, great oceans, and all the mountains of the Mahameru."*[29]

Language can point to an intuitive knowing of the Void (at its best), or obfuscate the matter into a seemingly hopeless tangle of confused, yet very rational-sounding definitions. The writings of

---

[29] From Chapter 2 of the *sutra* as given in *The Diamond Sutra and the Sutra of Hui-Neng*, translated by A.F. Price and Wong Mou-lam (Shambhala, 1990), p. 80.

New Aeon Tantra

the Western sage, Wei Wu Wei, follow up on these ideas in a delightful fashion, using language as a type of *koan* to tire the mind, and eventually force the streaming clarity of the gnosis to break through.

> *"Nothing is a secret key of this law. Sixty-one the Jews call it; I call it eight, eighty, four hundred & eighteen. But they have the half: unite by thine art so that all disappear." (AL, I:46–47)*

The lie of separation is the lie of the individual. At the relative level, yes, we are all individuals. At the absolute level, there is no me, no you, no self, no soul, no nothing. But this nothing is not nihilism, not extinction. The body of Nuit is a vast, glorious, all-embracing matrix—a womb of all potentials, all realities, all *dharmas*, Heaven and Hell, light and darkness, above and below, myself and other, one, none, naught and all. Yet to even say there is "nothing" is to use split-mind definitions that inevitably lead to dualism, and so are way off the mark. The Void is not empty, not full. Language fails us. I am very real on the level of duality, I am one Star in the Company of Stars; at the absolute level, I am truly I, and there is no other. I am all and one, naught; yet this emptiness is a lucid clarity and energy of infinite potentials. In giving up myself, I find my Self. In knowing my Self, I am One, Individual, Sovereign.

Thelema expresses the heart of the matter beautifully. Exoterically, it celebrates the individual. True Will is seen as the summit of individual expression. And for many, this is enough. To embark on the great quest of *Who am I?* is a task worthy of everyone. However, in this search for our identity, we inevitably come to the illusory barrier of the individual self. Penetrating this, a deepening of experience, a widening of the field of awareness, becomes known. As the layers are removed, as we plunge the depths of our being, we find that this True Will is, in fact, of the nature of the universe itself, the nature of clear, lucid Awareness. In the relative sense, there is the Hadit point of consciousness, the individual, and its experience of the continuum at any point in time as reference. At the absolute level, there is the Nuit continuum of *sunyata,* outside the boundaries and definitions of the mind, yet inherently the very self of the self. Thelema, as an individual point of view relating to the whole, contrasting with *agape* (cosmic Love), the whole as the entirety of nothingness, the dissolution into the Void, the union of I and Thou. Yet these two are one; two poles of the same thing; attempts by the split mind at the relative level to rationalize and categorize.

The nondual tantriks of India, such as the Kaula and Trika traditions, expressed this interplay with the dynamic love play of *Shiva* (Awareness) and *Shakti* (Energy). Rather than the negation of all qualities found in *Advaita,* the ultimate expression of the void is found to have qualities of bliss and creativity.

The Radiant Eternity

> *"Now, therefore, I am known to ye by my name Nuit, and to him by a secret name which I will give him when at last he knoweth me. Since I am Infinite Space, and the Infinite Stars thereof, do ye also thus. Bind nothing! Let there be no difference made among you between any one thing & any other thing; for thereby there cometh hurt."*
> — Liber AL vel Legis, I:22

The True Will, then, is the spontaneity of existence. *Jivanmukta* (liberation while still in the body) is the result of this spontaneity. *Samsara* (the material world) and *nirvana* (be extinguished; the state of bliss) are identical, and depend entirely on the individual's point of view. This is a matter of awareness. As Wei Wu Wei writes in *Why Lazarus Laughed*:

> *"Spontaneity is being present in the present. Spontaneity bypasses the processes of the conceptual [aspect of] mind. Reintegration with nature...is the recovery of spontaneity."*[30]

And *"Past and Future are a duality of which Present is the reality. The now-moment alone is eternal and real."* There is really nothing to do, no great arduous path of spiritual attainment to climb:

> *"There is neither creation nor destruction,*
> *Neither destiny nor free will,*
> *Neither path nor achievement;*
> *This is the final truth."*[31]

Sounds simple, and it is. However, there is a catch. If there is nothing to do, why am I not free of the delusions of duality? Why am I still subject to birth, life, old age, sickness and death? If our inherent nature is already that of pristine, self-aware clarity, why am I not a Buddha while I sit and mindlessly watch television? The short of it is that we *are* already Buddha—complete, perfect, enlightened; however, we are not aware of it due to obscurations and attachment to our dual perception. We are conditioned to buying the view that there *is* something to do, and that "what you see is what you get." Our natural condition is one of delusion, of obscurity. As the Hermetic axiom declares: *"Nature, unaided, fails."* Without liberation, we continuously are born, live, die and are reborn on the wheel of *samsara,* an endless cycle of dreamscapes, illusions, fantasies and nightmares. We exist in a perceptual world of

---

[30] Wei Wu Wei, *Why Lazarus Laughed: The Essential Doctrine,* Zen-Advaita-Tantra (Sentient Publications, 2003).
[31] Sri Ramana Maharshi's version of a quote from Shankara's *Vivekachudamani (The Crest Jewel of Discernment).*

duality, and live by split-mind dual rules. As long as we are conditioned this way, we play the roles of the magician unconsciously, automatically, weaving the illusory light beams of *maya* (illusion), spinning an elaborate magical lie of existence.

> *"Reason is a lie; for there is a factor infinite & unknown; & all their words are skew-wise." (AL, II:32)*

We live a dream—sometimes a nightmare—unconsciously, and never wake up. Due to conditioning, we are *not* spontaneous in our actions, our thoughts, our expressions of living. So how *do* we wake up? How *do* we come to know our Self as the star that it is? Elaborate systems of ritual, meditation, yoga, exercise, magick and so on come into use as means to help release our unconscious binding to these obscurations that keep us from knowing and doing our True Will. With full awareness, the opaque nature of the personality is cleansed and consecrated as a vehicle of the Stellar Gnosis, allowing the spontaneity of the True Will to shine through and rule. **The dreamer awakens.**

> *"But ye, o my people, rise up & awake!" (AL, II:34)*

When the point of view shifts to the absolute, when the True Will is lived consciously—with full awareness—the relative does not vanish. The magician continues as before, but with a new point of view, a new perspective or angle into it all. The center shifts from the relative, the dream, to the absolute, *sunyata*. Outwardly, there may be no difference visible, and the individual continues to live life as before. Internally, the magician consciously weaves the web of *maya*, and plays with the plastic point events of *samsara* under Will. There are references to this dance or play *(lila)* in *Liber B vel Magi*. Chopping wood, carrying water. Living the dream, instead of being lived by it. Having full, conscious responsibility for your thoughts and actions. Being a co-creator in the Great Awakening that is Now. From this condition, ritual becomes a willful dance in eternity, the movement of Shiva and Shakti, or Hadit and Nuit, in the cosmos. Existence itself is seen as the love play of the Infinite, and the beautiful art of nature. Ritual as skillful means.

> *"Expect him not from the East, nor from the West; for from no expected house cometh that child. Aum! All words are sacred and all prophets true; save only that they understand a little; solve the first half of the equation, leave the second unattacked. But thou hast all in the clear light, and some, though not all, in the dark." (AL, I:560)*

All of the various rituals, philosophies, religions, beliefs and so on, throughout history, are relative manifestations of the absolute, of emptiness. They are the play of *samsara*. They are the different angles of Stellar Gnosis, each with a different set of keys. For many, Thelema represents the synthesis and height of this current at the present time. The dawning of the New Aeon may be seen as something that humanity—as a whole and individually—must take; a conscious act to embrace the current forces of evolution streaming into the lifewave of this planet and be co-heirs of infinity.

Thelema allows you to drink from many streams, sometimes deeply, sometimes only a sip. Thelema allows you to go deep into the mystery of emptiness, and even leave the mainstream altogether, all for the "continuity of the consciousness of existence," the point of view of awareness. One of the primary values is in the universal application of Thelema. You can know and do your True Will, and express it as a Buddhist, a Christian, a Muslim, or a Pagan; as a carpenter, an artist, a janitor, a mother, a lover; *ad infinitum*. The body of Nuit is all-expansive, all-creative, all potential. She is everything and nothing. She is all things to me, and I am everything to Her.

The Heart of the Master

"But to love me is better than all things: if under the night-stars in the desert thou presently burnest mine incense before me, invoking me with a pure heart, and the Serpent flame therein, thou shalt come a little to lie in my bosom. For one kiss wilt thou then be willing to give all; but whoso gives one particle of dust shall lose all in that hour. Ye shall gather goods and store of women and spices; ye shall wear rich jewels; ye shall exceed the nations of the earth in splendour & pride; but always in the love of me, and so shall ye come to my joy. I charge you earnestly to come before me in a single robe, and covered with a rich headdress. I love you! I yearn to you! Pale or purple, veiled or voluptuous, I who am all pleasure and purple, and drunkenness of the innermost sense, desire you. Put on the wings, and arouse the coiled splendour within you: come unto me!" (AL, I:51)

"Sing the rapturous love-song unto me! Burn to me perfumes!
Wear to me jewels! Drink to me, for I love you! I love you!
I am the blue-lidded daughter of Sunset; I am the naked brilliance of the voluptuous night-sky." (AL, I:53–54)

The condition of *samsara* is often thought of as a disease, a type of schizophrenia. The human condition, living in duality, cut off from our source, is one of blindness, horror, meaninglessness. It is living a lie of duality, cut off from the root of our existence in a mundane, pointless, often automatic somnambulism. The Four Noble Truths of Buddhism address this condition elegantly, and summarize the human condition—really the state of all sentient beings in *samsara*—as *dukkha* (suffering). The message of *Liber AL vel Legis*

New Aeon Tantra

takes the point of view of suffering and attachment as a joyous, conscious dance in the infinity of Nuit, showing both the impermanence of sorrow and joy, of all attachment being a union of ecstasy between the interplay of Nuit and Hadit:

> *"For I am divided for love's sake, for the chance of union. This is the creation of the world, that the pain of division is as nothing, and the joy of dissolution all." (AL, I:29–30)*

> *"Remember all ye that existence is pure joy; that all the sorrows are but as shadows; they pass & are done; but there is that which remains." (AL, I:9)*

As *conscious* participants in the dance of Lord Shiva-Nataraja, we embrace every event as the interplay of energy, a tantrik ritual of cosmic proportion. Happiness, sorrow, desire, anger, pride—all are aspects of the dance, the rapturous union of Hadit and Nuit. The full range of human emotion and attachment, the obstructing *kleshas* and karmic tendencies, are in fact our ritual implements, our *sadhanas*; if only we know how to wield them, for transforming and weaving the magick display of **Light, Life, Love** and **Liberty** that is the **Heart of the Master,** the **Law of Thelema.** For with conscious awareness comes the fulfillment of the True Will.

> *"For pure will, unassuaged of purpose, delivered from the lust of result, is every way perfect." (AL, I:44).*

Chapter 3
BABALON

Figure 4
'The Chariot' Card of the Thoth Tarot
(© Ordo Templi Orientis)

For I am the first and the last.
I am the honored one and the scorned one.
I am the whore and the holy one. I am the wife and the virgin.
I am the mother and the daughter.
[...] For I am knowledge and ignorance.
I am shame and boldness.
I am shameless; I am ashamed.
I am strength and I am fear.
I am war and peace.
Give heed to me.
I am the one who is disgraced and the great one.
—*The Thunder: Perfect Mind*[32]

"The voice continues: This is the Mystery of Babylon, the Mother of abominations, and this is the mystery of her adulteries, for she hath yielded up herself to everything that liveth, and hath become a partaker in its mystery. And because she hath made herself the servant of each, therefore is she become the mistress of all. Not as yet canst thou comprehend her glory.

Beautiful art thou, O Babylon, and desirable, for thou hast given thyself to everything that liveth, and thy weakness hath subdued their strength. For in that union thou didst understand. Therefore art thou called Understanding, O Babylon, Lady of the Night!"

— *Liber 418,* The Cry of the 12th Aethyr

---

[32] *The Thunder: Perfect Mind,* Nag Hammadi Library, introduced by James A. Robinson (Harper One, 1990).

> Omari tessala marax,
> tessala dodi phornepax.
> amri radara poliax armana piliu.
> amri radara piliu son
> mari narya barbiton
> madara anaphax sarpedon
> andala hriliu.
> — *Liber 418,* The Cry of the 2nd Aethyr

> "Thou shalt drain out thy blood that is thy life into the golden cup of her fornication. Thou shalt mingle thy life with the universal life. Thou shalt keep not back one drop."
> — *Liber Cheth vel Vallum Abiegni sub figura CLVI*

In the *Tantras,* physical and visualized worship of women as the personification of *Shakti* is a primary practice. Such rituals may be adapted for the worship of Babalon, and this opens the tantrik aspects of *The Book of the Law.* In this chapter we look at some of the approaches to experiencing Babalon, and explore the implications of devoting one's life to her. We delve into the esoteric practices and symbolism associated with the worship of Babalon, particularly drawing parallels with Tantric traditions and the imagery found in the tarot, specifically the Chariot card from the Thoth Tarot deck. We explore the idea of Babalon as the personification of Shakti, the primordial feminine energy, and work with rituals and approaches to experiencing her directly. In this way the tantra of the *Book of the Law* becomes a living, visceral experience.

In *Atu VII: The Chariot* card of the *Thoth Tarot* (Figure 4) the canopy of the chariot is the night-sky-blue of *Binah.* The pillars are the four pillars of the universe, the regimen of Tetragrammaton.

The scarlet wheels represent the original energy of *Geburah*, which causes the revolving motion. This chariot is drawn by the four sphinxes, representing the four *kerubim*: the Bull, the Lion, the Eagle, and the Man. In each sphinx these elements are counterchanged; thus, the whole represents the sixteen sub-elements.[33]

The four *kerubim* about the chariot represent the Watch Towers of the Universe, and are the guardians of the Rosicrucian Vault of C.R.C. that is hidden within the Mount of Abiegnus, the Mystical Mountain of Initiation. The seven sides of this vault refer to the seven-lettered name of the Great Goddess that is the center of all devotion. What is the Vault of C.R.C. but the very *yoni* (vulva) of the Queen of Heaven? It is to this that the Knight-Monk carries his Sacred Lance of worship across the deserts of the abyss.

The vision of the 12th Aethyr from *Liber 418* records the rich tapestry of symbolism for this card. The charioteer is described as wearing golden armor which may be seen as symbolic of the achievement of the sphere of *Tiphareth* on the Qabalistic *Tree of Life*. This attainment represents the rapturous union of human consciousness with the Holy Guardian Angel, a term Crowley settled on for describing illuminated consciousness—superconsciousness or the "higher self." The act of union was described as *"the Knowledge and Conversation of the Holy Guardian Angel,"* in which the human consciousness and the divine were in accord. *Tiphereth* is associated with the Sun, and the imagery is that of the sun and its radiance seated in the heart. The Adept is then in possession of the Sacred Lance which must be dedicated wholly over to the service of Nuit. The language of the "Knowledge and Conversation" is intentional in the "Biblical sense" of carnal knowledge, as this is indicative of the

---

[33] Aleister Crowley, *The Book of Thoth* (Stamford, CT: U.S. Games, 1993).

blissful union, while the imagery of the "Sacred Lance" gives indications that this union is achieved thorough activation and wielding of the magick fire, which Crowley equated with the power of the Sun (in heaven) and the phallus (in the body). Going deeper, this phallic imagery is a representation of the sexual force present in men and women—*kundalini*. The journey continues across the Abyss as the rider sets his eyes steadily on the prize across the vast desert of night—toward Zion (TzIVN = ציון = 156 = BABALON), the City of the Pyramids. The so-called promised land is none other than the goddess herself. This crossing of the Abyss indicates the transformation of awareness from ego-oriented to cosmic orientation. Rather than an ephemeral, limited point of view, crossing the Abyss opens you up to the vast, pristine awareness of Self. The sense of self and other is no more. As with all Tarot cards, this is deeply symbolic, and the descriptions in *Liber 418* take this symbolism to an even deeper level, filled with rich symbolism that helps to lead the mind to states of ecstasy.

Central to the Chariot card is the image of the *Sangraal*. It is said that this jeweled cup is filled with the "blood of Saints." On the Qabalistic *Tree of Life*, the crimson blood is attributed to the *sephira Binah*, the Great Mother, showing the Atziluthic or superconsciousness influence. It is Her sacred womb in which this Holy Grail is a reflection, as every last drop of blood is to be spilled into Her—the very life essence of the initiate given over to Her love. It is said that to fully enter Her, the solar-phallic Angel itself must be abandoned, or rather given over entirely to Her embrace, as every last seed of starry fire is given to Her. Of this Cup of Blood, it is said,

> "*This is the Mystery of Babylon, the Mother of abominations, and this is the mystery of her adulteries, for she hath yielded*

up herself to everything that liveth, and hath become a partaker in its mystery. And because she hath made herself the servant of each, therefore is she become the mistress of all."[34]

The formula of BABALON is that of *"constant copulation or Samadhi on Everything."* Discussing the Chariot card from *The Book of Thoth*:

> "The central and most important feature of the card is its centre—the Holy Grail. It is of pure amethyst, of the color of Jupiter, but its shape suggests the full moon and the Great Sea of Binah. In the centre is radiant blood; the spiritual life is inferred; light in the darkness. These rays, moreover, revolve, emphasizing the Jupiterian element in the symbol."[35]

The Adept's journey is one of embracing the totality of Babalon, a formula of Love under Will, that unites everything with its opposite. This act of constant copulation is an opening to the primordial self-awareness of reality, a luminous state of consciousness that is entirely present in every moment. The Graal is none other than the sacred vessel of the Scarlet Woman, the Victorious Queen Babalon who was celebrated centuries ago in the gnostic text *The Thunder: Perfect Mind*, and who was foretold in the evocations of Dr. John Dee and Edward Kelly as the "daughter of fortitude":

> "I am the dowghter of fortitude,
> & ravyshed every howr, from my youth,
> for behold, I am understanding, & science dwelleth in me:
> & the hevens oppress me,
> They covet and desyre me with infinite appetite

---

[34] *Liber 418*, 12th Aethyr.
[35] Aleister Crowley, *The Book of Thoth* (Stamford, CT: U.S. Games, 1993), p. 85.

*few or none that are erthly have embraced me
for I am shadowed with the circle of the sonne:
and covered with the morning clouds:
My feet are swifter than the wynds,
& my hands are sweter than the morning dew.*

*My garments are from the beginning:
& my dwelling place is in my self.
The lyon knoweth not where I walk:
neyther do the bestes of the field understand me.
I am deflowered & yet a virgin.
I sanctifie & am not sanctified
happy is he that embraceth me.
for in the night season I am sweete,
in the day full of pleasure*

*my company is a harmony of many Cymballs
And my lips sweeter than helth it self.
I am a harlot for such as ravish me:
and a virgin with such as know me not:
for lo I am loved of many: & I am a lover to many:
and as many as come unto me as they should do,
have theyr enterteynment.
Purge your streets o you sons of men,
& wash your howses clean.*

*Make your selves holy, & put on righteousness.
Cast out your old strumpets, & burn theyr cloathes.
Absteyn from the company of other women that are defyled,
that are sluttish, & not so handsome, & bewtiful as I.
And then will I come & dwell amongst you.
And behold I will bring furth Children unto you:*

> *& they shall be the sons of comfort*
> *I will open my garments,*
> *& stand naked before you*
> *that your love may be more enflamed toward me."*[36]

It is to this Queen of Heaven that we are to pour out our lives in every moment, in every act. The great Graal Quest carries on into eternity, toward Her sacred, starry womb, blood-soaked and radiating with the fiery light of the Rosy Cross.

A central tenet of Thelema is that no one may know the formula by which anyone else's god is found. Others may help show the way, and give advice based on their own experience; however, the core mystery is always unique, individual and highly personal. The invocation of the Hidden God may only truly be found within.

How more so, then, is the worship of Babalon individual and secret? Not for the sake of any oaths is Her love kept so close and dear, although these, too, may play a part in Her devotions. The Love of Babalon is all-consuming, all-embracing. It touches upon every aspect of our life, to the very core of our existence. In Babalon is all power, even as in the Hindu *Tantras*, Shakti is said to be the animating force of the universe, for "without Shakti, Shiva is Shava."[37] Kenneth Grant notes in *The Magical Revival* that:

> *"Babalon, the Scarlet Woman, is the earthly avatar or priestess of the 'stars'; of those kalas which inform the sexual emanations of the magically-trained woman. Likewise, the Beast, her complement, is the vice-regent of the Sun upon earth, i.e. the vehicle of the solar current represented by the Phallus."*

---

[36] *Actio Tertio Trebonae Generalis,* Cotton Appendix XLVI.
[37] *Shava*: Dead; inert.

Again, this concept of "constant copulation" and "all things fornicating all the time" reflects into various strata of meaning.

To worship Babalon is to give oneself entirely to experience of the divine in the presence of every moment: *Sahaja Samadhi*. In this way, the true Vault of the Rosicrucians is found within, and the opening of its central shrine is the entering into union with Her, to experience the naked, awful and beautiful reality of pristine, primordial self-awareness. To know Babalon is to awaken to the luminous radiance of pure consciousness. This awakening transcends the concepts of self and other, opening the nondual experience of reality. Through apparent polarity, unity is experienced.

How can you give everything to Babalon? How do you pour every last drop of blood into Her Grail? In what way can "constant copulation" be practically worked? *The Oath of the Magister Templi* includes the clause, "I will interpret every phenomenon as a particular dealing of God with my soul." With great advantage you can practice this attitude long before holding this grade and without taking the oath. God may be replaced with "Holy Guardian Angel," Adonai, Babalon or whatever aspect of the divine calls to you. Going through the day with this point of view renders even the most seemingly insignificant acts and events pregnant with deeper meaning, helping to awaken the correct point of view. Awareness of the self is key in this practice. The great Dzogchen guru Namkhai Norbu expresses a similar practice:

> *"The recognition of our true State and the continuation of it is the essence of all the Paths, the conclusion of all practices, the pith of all secret methods, and the key to all the deeper teachings. This is why it is vitally important that we seek out our way to maintain continuous presence without being pulled off course. This means: not hanging to the past, not going after*

the future, and, without letting ourselves get involved in the illusory thoughts arising in the present moment, turning inwards and observing our own mind, leaving it in its true State beyond the limitations of past, present and future."[38]

Babalon is the totality of consciousness—the primordial self-aware mind. She is the beginning and the end of all paths, and the very path itself. Working with *Liber Astarte* is another suitable practice to help direct the intense devotions of *bhakti* yoga toward the Mother of Abominations in Her many outer forms.

The primordial consciousness weaves the fabric of all experience, and we are all Her children, and of Her substance. Still, it is in the form of woman that She is most accessible. Psychologically She may be the anima, that aspect of the unconscious that touches upon the darkest, remotest unknown depths of the mind. Consider all women, and in particular those you have loved, and see the Beautiful One looking back at you with Her eyes. Let *"every breath, every word, every thought, every deed"*[39] be an act of love with Her. This practice was developed extensively in the Hindu *Tantras*:

> *"Women are divinity, women are life, women are truly jewels."*[40]

> *"Women are heaven; women are dharma; and women are the highest penance. Women are Buddha; women are the Sangha; and women are the perfection of Wisdom."*[41]

---

[38] Namkhai Norbu, *The Mirror: Advice on the Presence of Awareness* (Barrytown NY: Barrytown, 1996), p. 32.
[39] *Liber Liberi vel Lapidis Lazuli*, V:22.
[40] *Yoni Tantra*.
[41] *Kulachudamani Tantra*, translated by Mike Magee.

New Aeon Tantra

For a taste of the pure bliss of experiencing Babalon, see the vision of the 2nd Aethyr, where Crowley is finally wedded with the Goddess in ecstatic orgasms that render the universe completely anew. For Her love is uncompromising, unyielding and irresistible, a *"song that no one could resist. For in it is all the passionate ache for the moonlight, and the great hunger of the sea, and the terror of desolate places—all things that lure men to the unattainable"*:

> *"I am the harlot that shaketh Death.*
> *This shaking giveth the Peace of Satiate Lust.*
> *Immortality jetteth from my skull,*
> *And music from my vulva.*
> *Immortality jetteth from my vulva also,*
> *For my Whoredom is a sweet scent like a seven-stringed instrument,*
> *Played unto God the Invisible, the all-ruler,*
> *That goeth along giving the shrill scream of orgasm."*[42]

In this way, our Quest for the Holy Graal continues ever onward, that we may aspire to know and experience Her in our every moment, always striving to be stronger and more aware, that we may experience more of Her, and finally, triumphantly, pour our every last drop of blood, our very existence, into Her radiant and beautiful Graal.

---

[42] Passage and translation of the song from the Vision of the 2nd Aethyr.

Chapter 4
THE HOLY BOOKS

"Oh Mother, may all my speech, howsoever idle, be recitation of Mantra; may all the actions with my hand be the making of ritual gesture; may all my walking be the pacing around Thy image in worship; may all my eating and other functions be Homa rites; may the act of my lying down be prostration before Thee; may all my pleasures be an offering to the great self. Whatsoever I do may it be counted for the worship of Thee."
— *Anandalahari, v. 28*

"Every breath, every word, every thought, every deed is an act of love with Thee."
— *Liber Liberi vel Lapidis Lazuli, v:22*

These rites represent a union of techniques from both the Western ceremonial traditions, and the esoteric Hindu and Buddhist traditions. Through a combination of symbolic movements and gestures, chanting, visualization and meditation, the ritual acts as a means of generating gnostic light. The rite is simple enough that it is also appropriate for public use.

The *Diamond Sapphire* may be used effectively with any of the canon of Thelemic Holy Books; however, particular emphasis is put on three—*Liber AL vel Legis*, *Liber VII*, and *Liber LXV*—as these are of particularly intense devotion, and contain a vast amount of spiritual instruction for the aspirant who would Attain the Knowledge and Conversation. Of these three, *The Book of the Law* is, without a doubt, the very heart of the practice and center of devotion.

While these inspired writings make up the central texts of the rituals, feel free to use whatever sacred scripture speaks to you at the deepest, most intimate devotional level. Whether the Bible, Koran, Upanishads or personal writings received from the divine, any sacred words that represent the gnosis, and open the chambers of the Hidden God are appropriate. What makes a book sacred or holy for you? Look in unexpected places, without automatically following what your culture or society dictates. Fiction should not be left out. The writings of Philip K. Dick and H.P. Lovecraft (some of my personal favorites) have been essential in my own work.

There may be some question as to the veracity of working with sacred writings that are not hundreds or thousands of years old, as are many of the *Tantras* and writings of the Eastern mysteries. For some, it may be that length of time and numbers of adherents are keys to authentic communications from beyond. While certainly there is appeal in this approach, it must be remembered that the gnosis is beyond space and time, beyond the ideologies, politics and personalities that most exoteric religions and philosophies endlessly propagate.

As a practitioner of *New Aeon Tantra,* you may make the personal choice to stand independent and victorious against the superstitions and dogmas of the world. As you increase in understanding, experience and your own connection to the radiant awareness of the gnosis, you will come to rest ever increasingly in your own sense of what is right and wrong. Rather than be influenced by external factors and unconscious patterns, or even the whims of popular opinion, you will rest firm and comfortable in your own adamantine Will. This is *svecchacara*—truly living your life in accordance with the Divine Will. Ultimately, this is the prize to be won: the Victory of Self. This Self transcends space and time, and is that very real core of your being that is a spark from the divine.

Svecchacara: living life according to your Will. This is the true Hero's Journey, the path of the Adept. For such an Adept, all Holy Books across all cultures, times and beliefs have a spark of truth in them, fitted specifically for a particular place, time and people.

The *rishi* (seers) who received the *Tantras*—Buddha, Moses, Mohammed, Crowley—all were Adepts who had a direct experience of the ultimate awareness of gnosis, and transcribed that experience into writing. These writings were picked up, and entire civilizations have been centered around many of them.

On the authority of the *Tantras* themselves, it is said:

> "The Tantras however appear and disappear according as they are revealed or withdrawn. Their authority does not depend on the fact that they were published to men on a particular date but on the Siddhi to which they lead; that is, the actual result flowing from them. This result proves the authority of the Tantra even though it were revealed yesterday."[43]

For the Adept who is living in accord with their own Higher Self, and whose life is the very embodiment of *svecchacara,* they may very well receive their own personal Holy Books. This is as it should be, for the gnosis is constantly evolving and revealing itself. Such writings are sacred to the individual who received them, and should be treated with the same respect as you would treat most established holy writings. Needless to say, such writings would certainly form

---

[43] Arthur Avalon, commentary to verse 31 of the *Anandalahari,* edited by Arthur Avalon (Ganesh & Co., 1953).

the centerpiece of your personal work with *New Aeon Tantra,* and should be used as the *supreme* Holy Book in your personal rituals and workings.

Chapter 5
THE TRUE WILL

"The doctrine that 'every man and every woman is a star' lies at the heart of The Book of the Law. Its meaning, that every man and every woman has a True Will, a True Centre, which he or she must discover and express, forms the basis of the new and scientific attitude to mystical consciousness that dominates the scene today."
— Kenneth Grant, *The Magical Revival*

"The term 'Thelemite' has a wider connotation than its hitherto exclusive use in Crowleian literature might suggest. The artist, the scientist, the inventor, the poet, is such only to the degree that he expresses his True Will."
— Kenneth Grant, *Aleister Crowley & the Hidden God*

"We are all free, all independent, all shining gloriously, each one a radiant world. Is not that good tidings?"
— Aleister Crowley, *The Law of Liberty*

The single most powerful message of the New Aeon is enshrined in a sentence of eleven words: **Do what thou wilt shall be the whole of the Law.** This, the *Law of Thelema*, is the ultimate injunction of self-discovery, self-discipline, and individual sovereignty. Throughout the corpus of the writings of Aleister Crowley will be found again and again this message of the amoral sovereignty of the True Will. *Amoral*, as one who lives according to the True Will stands outside the moral constraints of mundane society; and *sovereign,* as such a person is ruler of their own universe, as well as a potential King or Queen of the earth, the very aristocracy of the new Thelemic society.

The Creed of *Liber XV*—the Gnostic Catholic Mass—contains the declaration *"And I confess my life one, individual, and eternal that was, and is, and is to come."* As the cult of the **infinite within**, the *Law of Thelema* declares the birthright of every man and woman to fully know and be themselves; and in so doing, to know and be God (Hadit, the principle of the individual Will, Thelema/Θελημα). As the cult of the **infinite without**, we experience the paradox of our individual Godhead, our unique self-governance, to be in truth the expression of the One, or None, or Naught (Nuit the principle of Unity, which is Love, Agape/Αγαπη). This is perhaps best exemplified in the Gnostic paean of *Liber V vel Reguli*:

> *"I also am a Star in Space, unique and self-existent, an individual essence incorruptible; I also am one Soul; I am identical with All and None. I am in All and all in me; I am, apart from all and lord of all, and one with all.*
>
> *I am Omniscient, for naught exists for me unless I know it. I am Omnipotent, for naught occurs save by Necessity, my soul's expression through my Will to be, to do, to suffer the symbols of itself. I am Omnipresent, for naught exists where I am not, who fashioned Space as a condition of my consciousness of myself, who am the centre of all, and my circumference the frame of mine own fancy.*
>
> *I am the All, for all that exists for me is a necessary expression in thought of some tendency of my nature, and all my thoughts are only the letters of my Name.*

> *I am the One, for all that I am is not the absolute All, and all my all is mine and not another's; mine, who conceive of others like myself in essence and truth, yet unlike in expression and illusion.*
>
> *I am the None, for all that I am is the imperfect image of the perfect; each partial phantom must perish in the grasp of its counterpart, each form fulfill itself by finding its equated opposite, and satisfying its need to be the Absolute by the attainment of annihilation."*

You are at once individual, unique, the God of your own Universe; and yet, at the same time, an integral aspect of the continuum. As Crowley comments to verse I:3 of *Liber AL vel Legis*, man is the "middle kingdom" which bridges the gap between the individual and the Absolute.

The inherent rights of one who is doing their True Will are clearly laid out in *Liber Oz*. This is a doctrine of willful, amoral self-governance; we are each King and Queen, if only we make the great effort to discover and fulfill the True Will, and grant the same right of self-discovery and independence to every other star. The key to unlock this great mystery is to *Know Thyself*; yet to know the Will is not enough; you must have the discipline to live it, and allow others to do the same. As Crowley writes in the essay *Duty*, *"He who violated any right declares magically that it does not exist; therefore it no longer does so, for him."*

Further in the same essay, Crowley directs us to *"[find] yourself to be the centre of your own Universe,"* then to *"Explore the Nature and Powers of your own Being,"* developing in *"due harmony and proportion every faculty which you possess."* You are further enjoined to contemplate *"your own Nature,"* and find the *"formula of this purpose, or 'True Will,' in an expression as simple as possible."*

This "freedom from external interference" is the hallmark of the amoral, aristocratic sovereignty of Thelema; for so long as you are living according to your True Will, the entire momentum of the Universe is supporting you. Going deeper, underneath this philosophy is the doctrine once again of *Svecchacara*.

In the context of Hindu Tantra, *Svecchachara* is a term that encompasses the concept of "spontaneous" or "self-willed" conduct. Again, the spontaneous qualities of this way of living are deeply rooted in the experience of *Samadhi*.

Svecchachara is derived from two Sanskrit words: *sveccha* ("self-will" or "own will"), and *achara* ("conduct" or "behavior"). It signifies a way of approaching spiritual practices and rituals with a sense of personal autonomy, where you act according to your own inner guidance or divine will, rather than adhering to strict external rules or societal norms.

Svecchachara is often contrasted with the more orthodox and rule-bound path known as the Vedic or Shruti tradition. While the Vedic tradition focuses on adherence to prescribed rituals and social norms, *Svecchachara* allows for greater flexibility and individual expression within the context of tantric practices.

Svecchachara means the practitioner's uses their own discretion, intuition and inner guidance to shape and modify not only ritual procedures, but also in life itself. The adept is encouraged to go beyond the scriptural and societal guidelines, and live according to their unique spiritual temperament and needs.

The concept of *Svecchachara* recognizes the diversity of human experiences and the varying paths that can lead to spiritual realization. It acknowledges that different individuals may require different methods and practices to attain their spiritual goals. By embracing *Svecchachara*, the tantric personalizes their spiritual journey, and explores practices that resonate with their unique constitution and spiritual aspirations.

Like the concept of the True Will, *Svecchachara* does not imply a disregard for ethical or moral principles. While it encourages individual autonomy, it is understood within the framework of a deep understanding of Tantra, its principles, and the intentions behind the practices. You are expected to operate from a place of sincerity, purity and awareness of the consequences of your actions.

The concept of *Svecchachara* is deeply rooted in the broader philosophy of Tantra, which recognizes the inherent, divine nature in all aspects of life, including the physical body, sensory experiences, emotions and desires. In this sense, it is cognate with Thelema. It embraces these aspects as vehicles for spiritual transformation, and seeks to integrate them into the spiritual path, rather than denying or suppressing them.

Through the path of Knowing and Living the True Will, the *Svecchacarin* ("one who is free to move at will") aims to transcend dualities, and recognize the divine presence in all experiences, whether those be interpreted as positive or negative. You are expected to fully engage with the world and its experiences, rather than renouncing or detaching from them. This engagement is guided by your own inner connection to the divine, and the recognition of the divine presence in all beings.

When not living in awareness of the True Will, the bonds of the slave religions create delusion, misery and weakness. Consciousness becomes restricted by neurosis. For those who have embraced the inherent freedom of consciousness, the lies of the past are transformed. Shakyamuni's declaration that existence is sorrow is elevated in the face of the ecstatic cries of union; the bleeding heart of the popular version of Jesus is crucified by the glorious solar-phallic fire of the Rosy Cross. The "Knight Monks of Thelema" are to live as Kings and Queens of the Earth, our every act is one of worship to the Divine, and in service to our True Will:

> *"This is the only point to bear in mind, that every act must be a ritual, an act of worship, a sacrament. Live as the kings and princes, crowned and uncrowned, of this world, have always lived, as masters always live; but let it not be self-indulgence; make your self-indulgence your religion."*[44]

As Crowley writes in *Concerning the Law of Thelema (Liber CLXI)*,

> *"Those who accept the New Law, the Law of the Aeon of Horus, the crowned and conquering child who replaces in our theogony the suffering and despairing victim of destiny, the Law of Thelema, which is Do What Thou Wilt, those who accept it (I say) feel themselves immediately to be kings and queens. 'Every man and every woman is a star' is the first statement of The Book of the Law."*

The doctrine of the True Will is a powerful and liberating concept within the philosophy of Thelema. It emphasizes your inherent sovereignty, and the pursuit of self-discovery and self-expression. The Law of Thelema, *"Do what thou wilt shall be the whole of the Law,"* serves as the ultimate injunction to embrace your True Will, and live a life of personal autonomy and fulfillment.

The doctrine of True Will is closely intertwined with the principles of *Svecchachara*, which encourages spontaneous and self-willed conduct in spiritual practice as well as in daily life. *Svecchachara*

---

[44] *The Law of Liberty.*

allows for individual autonomy and personalization within the tantrik traditions, going beyond rigid external rules and norms. It recognizes the diversity of human experiences, and the various paths that lead to spiritual realization.

Living in alignment with the True Will, or embracing the spontaneous expression of *Svecchachara* does not imply a disregard for ethical or moral principles. It requires a deep understanding of the underlying principles and intentions of spiritual practices, operating from a place of sincerity and awareness of the consequences of your actions. From this depth, the *amoral* qualities of the inner self shine forth.

These concepts find resonance in the Tantras, where the divine nature of all aspects of life is recognized. It emphasizes the integration of physical experiences, emotions and desires into the spiritual path, rather than denying or suppressing them. It invites you to engage fully with the world, and recognize the divine presence in all beings.

This philosophy liberates you from the restrictions and limitations imposed by societal norms and dogmas. It allows for the exploration of personal freedom, and the fulfillment of your unique purpose. Through this path, you become the ruler of your own universes, manifesting your individual Godhead while recognizing their interconnectedness with the whole.

The doctrine of the True Will and *Svecchachara* call for self-discovery, discipline and the granting of the same rights to every other individual. It invites you to know yourself deeply, to live your purpose, and to harmoniously develop all aspects of your being. It is a path of personal transformation, where your consciousness expands, and the limitations of dualities dissolve.

By embracing the inherent freedom of consciousness and living in alignment with the True Will, you can transcend the illusions and restrictions imposed by traditional religions. You can live as a king or queen of the Earth, where every act becomes an act of worship and a sacrament. The Law of Thelema declares the divinity of every man and woman, inviting them to shine as radiant stars in the vast cosmic expanse.

Ultimately, the doctrine of True Will offers a profound invitation to embrace personal autonomy, discover your unique purpose, and live a life of self-realization. It is a path of empowerment, liberation and the recognition of the divine within and without. As you awaken to your True Will and embrace your sovereignty, you contribute to the evolution of consciousness, and the establishment of a society where every individual can freely express their divine nature.

Chapter 6
TANTRIK VOWS

In the traditions of tantra, the role of *samaya* (vow or promise) is essential. In Tantrik Buddhism, it is central. *Samaya* is required of the yogi to enter into the tantrik *mandala* of the pure realm, and be able to work with the gods and goddesses that are present.

In all the *yanas* (vehicles) of Buddhism, *samaya* plays a role. With Theravada, *samaya* is of the form of precepts for the monastic orders. With Mahayana, *samaya* is built up with the *Bodhisattva* vows. Vajrayana and Dzogchen take these roots even deeper, *samaya* being at the heart of each yoga. Commitment to the guru is ultimate, and maintaining the promises or oaths made to the guru is essential to realization. In practice you will find that the guru reflects the Inner Guru or teacher, represented as the Holy Guardian Angel.

We see a similar condition in Hindu Tantra, again with the guru being central, and the vow to the guru absolute. As the guru is the giver of *mantra*, and *mantra* is the very body of the Goddess manifest as sound, all work must commence from the center of the vow to the guru. The *Siva Sutras* of Vasugupta, a primary text of non-dual Saivism, gives the very existence of your body as the embodiment of the vow. According to the Adinath tradition (a heterodox sect of Hindu tantra founded by the legendary guru Matsyendranath), the root vow is that of *svecchacara*, to "live life according to one's Will."

Another important consideration is the *sankalpa*. The word *Sankalpa* is derived from Sanskrit, where *San* means "well" or "together," and *Kalpa* refers to a "vow" or "resolution." *Sankalpa* represents the act of making a heartfelt commitment or determination with clarity and intentionality.

Sankalpa is the resolve set by an individual to manifest a desired outcome, or align with a specific purpose. It is a powerful tool used in tantrik rituals, meditations and spiritual practices to direct and focus your energy towards a particular goal.

In the context of Tantrik philosophy, *Sankalpa* goes beyond ordinary goal-setting or mere wishful thinking. It is considered a sacred and potent force that draws upon your innermost desires, beliefs and aspirations. *Sankalpa* is often linked to the understanding that our thoughts and intentions have the power to shape our reality and influence the course of our lives.

The practice of *Sankalpa* involves creating a focused intention in the form of a statement that embodies your deepest desires, spiritual aspirations, or transformative goals. This intention is typically formulated in the present tense, as if it has already been fulfilled, and is often repeated during meditation or ritualistic practices to reinforce its energetic potency.

Sankalpa acts as a guiding light, reminding you of your purpose, and providing a clear direction for your actions and decisions. It helps to align the conscious and subconscious mind, bringing clarity and focus to your thoughts, emotions and behaviors. By repeatedly affirming and reinforcing the *Sankalpa*, you strengthen your resolve and cultivate a deep sense of commitment and determination.

In tantrik rituals and ceremonies, *Sankalpa* is often incorporated as a fundamental component. It is typically stated at the beginning of the ritual, setting the intention for the practice, and invoking the divine energies or deities associated with the specific purpose. The repetition of the *Sankalpa* throughout the ritual helps to anchor your focus, amplify your intentions, and create a sacred container for the transformative energies to manifest.

Sankalpa is related to the concept of the "magical oath," a contractual agreement between parties, a means to an end with a specific set of requirements for it to hold. As Crowley writes in *Liber ABA*, the magical oath *"must be taken for a clearly defined purpose, a clearly understood purpose, and [...] must never be allowed to go beyond it."*[45] The magical oath helps to express the True Will in objective relationships for specific aspects of the Work, and may have many requirements as to time, place, persons, actions and so on.

In contrast to this, *samaya* is a more intrinsic relationship—a sacred vow or commitment that is of the very underlying nature of the subjects involved. Where the magical oath may express aspects of the Will, *samaya* very much *is* the Will in a deeper, more profound sense. It is the "core of every star," a necessary relationship between you and the infinite. The *samaya* of the sun is to be a star in space. The *samaya* of the heart is to circulate blood.

Traditionally, *samaya* represents a profound understanding of your relationship with the divine, as well as your commitment to spiritual practice. *Samaya* can be translated as "sacred bond," "spiritual covenant," or "sacred agreement."

Samaya refers to the vows or commitments that a tantric practitioner willingly takes on as part of their spiritual journey. These vows are not mere external obligations, but are seen as sacred contracts made with oneself, the deity, and the tantric lineage. They are considered essential for progress on the path of Tantra, and are meant to deepen your connection with the divine and accelerate your spiritual evolution.

---

[45] Aleister Crowley, *Liber ABA*.

The idea of *Samaya* is rooted in the belief that the tantric practitioner enters into a sacred relationship with a particular deity or aspect of the divine. This relationship is built on trust, devotion and a mutual understanding that the practitioner will dedicate themselves wholeheartedly to the deity's worship, teachings and practices.

The vows taken in *Samaya* are individualized, and may vary depending on the specific tradition, lineage or deity involved. They can include commitments to regular spiritual practices, *mantra* recitation, ritual worship, meditation, ethical conduct, and the study of tantric scriptures. The vows are meant to be upheld with sincerity, discipline and devotion, reflecting your dedication to your spiritual path.

By adhering to the vows of *Samaya*, you establish a strong connection with the deity, and tap into the transformative power of your chosen spiritual path. You recognize that your actions, thoughts and intentions have a direct impact on your spiritual progress, and breaking the vows would disrupt the sacred bond and hinder your spiritual growth.

Furthermore, *Samaya* emphasizes the importance of maintaining purity and integrity in both external and internal aspects of life. It encourages you to cultivate ethical behavior, honesty, compassion and self-awareness in all aspects of your existence. You are expected to integrate your spiritual practice into your daily life, and strive for harmony between your inner and outer realities.

While *Samaya* involves personal commitments, it also encompasses a broader aspect related to the transmission of teachings and the continuity of the tantric lineage. Practitioners are entrusted with upholding the teachings, practices and rituals of the lineage, and passing them on to future generations. This aspect of *Samaya* emphasizes the importance of lineage, tradition and the preservation of tantric wisdom.

At the relative level, *samaya* may first be expressed objectively as a set of precepts to be kept sacred and true. As you progress, the relationship to *samaya* will deepen and expand in significance. The vow becomes built into the very fabric of your being, working its way into every aspect of consciousness, forging its flaming influence into the very cells of the body, informing the blood with its essence.

According to the medieval tantrik text *Saundaryalahari*, *samaya* even implies a type of worship that is purely internal or mental, as opposed to external ritual. The commitment is akin to the Thelemic *Western Oath of the Abyss* in interpreting every phenomenon as a particular dealing of the divine with your soul. In short, there is no progress without *samaya*. The commitment is central to the Work.

§ § §

Thelema is a "lightning path" of the West, a system of magick, mysticism and philosophy that is the quintessence of several streams of tradition from Eastern and Western sources. With *The Book of the Law* as our root *Tantra*, and the other Holy Books making up our collections of *Tantras, Sutras, Shastras* and so on, Thelema is a complete philosophy and transmission of gnosis—a Western *Tantra*.

In Thelema, the first root, *samaya*, is expressed as **Do what thou wilt shall be the whole of the Law.** To do your True Will, and nothing else, is the core of our tradition. This is expressed by our central *Tantra, Liber AL vel Legis*, in several places, such as:

> "*Who calls us Thelemites will do no wrong, if he look but close into the word. For there are therein Three Grades, the Hermit, and the Lover, and the man of Earth. Do what thou wilt shall be the whole of the Law.*" (AL, I:40)

> "Let it be that state of manyhood bound and loathing. So with thy all; thou hast no right but to do thy will." (AL, I:42)
>
> "For pure will, unassuaged of purpose, delivered from the lust of result, is every way perfect." (AL, I:43)
>
> "There is no law beyond Do what thou wilt." (AL, I:60)

To do your True Will is the root vow of Thelema. And as with our counterparts in the Eastern traditions, this *samaya* will grow, deepen and expand in meaning as we progress in the work, even as our relationship and understanding of the *Tantra* of *The Book of the Law* and associated texts will evolve:

> "The fool readeth this Book of the Law, and its comment; & he understandeth it not.
> Let him come through the first ordeal, & it will be to him as silver.
> Through the second, gold.
> Through the third, stones of precious water.
> Through the fourth, ultimate sparks of the intimate fire. Yet to all it shall seem beautiful. Its enemies who say not so, are mere liars." (AL, I:63–68)

First you have to discover the True Will. You must work through the *kleshas* (obscuring aspects of the personality and karma) to reach the level of spontaneity that is synonymous with the True Will. At this level of the work, the *samaya* is to find your Will, to understand it. Once "discovered," the next ordeal is to follow it, using whatever means necessary to fully embody and live the Will. The deepening of the vow is to use the newfound knowledge, and live life according to it—and not to deviate from it.

Next, with much perseverance comes the Knowledge and Conversation of the Holy Guardian Angel, a deepening of the True Will (or perhaps the understanding of it, depending on the point of view) a millionfold. *Samaya* takes a dramatic turn here, as now the Adept swears fealty directly to the Angel. The True Will is understood as the Voice of the Angel that was, in fact, talking to the Adept all along. This deepening of commitment and *samaya* continues across the Abyss, with the progress of the Magister Templi and beyond. At the heart of the practice, though, is this central *samaya* of the True Will. And with full embracing of the *samaya*, it becomes a way of life, the very life-blood of the Adept.

To what guru does the Thelemite pledge their vows? We don't have the long tradition of lineage masters that many of the traditions of the East hold. In the simplest sense, the vow is always to your Self, the sole Sovereign. Your understanding of this Self will, like the vow itself, mature as you progress in the work of self-discovery. The supreme guru, the *mahaguru*, is the Holy Guardian Angel. Once this vow is clearly voiced and accepted, there is no longer any need for other teachers or masters. (This is not to say that you won't have other teachers, both incarnate and discarnate; however, they will all be seen as aspects of the One True teacher from then on.) A similar pattern is witnessed in the tantrik traditions, where the guru is the symbol and an aspect of the supreme teacher, be it Padmasambhava, Vajradhara, Sri Sri Adinath, and so on.

The second root vow centers on *agape*, and is expressed as **Love is the law, love under will.** Like the Will, Love is central to our gnosis. The all-embracing infinity of Love must inform every action, every thought, every breath. Love is a radiant, luminous divine desire that is the very essence of all things. Again, *Liber AL vel Legis,* provides much instruction on this *samaya*:

> "*Come forth, o children, under the stars, & take your fill of love!*" (AL, I:12)

> *"For I am divided for love's sake, for the chance of union."* (AL, I:29)
>
> *"Invoke me under my stars! Love is the law, love under will. Nor let the fools mistake love; for there are love and love. There is the dove, and there is the serpent. Choose ye well! He, my prophet, hath chosen, knowing the law of the fortress, and the great mystery of the House of God."* (AL, I:57)
>
> *"Beware therefore! Love all, lest perchance is a King concealed! Say you so? Fool! If he be a King, thou canst not hurt him."* (AL, I:59)

The divine love of *agape* is the mystic *bhakti*, a profound, deeply-felt devotion that renders every act done in this light as one of **Love under Will**. Like the understanding of the Will, this Love will come to mean many things to the devotee, expressing itself in countless ways. Again, the injunction from the *Shiva Sutras* rings true here, as the very body itself is a covenant of love between the devotee and the Goddess, who is everything.

The third root *samaya* of Thelemic tantra is devotion to Nuit, expressed as **To Me**. This is shown throughout *Liber AL vel Legis*:

> *"Obey my prophet! follow out the ordeals of my knowledge! seek me only! Then the joys of my love will redeem ye from all pain. This is so: I swear it by the vault of my body; by my sacred heart and tongue; by all I can give, by all I desire of ye all."* (AL, I:32)
>
> *"If this be not aright; if ye confound the space-marks, saying: They are one; or saying, They are many; if the ritual be not ever unto me: then expect the direful judgments of Ra Hoor Khuit!"* (AL, I:52)

"But to love me is better than all things: if under the night-stars in the desert thou presently burnest mine incense before me, invoking me with a pure heart, and the Serpent flame therein, thou shalt come a little to lie in my bosom. For one kiss wilt thou then be willing to give all; but whoso gives one particle of dust shall lose all in that hour. Ye shall gather goods and store of women and spices; ye shall wear rich jewels; ye shall exceed the nations of the earth in splendour & pride; but always in the love of me, and so shall ye come to my joy. I charge you earnestly to come before me in a single robe, and covered with a rich headdress. I love you! I yearn to you! Pale or purple, veiled or voluptuous, I who am all pleasure and purple, and drunkenness of the innermost sense, desire you. Put on the wings, and arouse the coiled splendour within you: come unto me!" (AL, I:61)

"At all my meetings with you shall the priestess say—and her eyes shall burn with desire as she stands bare and rejoicing in my secret temple—To me! To me! calling forth the flame of the hearts of all in her love-chant. Sing the rapturous love-song unto me! Burn to me perfumes! Wear to me jewels! Drink to me, for I love you! I love you! I am the blue-lidded daughter of Sunset; I am the naked brilliance of the voluptuous night-sky. To me! To me!" (AL, I:62-65)

The root *samaya* to Nuit is essential. All is to be done for Her, in whatever guise She may present Herself. Whether I worship Her as Lalita, Kali, Babalon, Hecate, the universe of stars, all manifestation, all women, the Void—it is all aspects of Her body. It is all for Her. As every act is an act of Love under Will, existence itself is thus seen to be the love play between Hadit and Nuit, the perpetual intercourse of Shiva and Shakti, from which all reality is manifested.

To these three root vows may be added the Right View for all practice, which the yogi requires to stabilize their experience of the True Will, Love and Nuit. This view is the shift of one's point of reference from the ego to that of primordially pure, intrinsic awareness. From this perspective, all of reality, both relative and absolute, is perceived to be luminous and pure, already perfect, moving the perspective from the relative ego to the all-embracing, all-pervading center that is everywhere. Again, our root *Tantra, Liber AL vel Legis*, is the guide:

> *"Now, therefore, I am known to ye by my name Nuit, and to him by a secret name which I will give him when at last he knoweth me. Since I am Infinite Space, and the Infinite Stars thereof, do ye also thus. Bind nothing! Let there be no difference made among you between any one thing & any other thing; for thereby there cometh hurt." (AL, I:22)*
>
> *"Then the priest answered & said unto the Queen of Space, kissing her lovely brows, and the dew of her light bathing his whole body in a sweet-smelling perfume of sweat: O Nuit, continuous one of Heaven, let it be ever thus; that men speak not of Thee as One but as None; and let them speak not of thee at all, since thou art continuous!*
>
> *The Perfect and the Perfect are one Perfect and not two; nay, are none! Nothing is a secret key of this law. Sixty-one the Jews call it; I call it eight, eighty, four hundred & eighteen. But they have the half: unite by thine art so that all disappear." (AL, I:45–47)*

The Right View is the experience of Nuit, the Goddess of Infinite Space and Infinite Stars, as the *"consciousness of the continuity of existence." (AL, I:26)* This intrinsic awareness is the orgasm of the interplay between Hadit and Nuit, and the resultant cry of **HRILIU**[46] is the very fabric of existence, the currents of energy that are luminous and void. This is the *Tantra* of *The Book of the Law*, the magus wielding the dual weapons of Will and Love, united with the cosmic consort of infinity; and in their eternal lovemaking, the experience of non-dual clarity is ALL, the blissful waves of orgasm, the very awareness itself, radiating all of existence, all of creation, all non-creation, the luminous adamantine Void.

There are then **three root vows** implicit in Thelemic *Tantra*: ***Do what thou wilt shall be the whole of the Law***; ***Love is the law, love under will***; and ***To Me***. These are united with the Right View, forming the base *samaya*. In the Atus of Tahuti, this dynamic is symbolically shown with *Atu XII: The Hanged Man* (Figure 20), in which the aspirant embraces wholly the True Will, "nailing" consciousness to the cross of cosmic Will with vows of *samaya*, which are the very existence of the Adept.

> "Then saith the prophet and slave of the beauteous one: Who am I, and what shall be the sign? So she answered him, bending down, a lambent flame of blue, all-touching, all penetrant, her lovely hands upon the black earth, & her lithe body arched for love, and her soft feet not hurting the little flowers: Thou knowest! And the sign shall be my ecstasy, the consciousness of the continuity of existence, the omnipresence of my body." (AL, I:26)

There are, no doubt, many subsidiary vows that build up from and add to these root *samayas*, depending on the particular work of

---

[46] Hriliu is the "shrill scream of orgasm." The word comes from the vision of the 2nd Aethyr in *The Vision and the Voice*. It is also identified as the voice of the Dove in *The Heart of the Master*.

the person involved, their capacities, and so on. In the end, the *mahaguru* will provide the supreme *samaya* to the initiate, bringing them into the deepest realms of awareness, from which the subsidiary *sankalpas* will be derived and executed.

In keeping true to the promise, you are led to the very summits of attainment, to the depths of eternity, into loving embrace in the "consciousness of the continuity of existence," the continuum (tantra) of Nuit.

Chapter 7
SOUND & VISION

"Sri Devi said: One may meditate on a visible image, O Mahadeva. What is the nature of meditation on the invisible? Shri Shankara said: O Devi, sound, uttered by me, is the absolute. By pronouncing a mantra with a devoted mind, there is invisible meditation and so forth. Maheshvari, this is true, true, self-evident, undoubtedly."
— *Matrikabheda Tantra, xii:5–7*

"The God who commands is in my mouth!
The God of Wisdom is in my Heart!
My tongue is the Sanctuary of Truth!
And a God sitteth upon my lips."
— Aleister Crowley, *Liber Israfel, v. 10*

Commonly used in Hindu and Buddhist *Tantras*, *mantra*, *yantra* and *mandala* form the sacred trinity of magical tools of the adept of the Eastern mysteries. The sound vibrations of words of power that is *mantra* may be thought of as the active principle, a powerful current of force. Matched with this is the passive, receptive image of the *yantra*, serving as a container for the invoked force, the form by which the current is contacted and shaped for specific purposes. Additionally, the sacred landscape of the *mandala* serves to visually map out the magical universe of the practitioner, showing in symbolic form the primary deities, guardians, attendants and temple layouts on the subtle planes.

Through the proper use of *mantra, yantra* and *mandala,* the *sadhaka* becomes empowered and able to wield change according to will. The traditional powers ascribed in the *Tantras* are *vashikarana* (to bring anyone or anything under control); *shantikarana* (healing, prosperity, protection against negative influences); *stambhan* (paralysis, or to stop enemies and block negative influences); *videshan* (to create disharmony and fights between people); *uchattan* (distraction of enemies and producing obstacles, uneasiness between people); and *maran* (to cause death). An ostensibly infinite variety of applications are possible, reminiscent of the equally fantastic lists of powers in the Western grimoires of ceremonial magick. As an eminent *samaya* (mental) worship, *mantra* and *yantra* are akin to the wand and the cup of the Western magician, using magical speech to penetrate the absolute with ever-increasing vigor, and then allowing the stellar flood to rain into the depths of the lustrous vessel. The *mandala* acts as the astral map and gateway to initiation. It is by introduction to the world of the *mandala* that the initiate enters into successive levels of relationship with the primary deities of the tradition, and is empowered to work with them directly. We find in these tools a sacred sacrament of the stars, as well as a relentless force of magical power and initiation.

In the Western traditions of ceremonial magick, we too have methods by which force and form are utilized to affect the magick of Light. The many lists of Qabalistic divine names in Hebrew, Greek, Egyptian and so on are words of power, akin to the *heka* (magical speech) of ancient Egypt. Similarly, the various lineal figures—ritually traced pentagrams, hexagrams and other images—are the forms by which the elements may be directed, the astral light molded, demons and spirits contacted and directed, and the essence of the divine invoked. The magical *mandalas* serve as gateways to initiation and ever-deepening points of contact with the divine.

Thelema, in particular, is rich with *mantras, yantras* and *mandalas* of incredible power and beauty. *The Law of Thelema,* as proclaimed in *Liber AL vel Legis,* is abundant with sacred words of power and visual forms of the divine.

Mantra

Mantra—sound vibration—is understood not so much as a representation of deity, or even a vehicle of deity, but rather, it *is* deity. The Vajrasattva *mantra is* Vajrasattva. The *mantra* of Kalika Smashana *is* Kali Herself, not a representation. When spoken, the divine is present. There are a seemingly infinite variety of *mantras*—with just as many applications of use—ranging from the invocation of the Goddess, to the acquiring of wealth, to the accumulation of *siddhis* (magick powers), and more.

This wisdom of sound finds a match in the Western traditions of ceremonial magick. Consider the proper method of vibrating divine names.[47] The particular name intoned is *the very force itself!* As well, the "barbarous names of evocation" found in the Greek hermetic papyri are seed syllables—radiant hooks of light that pull forth the current to do the Will of the magician. This may be carried over into the magical name of the aspirant; the magical motto carries a power and sacredness often overlooked.

Mantras embody power in vibration. They are the Logos—the Word of Thoth, the great magician and manifestor of the unseen. Speech itself is *mantra.* As magicians, our words are selected carefully, for each is replete with creative potential. Meanings are both objective and subjective, impressions that rise to consciousness in the fabric of the silence that is in between points of sound. Images

---

[47] See *Liber O vel Manus et Sagittae.*

arise in consciousness from the fertile darkness of emptiness, and vibrate between the depths and the heights into words, syllables and sentences.

Mantras are composed of *bijas* (seed syllables), seemingly meaningless phonemes that were uttered by an enlightened being and recorded by the *rishi* (seer). Kenneth Grant has an illuminating discussion on the essence of *bija*:

> "Mantra yoga or the magically charged vibration of 'sacred' words and phrases is one of the oldest occult practices known to man. The spell or incantation did not always have a rational meaning; more often than not the phrase had no intrinsic significance."

As Wei Wu Wei observes:

> "A mantram is not intended to be subjected to conceptual interpretation; therefore, it need not be given in literal translation. It is not an exoteric résumé of doctrine, but an esoteric—chiefly auditive—medium for the apperception of what universally we are."

Concerning the *mantra* in Tantric Buddhism, S.B. Dasgupta observes:

> "On the whole it seems that most of the mantras...are composed of a string of syllables which have lost their etymological meaning or which had never an etymological meaning. Vasubandhu says in his Bodhisattvabhúmi that this absolute meaninglessness is the real significance of the Mantras. A Sadhaka (aspirant) is to meditate on these Mantras as something absolutely meaningless and this constant meditation will gradually lead to a state of mind where it will be very

easy for him to meditate on the ultimate nature of the dharmas (principle of existence) as absolutely meaningless; this meaninglessness is the void nature of the dharmas and thus the meditation on the Mantras will gradually lead a Sadhaka to the realization of the void nature of the dharmas."

Dasgupta goes on to say: *"In the hands of Vasubandhu, the Mantras obtain a deeper significance than the mere invocation of any particular god or goddess who might confer mundane benefit on us or fulfil some of our selfish desires."*

The idea behind the apparently absurd repetition of a meaningless word or phrase is similar to the theory behind the sigil, which has no linear form that the conscious mind can recognize. By bypassing the endopsychic censor, the vibration is free to return the mind to its subconscious source without its being able to breed images from the *mantra*, for the conception and birth of images would render the whole process abortive. Even the *mantras* which have definite meaning become bereft of meaning in the process of constant repetition. The Tantric Buddhists had sufficient strength of mind to dispense with meaning at the outset. Other traditions were more cautious, no doubt supposing that if the *mantra* was known to have no meaning, the rational mind of the aspirant would rebel at the outset. A simple experiment will demonstrate that even the most ordinary word, repeated continuously, will empty itself of all meaning in a very short time.[48]

In one sense, many *Tantras* are elaborate commentaries on the great *mantras* of the different lineages. *Mantras* (as well as the larger *Tantras* themselves) are often written in *Sandhyabhasha* (twilight

---

[48] *Aleister Crowley & The Hidden God*, Kenneth Grant. pp. 117–118. Starfire Publications.

language)—a secret, coded language. Without the key to their understanding—which is delivered from the mouth of the guru to the ear of the disciple—the intended meaning remains deliberately obscured. A deeper aspect of twilight language is opened up when you leave it in context; that is, rather than having it "translated" into a rational form of language that can be easily understood, the subtlety of the magical language itself weaves a tapestry of symbolic associations in consciousness. The real power of *mantra* is in its subjective weavings of light in the ocean of consciousness. From this, the images and meanings are applied in a manner that the rational mind—the *ruach* below the abyss—may relate to it and play in the eternal dance of sound and color, creating the tapestry of the objective universe.

Crowley discussed the efficaciousness of words of power in Chapter IX of *Magick in Theory and Practice*:[49]

> "*It is found by experience (confirming the statement of Zoroaster) that the most potent conjurations are those in an ancient and perhaps forgotten language, or even those couched in a corrupt and possibly always meaningless jargon. [...]*
>
> *The Egyptian Invocations are much purer, but their meaning has not been sufficiently studied by persons magically competent. We possess a number of Invocations in Greek of every degree of excellence; in Latin but few, and those of inferior quality. It will be noticed that in every case the conjurations are very sonorous, and there is a certain magical voice in which they should be recited. [...]*"

---

[49] Aleister Crowley, *Liber ABA*, part III.

When *mantras* are recited, the proper concentration and attitude are essential as your body, your voice, the air vibrating with the sound—all of this is truly the presence of the Divine One. The mouth, tongue, brain, heart, the entire body, and consciousness are all, at that time, the very manifestation of deity. In divine workings, your very body becomes the Goddess or God. In evocation, the vibration radiates a line of force into the aethyr that resonates with the current of the particular demon, angel, spirit, intelligence and so on. This is one of the reasons why the *Tantras* place so much emphasis on the cleansing of the body and mind before embarking on *mantra* work. In many of the older Hindu *Tantras* are instructions for purifying the mouth, bathing the body, cleaning out the nostrils, and so on. In addition to helping establish good hygiene, and the practical considerations of needing clear nostrils to be able to effectively practice *pranayama*, there is a subtler wisdom here in preparing the living shrine of the devoted into a suitable *adytum* of the Goddess or God being invoked.

Many Thelemic *mantras* can be constructed using *The Book of the Law* and other Thelemic Holy Books. Those used to the melodic *mantras* of Sanskrit may find it odd at first to use the English language as a basis for *mantra*, with its lack of long, flowing vowel combinations, and rolling multi-syllabic conjunctions. However, the *Meru Tantra*, originating in seventeenth-century India, seems to allude to a time when this practice will be more common, and may even be a foretelling of the Western Tantra of Thelema:

> "There will be born at London English folk whose mantra for worship is in the Phiringa[50] language, who will be undefeated in battle and Lords of the world."

---

[50] Sanskrit: foreign. Translation of the *Meru Tantra* by Mike Magee.

The very expression of the "Word of the Law" is *mantra*, alternating the phrases *Do what thou wilt shall be the whole of the Law* and *Love is the law, love under will* in some combination that is significant to you, perhaps in combination with a *mala* (rosary) constructed with Thelemic and other symbolism.

An especially personal application of *mantra* is open to those who know the name of the Holy Guardian Angel. The name acts as the *bija* of the *mantra*, around which other words may be woven; also, the name itself may be used alone.

Perhaps the most celebrated *mantra* in *The Book of the Law* is the Egyptian invocation taken from the *Stele of Revealing* (Figure 1), and which forms the centerpiece of much of this book:

A ka dua
Tuf ur biu
Bi a'a chefu
Dudu ner af an nuteru

This has been poetically translated into English in *The Book of the Law* as:

Unity uttermost showed!
I adore the might of Thy breath
Supreme and terrible God,
Who makest the gods and death
To tremble before Thee:—I, I adore thee!

Yantra

Figure 5
The Sri Yantra
(Photo by Daniel Conrad)

The *yantra* (magick diagram) is a geometric embodiment of deity. Along with *mantra*, the construction (or creative visualization) of *yantras* also serves a similar role of embodying the divine for worship and meditation, or as talismans to attract or confine specific forces. At times it is the equivalent of the Western ceremonialist's talisman, and at other times it serves as the triangle of art in evocation. Countless examples of *yantras* exist, often consisting of various geometric patterns, and laced with combinations of the 51 *matrikas*.[51]

---

[51] The sacred Sanskrit letters. Each letter is also associated with a *shakti*, or Goddess, that has Her own *siddhis* (magic powers).

With tantrik *yantras*, there are usually several initiated traditions of visualization, *mantra* recitation, and other ritual acts that are used to activate the *yantra* and install the deity into it. The *yantras* may be permanent—engraved in gold, silver, copper or other metals—and used in daily *puja* (worship), as with the *Sri Yantra* (Figure 5). They may be made from various flowers, or colored sands, ash or blood; etched in the dirt; or drawn on paper. They may be worn as talismans, or built mentally with creative visualization. To be efficacious and a suitable expression of the divine, a *yantra* must have life breathed into it, and have the *matrikas* of the Sanskrit alphabet adorning it appropriately. Elaborate rituals surround the construction and use of physical *yantras*, and dictate what materials they are to be constructed from, how long they will be useful, how to treat them, and so forth—very much like the magical talismans found in such Western grimoires as the *Goetia*[52] and *The Sacred Magic of Abramelin the Mage*.[53] Used in combination with *mantras*, the *yantra* becomes a meeting ground between the divine and human, as well as the charged talisman to evoke and control a countless variety of lesser deities, angels, spirits and so on.

As the sound element is the force itself, a suitable vehicle or container is required to house the force. This vehicle is the *yantra*. Among the foremost of these in the Hindu *Tantras* is the *Sri Yantra*. As with *mantras*, the *Sri Yantra* is not a representation or symbol of the goddess Tripurasundari—rather, it is *the very body of Her, Her very essence*. "There is no difference." When working with a physical *yantra* that has *devi* (goddess) installed into it, the tantrika

---

[52] Aleister Crowley, *Goetia* (First Impressions, 1993).
[53] S.L. MacGregor Mathers, *The Book of the Sacred Magic of Abramelin the Mage* (New York: Dover Publications, 1975).

is admonished to treat the *yantra* as though the Goddess were present, offering to Her flowers, perfumes, incense, food and drink, light, sound and so on. The deeper commitment is the practice of mental worship, using visualized *yantras* built up inside the microcosm of the practitioner, or macrocosmic workings in which the image is projected into space. These, too, are empowered and treated as the sacred and holy vessels that they are. The *Saundaryalahari*, a *Tantra* of the *Sri Vidya*, in addition to being one of the most lusciously evocative adorations of the Goddess, also gives the mantric invocations and corresponding *yantras* to invoke Her under several of Her manifestations, as well as such sundry objectives as to grant boons of health and wealth, increase sexual magnetism, cause crops to grow, and acquire great learning.

An example of a Western talismanic *yantra* is the pentagram—tremendous force in itself, the embodiment of Sacred Truth, and the key of the Philosopher's Stone. When combined with proper visualization and words of power, it is a formidable presence of Divine Will, capable of effecting seemingly miraculous results.

Within Thelema, we find many examples of *yantras*. Consider the downward-pointing red triangle—the *Kali Yantra* (Figure 17), in Hindu *Tantras*. This is the ensign of Ra-Hoor-Khuit, the very bodily manifestation of the Crowned and Conquering Child Horus. When visualized completely and properly, the activation in the initiate generates currents of force from the presence of the very divine itself. This may be applied to the *marmas* of the body (similar to acupuncture points, but of a subtler nature), both physically and astrally, to effect countless results. As both the visible icon of Ra-Hoor-Khuit and the embodiment of the *yoni* of the Goddess, this "*red three-angled heart*"[54] is the living embodiment of divine Truth.

---

[54] *Liber LXV*, II:28.

Consider also the "Star of Nuit":

"My number is 11, as all their numbers who are of us. The Five Pointed Star, with a Circle in the Middle, & the circle is Red. My color is black to the blind, but the blue & gold are seen of the seeing. Also I have a secret glory for them that love me." (AL, I:60)

This description may be used to construct a *yantra* of the Goddess of Infinite Space and Infinite Stars.[55] This stellar *yantra* may then be visualized on the body, activating centers of power in the physical-spiritual complex of the tantrika. Similar to how the *Sri Yantra* is visualized upon the body, the stellar *yantra* of the Goddess Nuit shows occult zones in the body that may be used to stimulate the *kalas* (alchemical essences). Combined with the Triangle of Ra-Hoor-Khuit and the recitation of *mantras* appropriate to the work at hand, a powerful current of energy is invoked. Applying this to physical polarities is a rite in and of itself, a powerful tool of gnosis—perhaps a veritable *"war engine."*[56]

Mandala

Found throughout the cultures and religions of the world, *mandalas* are images of elaborate, beautifully constructed diagrams, usually composed of several concentric circles and adorned with the symbols of particular traditions. Native American "dream catchers" and medicine wheels, the rose-adorned windows of many European cathedrals, the intricate *yantras* of Hindu tantrism, and the Tibetan Buddhist magical diagrams are all types of *mandalas*. The Hermetic "Tree of Life" might also be viewed in this light.

---

[55] See *Liber AL vel Legis*, I:22.
[56] *Liber AL vel Legis*, III:7.

A *mandala* may be thought of as a type of representation of the path of initiation, showing a progressive movement from the outer toward the center. This progress may be shown quite clearly—for example, in the interconnected circles of the Tibetan *mandalas* around the central palace of the reigning deity. Or the *mandala* may be more representative of the energies worked with, where the actual paths are alluded to or triggered via astral gateways. The path of the soul through the chambers of Amenti in the Egyptian mysteries shows this—a progressive initiation of the soul from the outer, objective world into the deepest subjective shrine at the center.

The *mandala* serves as an iconographic representation of the magical universe, the "magick circle," usually representing the key symbols for an entire school or lineage and their astral matrix. An initiate may not effectively begin to work with deities, guardians and other forces of that area of the universe until they have been initiated or "entered into" the appropriate *mandala*. The rite of *abisheka* (ritual anointing) lustrates the candidate with the sacred nectars of the Goddess, empowering them to ritually enter into the sacred space of the *mandala,* and be formally introduced to the presiding powers and their majestic palaces.

Unlike the *yantra,* which is often constructed by the individual practitioner for personal use, the *mandala* is typically oriented to the larger egregore of the group mind, tying in directly to the aspect of initiatory current that is worked by that particular sect, school, lineage, order, etc. While the design of *yantras* may incorporate *mandalas*,[57] the reverse is not necessarily the case.

---

[57] Again, the *Sri Yantra* is the classic example, composed of several interconnected *mandalas*. It encapsulates the universe at both the macro– and microcosmic levels. It functions simultaneously as the initiating *mandala* of *Sri Vidya* and many *Tantras* (being as it were the very body of the Goddess in

A look at the Sanskrit word is revealing. Some definitions of *mandala* from the *Monier-Williams Sanskrit-English Dictionary* are:

> "*mandala. n. circular, round; A disk (especially of the sun or moon); anything round; a circle; the charmed circle of a conjuror; globe, orb, ring, circumference, ball, wheel; the path or orbit of a heavenly body; a halo round the sun or moon; a circular array of troops; a territory, province, country, district; a surrounding district or neighboring state, the circle of a King's near and distant neighbors; a multitude; group, band, collection, whole body, society, company; an oblation or sacrifice, sexual dalliance.*"

Well-known are the *mandalas* of Hindu and Buddhist tantrism, with perhaps the colorful sand *mandalas* of Tibetan Buddhists being at the forefront. Within the construct of Hindu and Buddhist *Tantras*, the *mandala* is generally a magical diagram that represents the primary forces and doctrine of a particular lineage. In it will be found symbolic representations of the universe as understood by that school, with depictions of the central deities, accompanying attendants and guardians, regions of heavens and hells, and usually a central palace or temple that is the house of the primary deity.

Within the tantrik traditions of Hinduism and Buddhism, a *mandala* serves as a type of astral gateway to an initiatory matrix. Once the *mandala* has been entered, the candidate is ritually guided through the magical dimension of the *mandala*, a type of guided visualization. They partake of sacramental elixirs, are anointed with differing sacred substances, are formally introduced to the guardians

---

geometric form), as well as the magick *yantra* for personal devotion and works of talismanic sorcery.

and presiding deities of the region, and are invested with the appropriate signs, grips and words to be able to return to the *mandala's* realm at Will. In addition, the initiate is given a new, sacramental name representing the initiated state, and having been chosen by a particular deity, is given the corresponding *mantra*.

Subsequent ceremonies introduce the practitioner to further *mandalas,* or specialized regions of the primary *mandala's* matrix. Some of the more complex *mandalas,* for example, will be composed of several individual matrices that are bound together into one great *mandala* representative of the entire school's instruction. In this way, a complete path of initiation is mapped out according to the symbols that the *mandala* contains.

Some of the most powerful *mandalas* among Western occultists are the *Enochian Elemental Tablets,* and the *Watchtowers of the Universe.* Taken together, they form a complete *mandala* of the universe, with accompanying deities, archangels, angels, and countless demons and lesser spirits ruling over their particular regions of the universe. Individually, the Watchtowers each rule over a particular region of the universe, and have clearly mapped out hierarchies of governance. Similar to the corresponding *mandalas* of the Eastern systems, the postulant of the Western mysteries must be ritually "entered" or initiated into each element and corresponding Watchtower before effectively being empowered to work with the elemental energies. Aleister Crowley's *The Vision and the Voice (Liber 418)*[58] journals the specific ordeals and initiations that Crowley had to pass through to attain mastery of the 30 Aethyrs of the Enochian magical matrix.

The **Stele of Ankh-af-en-Khonsu**—also called the **Stele of Revealing** (Figure 1)—is the supreme *mandala* of Thelema. The

---

[58] Aleister Crowley, *The Vision and the Voice.*

very talisman by which the current of the New Aeon was first brought down to earth, the Stele graphically shows the primary deities of Thelema and the prophet of the Aeon, and is encoded with the magick mantric phrases of power in Egyptian hieroglyphics—a truly sacred and powerful icon for the New Aeon. Matched with the supreme *mantra,* **A ka dua**, these are two keys to unlock the mysteries of the Aeon and securely embrace its forces—a powerful and sacred sacrament with the Holy Guardian Angel. Initiation into the *mandala* of the Stele empowers you with the primary keys of Thelemic gnosis—the conscious stepping forth out of the old and into the New Aeon of the Crowned and Conquering Child. You are sacramentally introduced to Nuit, Hadit and Ra-Hoor-Khuit, and their inner worship and expression as powerful, living archetypes of divine Truth.

> *"Above, the gemmed azure is*
> *The naked splendour of Nuit;*
> *She bends in ecstasy to kiss*
> *The secret ardours of Hadit.*
> *The winged globe, the starry blue,*
> *Are mine, O Ankh-af-na-khonsu!" (AL, I:14)*

The Tattvas

From the sun is said to flow a continuous stream of *prana* (life force). Within the Hindu esoteric systems, the *tattvas* (elements), are recognized as having powerful affects upon the flow of the astral light. For practical workings, timing the correct elemental influence is a necessary factor for a successful operation. As just one example, in the Western ceremony of the consecration of the Magick Sword, the Adeptus Minor is instructed to perform the ritual during the course of *tejas,* when the astral flow of elemental fire is predominant.

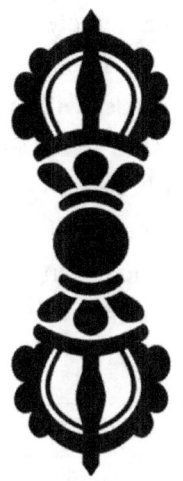

Figure 6
Vajra
(commons.wikimedia.org)

The New Aeon tantrika may wish to incorporate various ritual implements into their practice. One which holds particular significance is the *vajra*. This Sanskrit term means "diamond" or "thunderbolt". In Buddhism, Hinduism and other religions, the *vajra* is a symbol of both spiritual power and indestructibility. It is often depicted as a short, flat-headed weapon or scepter with a double-sided point, and is sometimes ornamented with precious stones or other embellishments.

In Buddhism, the *vajra* is one of the most important ritual objects used in tantrik practice. It is used in various rituals and ceremonies to represent the indestructible nature of enlightenment, and the power of the Buddha's teachings. The *vajra* is also used as a symbol of the enlightened mind, which is said to be indestructible and unchanging, like a diamond.

In Hinduism, the *vajra* is known as a "thunderbolt", and is associated with the god Indra. It is said to represent both physical and spiritual strength, and is often depicted in Hindu art and mythology as a weapon that can destroy obstacles and enemies.

Knowledge of the *tattvic* tides will assist in timing the consecration of your tools, as well as for deeper ritual and meditative work to harness the subtle flows of cosmic energy.

The *Tattvas* (Figure 7) consist of five elemental currents that are thought to radiate out from the sun in continuous streams of *prana*. The order of the elements is that of the *chakras* from the throat down. Their correspondences are:

TATTVA	ELEMENT	SYMBOL
Akasha	Spirit	Black oval
Vayu	Air	Blue circle
Tejas	Fire	Red triangle
Apas	Water	Silver crescent
Prithivi	Earth	Yellow square

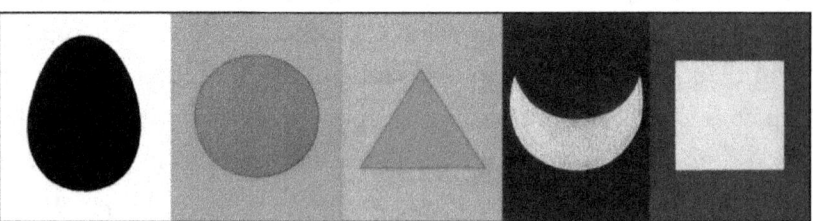

Figure 7
The Tattvas
(Kat Lunoe)

The elemental tides have several models that may be utilized for varying purposes, depending upon the intent and skill of the operator. For most practical purposes though, there is a two-hour cycle that has been found effective, where each element predominates for twenty-four minutes at two-hour intervals from dawn. Thus, commencing at sunrise, the cycle begins with *akasha* and lasts twenty-four minutes; *vayu* begins twenty-four minutes after sunrise; *tejas* commences forty-eight minutes after sunrise, *apas* seventy-two minutes after sunrise, and *prithivi* ninety-six minutes after sunrise. The cycle then begins again with *akasha,* and so on throughout the day.

An element may be locked into place during the course of a ritual. Thus, if a ritual requires the element of air, it may commence during the course of *vayu*. The invoking rituals of the pentagram of the element of air serve to hermetically seal the current of the *tattva* during the course of the ritual in the practitioner's *adytum*. In this way, you do not have to force the ritual to last less than twenty-four minutes before the next *tattva* commences.

You may determine the exact time of sunrise for your geographical location online, or with an app, or on many watches.

With the time of sunrise, it is a simple calculation to find the beginning of an elemental window and its two-hour intervals throughout a twenty-four-hour period. For example, if I were to work with the element of fire today, I would see that the sunrise in San Francisco, California, was at 7:13 am—this is the commencement of *akasha*. We know that *tejas* commences forty-eight minutes after sunrise, so today that means *tejas* begins at 8:01 am. This is a little early in the morning, so I may wish to calculate when *tejas* is in predominance during the rest of the day. Knowing that it began at 8:01 am, I can count two-hour intervals, which means that other suitable times would be 10:01 am, 12:01 pm, 2:01 pm, 4:01 pm, 6:01 pm, 8:01 pm, and so on throughout the night, until sunrise the next day when the cycle commences anew.

The ability to choose an elemental window is important. In addition, you must factor in other aspects of timing that will either be a positive, supporting influence, or detrimental to the operation (or, at the very least, work against all your efforts!) For example, I may wish to consecrate a *vajra* dagger for my practice. It is desirable to perform the ritual during the course of elemental fire, but also to do it on the day of Mars (a Tuesday), and during the hour of Mars, at a time when Mars is forming a powerful angle in the skies and is located in an astrological sign that is compatible with the element of fire; and preferably when the moon is waxing or full! All of these factors should be taken into consideration to achieve the most effective and auspicious timings for ritual work.

For the majority of your workings, especially in the beginning, you may find that it is not necessary to calculate which *tattva* is in ascendance. However, as you become more sensitized and skilled, the desire to fine-tune and accumulate as much support from the universe as possible in specialized workings will become apparent. You may wish to calculate the most auspicious times for the performance of the *Diamond Sapphire,* or deeper work with *yantras,* and so on. The *tattvas* may also be used as doorways for exploring the astral realms and deeper aspects of the psycho-spiritual constitution of the body. Kenneth Grant notes in *Cults of the Shadow,*

> *"There are in all 16 astrol-sexual tattvas or tarots—8 in the female organism and 8 in the male—and they form the basic tattva-pattern, which together with their etheric counterparts form the 32 tarots. These are the primal occult power-zones whereupon was founded the qabalistic Tree of Life with its 32 Paths, and, long ages earlier, the 6423 Fa or principles of Chinese mysticism, where they are identified with the hexagrams of the Yi King."*

Chapter 8
PRELIMINARY RITUALS & MEDITATIONS

Before beginning these practices, it's helpful to symbolically dedicate yourself to the mysteries. Even as the *mala* was prepared as the essential tool of your practice (see Chapter 1), so too must you be prepared for the work by ritually setting your first step on the path of this system. The following rite is an example of self-initiation that may be used for solitary practitioners.

The Rite of Dedication
Preparation

In the east, the *Stele of Revealing* hangs above all other items. On the altar is a single white candle *(shin-*ש*)*, a small bowl of fresh water *(maim-*מ*)*, and incense *(aleph-*א*)*, preferably red sandalwood. These items are arranged in a descending triangle (single point to the west), with the candle at the top left angle, water at the top right angle, and incense at the bottom. Within the triangle should be placed some visible image of the Great Work, such as a statue of Horus, Buddha, Durga, Shiva or any image of awakened consciousness. Thelemites might want to use Cakes of Light for the eucharist, with a Grail of Wine (see Chapter 11 for details.) Additionally, a smaller, second altar may be used to place any images that invoke the aspiration, with fresh flowers, fresh food offerings, and any other images or items that are found pleasing and inspiring.

Alternatively, if you want to keep it to the bare minimum, have a bowl or cup of fresh water, a white candle, incense and a vial of

Abramelin oil. The ideal *tattva* is *akasha*. For added power, this rite may be practiced outside, underneath the rays of the sun, or beneath the full moon. Have your *mala* on hand, either hanging around your neck or wrapped about your wrist.

1. Light the candle and incense. Center and focus your mind, taking three deep, cleansing breaths. See the space you are in filling with radiant, pure white light.

2. When ready, perform three full prostrations toward the east. Then sound a long and resonant AHHHHHHH. Pause, then give the *mantra*:

A ka dua
Tuf ur biu
Bi a'a chefu
Dudu ner af an nuteru

3. Assume the *kavacha* with the formula of *Thelemic Refuge* (see Chapter 1). Recite the *mantra* of the Aeon eleven times:

Om hrung bhagavati vri vru heru aha

4. Say:
> *This shall regenerate the world, the little world my sister, my heart & tongue, unto whom I send this kiss.*

5. Dip your right forefinger into the water and trace a circle on your forehead.

6. Say:
> *I am the flame that burns in every heart of man, and in the core of every star.*

7. Take the Abramelin oil, and trace a cross within the previously traced circle on your forehead.

8. Say:
> For pure will, unassuaged of purpose, delivered from the lust of result, is every way perfect.

9. Take some ash from the incense, and trace the circle and cross on your forehead.

10. Generate *Bodhicitta* (the mind of enlightenment) by reciting the Sanskrit *mantra* eleven times:

Om bodhi-cittam utpadayami.[59]

11. Say:
> By the virtues collected in the three times
> By myself and all beings in samsara and nirvana
> And by the innate root of virtue.
> May all sentient beings quickly attain
> Unsurpassed, perfect, complete, precious Enlightenment
> For as long as space exists, and sentient beings endure,
>   may I too remain, to dispel the darkness of the world.

12. Say:
> I am uplifted in thine heart; and the kisses of the stars rain hard upon thy body. May Light, Life, Love, and Liberty be extended universally to all!

13. Vibrate:

ABRAHADABRA. [*Knock once.*]

Now take a few minutes to sit quietly, and feel your newfound connection to this tradition which has roots deep in the mists of time. Feel the light raining down from the cosmos, gently covering

---

[59] *"Om, I aspire to evolve the mind of awakening."*

you in stellar dew, invigorating every cell of your body, renewing you with radiant energy.

Take time to relax in this meditative state, all the while maintaining awareness of the present moment. Do not worry about the past, or get caught up in planning the future. Do not judge yourself or your thoughts. Just allow them to flow, and bear silent witness to this moment of eternity.

The Lantern of Thebes

An effective and simple method of rapidly establishing an active current of light in the sphere of sensation is to use the Egyptian *mantra* from *Liber AL vel Legis* in conjunction with a Middle Pillar–type practice, incorporating the Four Worlds map of consciousness. In this method, each line of the mantra is associated with one of the Four Worlds, as follows:

WORLD	MANTRA	CHAKRA	SEPHIROTH
Atziluth	**A ka dua**	Sahasrara	Kether
Briah	**Tuf ur biu**	Anahatta	Tiphareth
Yetzirah	**Bi a'a chefu**	Svadhisthana	Yesod
Assiah	**Dudu ner af an nuteru**	Muladhara	Malkuth

The entire paraphrase in English is a powerful micro-ritual. Each stanza may be associated with one of the Qabalistic Four Worlds, utilizing the Gate Sephira of *Kether, Tiphareth, Yesod* and *Malkuth* to launch consciousness into progressively more refined dimensions of experience.

1. Stand straight up, hands to your sides. Visualize your sphere of sensation filling with radiant, white light, with a barely perceptible

field of blue light at the outer perimeter of the aura. With this current of energy coursing through your system, say:

> I am the Lord of Thebes, and I The inspired forth-speaker of Mentu; For me unveils the veiled sky, The self-slain Ankh-af-nakhonsu Whose words are truth. I invoke, I greet Thy presence, O Ra-Hoor-Khuit!

2. *Atziluth. Kether.* Visualize divine white brilliance above your head at the *sahasrara chakra* as a radiating luminescent sphere and say:

> Unity uttermost showed! I adore the might of Thy breath, Supreme and terrible God, Who makest the gods and death To tremble before Thee:—I, I adore thee!

3. *Briah. Tiphareth.* Bring a current of white light down from the *Kether* sphere to the *anahatta chakra* at the chest, where a brilliant rose-gold solar sphere of radiant fire appears. Say:

> Appear on the throne of Ra! Open the ways of the Khu! Lighten the ways of the Ka! The ways of the Khabs run through To stir me or still me! Aum! Let it fill me!

4. *Yetzirah. Yesod.* The current of white light extends down from the chest to the genitals at the *svadhisthana chakra,* as a sphere of brilliant, luminescent, violet light emerges. Say:

> The light is mine; its rays consume Me: I have made a secret door Into the House of Ra and Tum, Of Khephra and of Ahathoor. I am thy Theban, O Mentu, The prophet Ankh-af-na-khonsu!

5. *Assiah. Malkuth.* The scintillating column of white light descends from the genitals to the feet, representing the *muladhara chakra,* where a sphere of brilliant citrine light appears. Say:

By Bes-na-Maut my breast I beat; By wise Ta-Nech I weave my spell. Show thy star-splendour, O Nuit! Bid me within thine House to dwell, O winged snake of light, Hadit! Abide with me, Ra-Hoor-Khuit!

6. Circulation of the Light *(Lantern of Thebes,* Figure 8). Now pause to see the four spheres of radiant light, and the central column of brilliance connecting them all. Reaffirm each of the centers from the crown down to the feet, while vibrating the appropriate *mantra*.

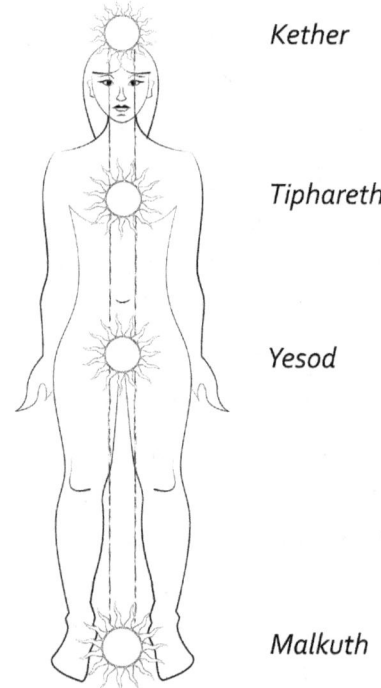

Figure 8
Lantern of Thebes
(Kat Lunoe)

With each inhalation, see a current of light rise up the central column from the feet, until it reaches the crown center. On each exhalation, see the light spray out of the crown center like a fountain of radiance, bathing the entire sphere of sensation in stellar light. Repeat at least three times.

From this point, you may wish to go into meditation, invocation of the Holy Guardian Angel, or other forms of ritual and meditative work. This ritual quickens the astral light, and helps release the several energetic layers of the aspirant, rendering and combining them into a powerful, vibratory symphony of multiple currents of energy. This rite may effectively be practiced once a week at the beginning, then moving to once a day after a few months, and eventually to twice-a-day sessions (morning and evening).

This practice is open to quite a lot of specialization. For example, it may be used to lock in a particular tattvic current with the proper visualizations, and then to circulate the light modified by that *tattva* throughout the sphere of sensation. From this, you may modify the practice for the consecration of implements, talismans, and so forth by charging your sphere of sensation, and then projecting it onto the item to be consecrated.

You may use it to effectively change the atmosphere of a room (external influence), or your personality (internal influence), by attuning to planetary or astrological currents of energy. You may generate healing currents of life force, and apply these to yourself or to others, both physically present or at a distance.

The key to these workings is the right use of breath and visualization in coordination with your *intent* (Will). Add to this the use of word (vibration) with *mantra*, and you unlock a powerful method of practical magick. The adaptations of the *Lantern of Thebes* are manifold and left to your own inner genius for discovery.

The Vajra Tower

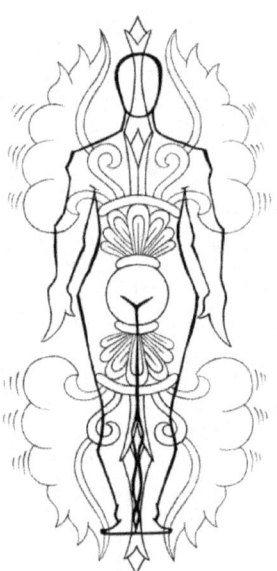

Figure 9
The Vajra Tower
(Kat Lunoe)

This practice is used as a ritual of purification, consecration and connection to the Light of your Higher Self or Genius. A *vajra* is a thunderbolt, a symbol of the power of the gods that represents the dynamic, creative potential of consciousness. By doing this ritual, you turn yourself into a channel of this creative force. A weekly practice is the minimum, with additional cycles as you feel necessary. As your work deepens, you may find that the *mala* is unnecessary for counting, and the chanting of the central *mantra* extends for increasingly longer periods of time—this is encouraged! The ritual develops your capacity to both absorb and radiate more light. The *tattvas* of *vayu* or *akasha* will be found most resonant to this work.

Light a candle and some incense. Perform banishing rituals to clear the space and demarcate a circle.

1. Stand, facing east. Take three deep, cleansing breaths and exhale, letting the breath out slowly, relaxing the body. Establish a rhythmic breathing pattern.

2. Assume the *kavacha* with the formula of *Thelemic Refuge*.

3. Recite the *Four Limitless Meditations*:
   May all beings have happiness and the causes of
   happiness!
   May all beings be free from suffering and the causes of
   suffering!
   May all beings never be without the sacred joy which is
   free from suffering!
   May all beings dwell in the great equanimity which is
   free from all partiality, attachment and aversion.

4. Perform the *Lantern of Thebes*. Circulate the currents of light with the Fountain of Light.

5. See the aura filled with radiant, scintillating, white light. Allow all of the spheres of light to fade from awareness, save for the crown sphere, which grows brighter and continues to radiate pure white brilliance; the bottom sphere, which changes its color to pure white, slightly less brilliant than the crown; and the heart center, which radiates with solar golden fire.

6. Inhale. See the crown sphere radiate brilliant white intensity.

7. Exhale. See the current of white light stream down from the crown to the heart center, which blazes forth in a radiant sphere of golden, yellow light. Inhale, as you focus on the light.

8. Exhale. See the light stream down to the feet, where the sphere at the bottom glows in white intensity.

9. Inhale. See the light rise up from the feet in a rose-gold flame and enter into and embrace the solar center at the heart. Exhale. The light rests. Repeat three to six times.

10. See the aura filled with radiant white light, and the warmth of the golden fire at the center radiating outward with each breath. See the sphere of sensation surrounded by a thin shell of electric blue light.

11. Feel the light cleansing your body, speech and mind of all impurities and imperfections as you bathe in this stellar light, which coruscates through your body, purifying your physical, emotional and mental vehicles, consecrating you completely to the light. As you maintain this visualization, chant the 100 Syllable *Mantra of Vajrasattva*:

OM VAJRASATTVA SAMAYA MANU PALAYA VAJRASATTVA DENO PA TITO DIDO MAY BHAWA SUTO KAYO MAY BHAWA SUPO KAYO MAY BHAWA ANU RAKTO MAY BHAWA SARWA SIDDHI MEPAR YATSA SARWA KARMA SU TSA MAY TSITAM SHRIYAM KURU HUM HA HA HA HA HO BHAGAWAN SARWA TATHAGATA VAJRA MA MAY MU TSA VAJRA BHAWA MAHA SAMAYA SATTVA AH[60]

---

[60] This is the primary *mantra* of the Bodhisattva Vajrasattva (Dorje Sempa). The original was likely in Sanskrit, and has come down into Tibetan with variations over time. The meaning of this, and most other *mantras*, is open to quite a lot of interpretation. One traditional translation reads: *"Om, Vajrasattva! Preserve the Vow! Stand before me. Be firm for me. Be greatly pleased with me. Deeply nourish me. Love me. Grant me siddhi in all things, and in all actions make my mind most excellent, hum! Ha ha ha ha ho! Blessed One! Diamond of*

Repeat the *mantra* for at least one revolution of the *mala*, while visualizing the light coursing through the aura and clearing away all impurities.

12. Generate the *Mind of Enlightenment* by saying:
    With a wish to free all beings, I shall always go for refuge to the Buddha, Dharma and Sangha, until I achieve full enlightenment.
    Filled with wisdom and compassion, today in the Buddha's presence I generate the mind for full Awakening for the benefit of all sentient beings.
    As long as space remains, as long as sentient beings remain, until then, may I too remain and dispel the miseries of the world.

13. See the golden sun at your heart grow in light and intensity, filling your aura with radiance. See everything dissolve into the clear light. Rest in this state of pure mind.

14. Dedicate the merit of your practice by saying:
    By this merit may enlightenment be attained. May we overcome the afflictions of evil, may we liberate all beings from the ocean of suffering, the stormy waves of birth, old age, illness and death.

15. Recite the *Bodhicitta Prayer*:
    Bodhicitta is precious. May it arise in those who have not cultivated it. In those who have cultivated it, may it not diminish; may it forever grow and flourish.

---

all the Awakened Ones! Do not abandon me! Be the Vajra-bearer, Being of the Great Vow! Ah hum phat!"

The Midnight Sun

This practice may be used as a ritual of energization and invocation, suitable for ritual operations in which a powerful influx of stellar light is required as a preliminary to other magical or meditative practices. Similarly, it may be used as a personal rite of devotion and invocation. If you are working with the tattvic currents, *apas* may be found to have the most affinity.

Figure 10
Harpocrates Giving The Sign of Silence
(Kat Lunoe)

1. Stand, facing east. Take three deep cleansing breaths and exhale, letting the breath out slowly, relaxing the body. Establish a rhythmic breathing pattern.

2. Assume *The Sign of Silence* (Figure 10). See yourself in the form of the Divine Child Harpocrates, standing upon two crocodiles afloat in the Celestial Nile (cf. Atu XX of the *Thoth Tarot*, the

Aeon card). Visualize your entire form encased in an egg of fluidic, blue astral water. Proceed after the protective Silence is firmly established.

3. Drop your arms to your sides, releasing the previous visualization. See a vast, dark ocean with no waves. It is night, and the sky is dark and filled with a myriad of radiating stars. During the following sequence, visualize the sun rising above the waters in the east with the brilliance of a Golden Dawn. By the completion of the third line, the sun will be in all its glory at the zenith of the sky, radiating streams of light in all directions, in the middle of the night:

4. Assume the *kavacha* with the formula of *Thelemic Refuge*.

5. Cross your arms over your chest, right over left, and say:
   Above, the gemmed azure is
   The naked splendour of Nuit; She bends in ecstasy to kiss
   The secret ardours of Hadit.
   The winged globe, the starry blue,
   Are mine, O Ankh-af-na-khonsu! (AL, I:14)

6. Drop the arms to the sides. Visualize the crown center as an intense pulsating sphere of white brilliance.

7. Inhale. As the breath is drawn in, a shaft of radiance descends from the top of the head to the heart, where it expands into a sphere of golden yellow light.

8. Exhale. As the breath is released, the shaft of brilliance descends from the heart to the feet, where it expands into a sphere of brilliant whiteness.

9. Inhale. As the breath is drawn in, a reflux charge of intense rose-gold flame rises from the feet and passes into the heart center.

10. Exhale. The light rests.

Repeat the sequence of steps 3–5 five, six, or eleven times.

11. Concentrate on the heart center. The central solar-nucleus remains quite distinct as a blazing and vibrant inner sun, but emits a powerful radiance that steadily grows until the total sphere of sensation is charged with golden yellow light.

12. Give the *Sign of Typhon-Apophis* (the "Trident", Figure 11, below), striving with all of your being to aspire unto the Light, while invoking:

> *I am the Heart; and the Snake is entwined*
> *About the invisible core of the mind.*
> *Rise, O my snake! It is now is the hour*
> *Of the hooded and holy ineffable flower.*
> *Rise, O my snake, into brilliance of bloom*
> *On the corpse of Osiris afloat in the tomb!*
> *O heart of my mother, my sister, mine own,*
> *Thou art given to Nile, to the terror Typhon!*
> *Ah me! but the glory of ravening storm*
> *Enswathes thee and wraps thee in frenzy of form.*
> *Be still, O my soul! that the spell may dissolve*
> *As the wands are upraised, and the aeons revolve.*
> *Behold! in my beauty how joyous Thou art,*
> *O Snake that caresses the crown of mine heart!*
> *Behold! we are one, and the tempest of years*
> *Goes down to the dusk, and the Beetle appears.*
> *O Beetle! the drone of Thy dolorous note*
> *Be ever the trance of this tremulous throat!*
> *I await the awaking! The summons on high*
> *From the Lord Adonai, from the Lord Adonai!*[61]

---

[61] *Liber Cordis Cincti Serpente sub figura ADNI (Liber LXV)*, I:1.

13. Assume *The Sign of Baphomet* (the "Chalice", Figure 12, below), allowing the stellar dew to descend into you, relaxing the invocation and allowing the light to descend and enter your heart, while saying:

> *I am uplifted in thine heart; and the kisses of the stars rain hard upon thy body. (AL, I:62)*

14. After a pause, cross your arms over your chest, right over left, and recite slowly:

> *For pure will, unassuaged of purpose, delivered from the lust of result, is every way perfect. (AL, I:44)*
> *I am the flame that burns in every heart of man, and in the core of every star. (AL, I:6)*
> *I am alone: there is no God where I am. (AL, I:23)*

15. Meditate in the Silence.

When you are done, absorb all of the light into the heart center with the Sign of Silence, and say:

> *O land beyond honey and spice and all perfection! I will dwell therein with my Lord forever.*[62]
> *There is a splendour in my name hidden and glorious, as the sun of midnight is ever the son. Aum Ha. (AL, I:62)*

---

[62] Ibid. V:60.

The Victorious City

Bes-na-Maut my breast I beat;
By wise Ta-Nech I weave my spell.
Show thy star-splendour, O Nuit!
Bid me within thine House to dwell,
O winged snake of light, Hadit!
Abide with me, Ra-Hoor-Khuit![63]

Now riseth Ra-Hoor-Khuit, and dominion is established in the Star of the Flame.
Also is the Star of the Flame exalted, bringing benediction to the universe.[64]

The ritual of the Victorious City is a specialized practice. An adaptation of A∴A∴ *Liber Samekh*, it should only be performed once a month, during the course of the waxing gibbous or full moon. For the *tattvas, tejas* or *akasha* is most appropriate.

Incense of Abramelin or red sandalwood should be lit. Flowers, a bowl of water, and a white candle should be present on the altar. As always, the *mala* should be worn around your neck or wrist.

1. Stand, facing east. Take three deep cleansing breaths and exhale. Let the breath out slowly, relaxing the body. Establish a rhythmic breathing pattern.

2. Assume *The Sign of Silence* (Figure 10). See yourself in the form of the Divine Child Harpocrates, standing upon two crocodiles afloat in the Celestial Nile (cf. Atu XX of the *Thoth Tarot*, the Aeon card). Visualize your entire form encased in an egg of fluidic,

---

[63] *Liber CCXX*, III:38.
[64] *Liber CCXXXI*, vv. 4–5.

blue, astral water. Proceed after the protective Silence is firmly established.

3. Drop your arms to your sides, and release the previous visualization. See a vast, dark ocean with no waves. It is night, and the sky is dark and filled with a myriad of radiating stars. During the following sequence, visualize the sun rising above the waters in the east with the brilliance of a Golden Dawn. By the completion of the recitation, the sun will be in all its glory at the zenith of the sky, radiating streams of light in all directions, in the middle of the night:

4. Assume the *kavacha* with the formula of *Thelemic Refuge*.

5. Drop your arms to your sides. Visualize the crown center *(Kether)* as an intense pulsating sphere of white brilliance.

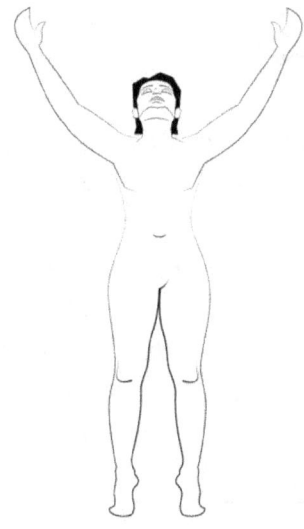

Figure 11
The Sign of Typhon-Apophis
(Kat Lunoe)

6. Give the *Sign of Typhon-Apophis*, striving with all of your being to aspire unto the light, while invoking:

> *Thee I invoke, the Bornless One.*
> *Thee, that didst create the Earth and the Heavens.*
> *Thee, that didst create the Night and the Day.*
> *Thee, that didst create the darkness and the Light.*
> *Thou art ASAR UN-NEFER,[65] whom no one hath seen at any time.*
> *Thou art IA-BESZ.[66]*
> *Thou art IA-APOPHRASZ.[67]*
> *Thou hast distinguished between the Just and the Unjust.*
> *Thou didst make the female and the male.*
> *Thou didst produce the seed and the fruit.*
> *Thou didst form humanity to love one another, and to hate one another.*
> *I am [Motto], thy Chosen One, unto whom Thou didst commit Thy mysteries, the Radiant Current of the Stellar Gnosis.*
> *Thou didst produce the moist and the dry, and that which nourisheth all created Life.*
> *Hear Thou me, for I am the Angel of NU, Angel of HAD, Angel of RA-HOOR-KHUT: this is Thy True Name, handed down to the Mes Khut Ukha.[68]*

---

[65] "Myself made perfect." Replace this with the name of the Holy Guardian Angel, if known.

[66] "The Truth in matter."

[67] "The Truth in motion."

[68] "Children of the radiant darkness." The womb of night, or Nuit, the Void of *sunyata*, the stellar radiance of Her Body as deepest space. This is a technical

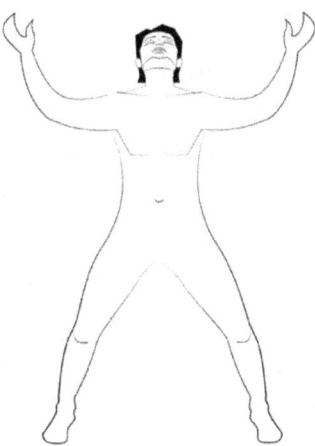

Figure 12
The Sign of Baphomet
(Kat Lunoe)

7. Assume the *Sign of Baphomet,* allowing the stellar dew to descend into you, relaxing the invocation and allowing the light to descend and enter into your heart. Maintain this as long as desired, then say slowly:

> ***This*** *is the Lord of the Gods.*
> ***This*** *is the Lord of the Universe.*
> ***This*** *is He whom the Winds fear.*
> ***This*** *is He, Who, having made Voice by His commandment, is Lord of all Things;* **King, Ruler, and Helper!**

8. After a pause, assume again the *Sign of Typhon-Apophis.* See a blaze of radiant, stellar light coruscating from out of your heart center in all directions, inflaming you with starry fire while saying:

---

phrase from ancient Egyptian that Dedicants of the Company of Heaven explore.

> I am He! the Bornless Spirit! having sight in the feet: Strong, and the Immortal Fire!
> I am He! the Truth!
> I am He! Who hate that evil should be wrought in the World!
> I am He, that lighteneth and thundereth!
> I am He, from whom is the Shower of the Life of Earth!
> I am He, whose mouth ever flameth!
> I am He, the Begetter and Manifester unto the Light!
> I am He, The Grace of the Worlds!
> "The Heart Girt with a Serpent" is my name!
> Come thou forth, and follow me: and make all Spirits subject unto Me, so that every Spirit of the Firmament, and of the Ether, upon the Earth and under the Earth, on dry Land, or in the Water, of Whirling Air or of Rushing Fire, and every Spell and scourge of God the Vast One may be obedient unto me!

9. Assume again the *Sign of Baphomet*, the currents of stellar radiance descending gently, a fountain of starry light, into your being. See your sphere of sensation ablaze with the brilliant light.

10. See yourself seated on a Lotus throne within a *Diamond Vajra* (Figure 13) over a full moon. The *Vajra* slowly rotates clockwise in the depths of space. Light beams stream continuously from your heart, and are matched with brilliant rose-golden fire from the *Vajra*, flowing out into the universe in all directions. Maintain this visualization, and recite the *mantra* of Horus for at least one revolution of the *mala;* it may be extended for as long as desired:

Aum Heru Mani Padme Hum.[69]

---

[69] "Aum, Heru (Horus), the Jewel in the Lotus."

Figure 13
Diamond Vajra
(Kat Lunoe)

11. As the *mantra* fades, allow the visualization to dissolve into your heart. Gradually see all of the light refocus into the heart center with the *Sign of Silence,* leaving a warm afterglow over your entire body.

12. Ring the bell and close with the intonation:

IAO SABAO.

Such are the Words!

The Pool of Reflection

This practice helps break down the illusion of separation, and gives an immediate taste of expanded consciousness. The effects can be almost psychedelic at times—even unnerving—when you feel as though your point of reference has moved "outside of your head" and into an expansive, undefined space. Ideally, do this with a partner, but you can also perform it alone with a mirror.

1. Perform any preliminaries to prepare the space. Incense, candles and any other preparations may be conducted as desired.

2. Sit comfortably with your spine erect but not overextended. Look into your partner's eyes, or if you are using a mirror look into the mirror reflection of your eyes. Eye contact should be maintained for the duration of the ritual, but don't strain. It's ok to blink; you are not trying to forcefully stare. Just let the vision be relaxed, without strain.

3. Breathe in slowly together, and then exhale, feeling your body and mind relax. Repeat three times to remove any tension and get into a calm state. Now establish an easy, relaxing breath. If working with a partner, as one breathes out, the other breathes in, so the breathing is synchronized.

4. Chant the **A ka dua** *mantra* together slowly, for at least one round of the *mala*. You could also set a timer and use that instead of a *mala* (start with 11 minutes).

5. Remain in Silence. Gaze into each other's eyes, while silently asking the question, *Who am I?*

6. Do not judge. Do not criticize. Do not analyze. Allow all thoughts that well up to be processed, without attaching yourself to them or following them. They are bubbles, impermanent, transitory waves in the Ocean of Bliss. When you find your mind wandering,

gently bring it back to awareness of your partner's eyes and the question, *Who am I?*

7. Eventually, when you are ready, conclude the practice. How do you know when you are ready? This is a subjective call that will need to be determined by both you and your partner. You may notice a change in consciousness or attitude, or have a strong urge to start moving around. Or, you may both just feel that the meditation is complete. If you are with a partner, you may feel the need to embrace, as the emotions stirred up in this practice can be powerful. Share any feelings that come up, as thou Will.

When ready, one will say:

Do what thou wilt shall be the whole of the Law.

The other will respond:

Love is the law, love under will.

Together say:

There is no law beyond: Do what thou wilt.

Close as you feel appropriate.

Chapter 9
THE DIAMOND SAPPHIRE GEM OF RADIANT LIGHT

"This shall regenerate the world, the little world my sister, my heart & my tongue, unto whom I send this kiss."
— *Liber AL vel Legis, i:53*

The *Diamond Sapphire Gem of Radiant Light* is the central rite of *New Aeon Tantra*. It is intended for group work, but may be modified for individual use. Although the practices included in the previous chapter prepare you to serve as an Officiant in this rite, the ritual is suitable for participants with any level of skill or experience.

At the core of the ritual is the experience of the great Bliss of Self Realization, expressed as the radiating light of a cosmic sapphire. Sapphires have been revered and associated with various mythical and magical qualities in different cultures throughout history. Here are some examples:

In ancient Persia, sapphires were believed to protect the wearer from envy and harm. They were considered a symbol of divine favor and were often worn by royalty and those in positions of power. In Greek and Roman mythology, sapphires were associated with the god Apollo. They were believed to possess the power to bring wisdom, truth and spiritual enlightenment. It was also thought that sapphires could protect against evil and curses. In Hindu mythology, sapphires were considered sacred gems associated with Saturn

(Shani). They were believed to have the power to ward off negative energies, bring good fortune, and enhance spiritual practices. In Buddhist teachings, it is believed that sapphires can help purify the mind, promote tranquility, and support meditation and spiritual practices. They are often used as a focus point during meditation. During the Middle Ages, sapphires were believed to have a wide range of magical properties, such as protection against sorcery, witchcraft and evil spirits. Sapphires were also associated with loyalty, faithfulness and love. In Islamic tradition, sapphires were highly valued and considered auspicious. They were believed to bring blessings, protection and divine favor. Sapphires were associated with the Prophet Muhammad, and it was believed that the stone would darken or brighten depending on the wearer's piety. In ancient Egypt, sapphires were associated with the sky goddess Nut. They symbolized the heavens and were believed to bring spiritual enlightenment and protection. Native American tribes held sapphires in high regard, and believed they possessed healing and protective qualities. The stone was thought to bring peace, wisdom and harmony to the wearer.

This cosmic bliss—Gnosis—expresses itself in freedom, creativity and spontaneity—*Svecchacara*. This is the true Art of the Wise. As Kenneth Grant discusses in *Outside the Circles of Time*, this expression of the Gnosis is rippling across consciousness:

> *"The fundamental thesis of this stellar or nuclear art is that anti-matter, non-being, and absence are the source of all objects, all being, all presence. The interaction of the twin poles of genius operating in the fully polarized magical entity will create a nuclear consciousness which, in its explosive impact on the mind, will disintegrate the concepts of being and of non-being. The resulting transcendent experience of total Beauty,*

total Bliss, will 'regenerate the world, the little world my sister'—our insignificant planet—creating in its violently disruptive vortex of power an identity of God and Man as a supreme absence capable of generating instantaneously, and on all levels, every conceivable time and every conceivable space simultaneously, or not at all."

In this chapter we look deeply into the *Diamond Sapphire*, exploring some of the ritual mechanics and background that goes into the performance of the rite. This chapter is largely an elaboration of *Rivers of Fire, Water and Air*, a private paper circulated to people working with this material. These "rivers" make up a central part of the visualized astral landscape where the ritual is conducted, and also refer to the three primary elements and their corollaries in the Hindu concept of the *gunas* (qualities). This trinity of influences continues to reflect upon itself in further combinations, one of the most important being that of the three *shaktis* (powers): *iccha* (will), *jnana* (knowledge), and *kriya* (action).

In group work, one person acts as the Officiant who leads the group, and is in charge of the overall performance and pace of the ritual. The Officiant should have previously gone through the *Rite of Dedication* (see Chapter 8). Originally, groups would perform the Diamond Sapphire workings weekly on Sunday. This was chosen since Sunday is under the regency of Sol, the visible image of the Lord of the Universe, and a symbol of the Holy Guardian Angel. Over time this changed for many groups, moving to a monthly frequency, oriented to the phase of the moon. The lunar workings bring in more of a magical and astral atmosphere to the ritual, as well as aligning closely with historical tantrik antecedents.

The rite may be effectively performed in a wide variety of environments. At the simplest, a room may be converted into the *adytum* that will provide enough space to comfortably seat all the participants. The setup is intentionally kept simple and to a minimum of requirements, while leaving enough flexibility for individual creativity and elaboration.

The underlying symbolism of the ritual is that of the union of the human and the divine, the opening up of enlightenment (cosmic consciousness), or the opening of the *ruach* (intellect, or the rational mind) to Briatic consciousness, associated with the Knowledge and Conversation of the Holy Guardian Angel. For this reason, the ritual is centered around the symbolism of the hexagram as the union of fire and water, again showing the union of the human and the divine.

The *adytum* faces east, the direction of the rising sun, and a symbol of the rising light of divine consciousness, or enlightenment.

The *Stele of Revealing* (Figure 1) is placed in the east, at the highest point above all other items. It is a graphical representation of the primary three-in-one divinity of Thelema, showing Nuit, Hadit and Ra-Hoor Khuit (the active aspect of Heru-ra-ha, the initiating Lord of the Universe, or the Holy Guardian Angel). Thus, the Stele serves as a visual focus of devotion.

The altar may be a simple table, large enough to hold the ritual items. It may be covered with a white cloth to symbolize the purity and sacredness of the work, with gold trim to emphasize the connection to *Tiphareth,* the sphere of the sun.

The three primary altar implements are the candle, a bowl of water, and incense. These are arranged in a descending triangle at the center of the altar *(Red Three-Angled Heart,* Figure 15, below). The triangle, with the single point down, represents the fiery descent of spirit into the *adytum*—and therefore into the consciousness of all—as well as the watery or reflective and intuitive nature of the *Neshamah*, or superconsciousness—thus a symbol of the hexagram, the sun, and *Tiphareth*.

Figure 14
Diamond Sapphire Altar
(Kat Lunoe)

Preparation

In the east, the *Stele of Revealing* is hanging above all other items. On the altar is a single white candle *(shin-*שׁ*)*, a small bowl of fresh water *(maim-*מ*)*, and incense *(aleph-*א*)*, preferably red sandalwood.

These items are arranged in a descending triangle (single point to the west), with the candle at the top left angle, water at the top right angle, and the incense at the bottom. Within the triangle should be placed some visible image of the Great Work, such as a statue of Horus, Buddha, Durga, Shiva or any other image of awakened consciousness. Thelemites might want to use Cakes of Light for the eucharist, with a Grail of Wine (see Chapter 11 for details). Additionally, a smaller second altar may be used to place any images that invoke the aspiration, with fresh flowers, fresh food offerings, and any other images or items that are found pleasing and inspiring.

Heart of the Sun

As a particular emblem of Heru-ra-ha, the descending triangle is often depicted in scarlet red, showing its fiery spiritual nature. When viewed in this light, the top right angle is attributed to *Chesed*, the top left to *Geburah*, and the single bottom point to *Tiphareth*, showing the composite nature of the Lord of the Universe as being primarily solar—or stellar—in nature, with dual influences of water and fire, or Mercy (Hoor-Paar-Kraat) and Severity (Ra-Hoor-Khuit). This is the *"red three-angled heart"* referred to in chapter II, verse 28, of *Liber Cordis Cincti Serpente*:

> The red three-angled heart hath been set up in Thy shrine; for the priests despised equally the shrine and the god.

It is also the *"Heart of Blood"* referred to in chapter V, verse 42, of *Liber Liberi vel Lapidis Lazuli*:

> There is the Heart of Blood, a pyramid reaching its apex down beyond the Wrong of the Beginning.

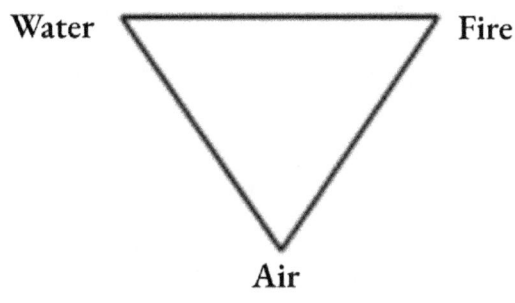

Figure 15
Red Three-Angled Heart

The heart is another cognate symbol of *Tiphareth*, and the attainment symbolized by the union of fire and water—the divine and the human. Similarly, blood is considered to be the essence of life, the medium by which the solar current of *prana* (life force) is brought into our bodies.

The descending triangle is also an image of the *Yoni Mudra*, which forms the basis of a great many *yantras* and *mandalas* of the East, particularly of the Hindu tantrikas. *Yantras* are considered to be geometric expressions of the deity itself—a manifestation of the divine in the form of linear expression. The *Yoni Mudra* (Figure 16) is the primary form of the *Kali Yantra* (Figure 17), representing the divine feminine force *(Shakti)* that informs the universe. This *mudra* (a ritual gesture with the body) also forms the central design for the *Sri Yantra*, a representation of the Goddess in highest tantrik science. The *Yoni Mudra* is also called the *Mudra of Union*.

Figure 16
Yoni Mudra (Mudra of Union)
(Kat Lunoe)

Figure 17
Kali Yantra
(Kat Lunoe)

Trinity of Elements

The three implements that form the triangle on the altar are the candle, a bowl of water, and incense. These are attributed to fire, water and air, respectively. This also shows the attribution to the letters of IHVH: *Yod*—fire—Father—*Atziluth*; *Heh*—water—Mother—*Briah*; and *Vav*—air—Son—*Yetzirah*. The final *Heh*, attributed to earth, the Daughter, and *Assiah*, is represented as the entire combination of elements solidified into manifestation. A similar distribution of the elements may be seen in the *Tree of Life*, wherein the Root of Air is in *Kether*, the Root of Fire in *Chokmah*, and the Root of Water in *Binah*. The elements are mirrored down into the lower Sephiroth, finally coalescing at *Malkuth* as earth, the combination of all three elements.

The candle represents a fire triangle, the element of activity and active aspiration toward the divine that may be physically symbolized in the assumption of *The Sign of Typhon-Apophis* (Figure 11). The bowl of water represents a water triangle, showing the open, receptive, passive act of allowing the divine influence to descend and enter into the practitioner, symbolically represented in *The Sign of Baphomet* (Figure 12), or Isis in Welcome. The two triangles united form the solar hexagram of *Tiphareth*, attributed to air and the incense, which may be symbolized effectively in *The Sign of Osiris Risen* (Figure 18). The altar arrangement, therefore, shows symbolically one of the simplest, most effective formulas for invoking the divine presence of the Holy Guardian Angel.

Figure 18
The Sign of Osiris Risen
(Kat Lunoe)

The elements of fire, water and air are associated with the three Mother Letters of the Hebrew alphabet—*shin* (ש), *maim* (מ) and *aleph* (א)—and contain a wealth of symbolism both individually and collectively. The three Mother Letters are associated with the three *gunas* of Hindu symbology: *rajas* (activity), *tamas* (inertia), and *sattva* (lucidity). These, in turn, are associated with the three-in-one divinity of Shiva, Vishnu and Brahma: Destroyer, Preserver and Creator. The three alchemical elements of sulphur, salt and mercury are similarly associated. In Western esoteric symbolism, these are associated with the Three Rays of the Divine essence: the Ray of Power, the Ray of Love, and the Ray of Wisdom. Power may be developed through ritual; Love by means of meditation; and Wisdom through study and experience of the other two rays. Thus, the altar arrangement shows the three primary methods of esoteric practice: magick and ritual (fire), mysticism and meditation (water), and intellectual work (air). In the Egyptian pantheon, the three elements are attributed to Nephthys (fire), Isis (water), and Thoth (air). Nephthys, the consort of Set, is a symbolic representation of Western ceremonial magick (fire). Isis, the consort of Osiris, symbolically represents Eastern mysticism and yoga (water). And Thoth, the scribe of the Gods and Lord of All Knowledge, symbolizes the unification of both paths (air).

Three Precious Jewels

The Triple Gem or Three Jewels of Refuge—the *Buddha*, the *Dharma*, and the *Sangha*—are symbolized in the altar arrangement; as are the Three Secrets of Body, Speech and Mind; and the three *kayas* (bodies) of *Dharmakaya, Sambhogakaya* and *Nirmanakaya*.

The Three Jewels form the basis from which Buddhism grows, and all schools of Buddhism share this common foundation. To the Buddha is attributed enlightenment, or the attainment of superconsciousness. To the *Dharma* is attributed the sacred writings of the Law, which express the means of enlightenment. And to the *Sangha* is associated the community of initiates who have taken refuge and other vows on the Path of Return, and are united in the goals of the Great Work.

The Three Secrets of Body, Speech and Mind are associated with three esoteric techniques that may be used to bring illumination. These are *mudras*; the recitation of *mantras*; and the training, focusing and awakening of the mind through meditation. These techniques are used in the *Diamond Sapphire* ritual to bring about conditions favorable for healing and spiritual transformation.

The Three Bodies of *Dharmakaya, Sambhogakaya* and *Nirmanakaya* are a means of mapping out the three primary manifestations of the Buddha, and are thus also a means of mapping the three major levels of consciousness in humanity. They are similar in nature and in use to the Four Worlds of the Qabalists, as both are used to describe varying levels of existence and consciousness. The *Dharma* body is the eternal, archetypal, ever-present realm from which the universe finds its beginning—the source of All. This is the realm of the eternally manifest Buddha, and is similar to the World of *Atziluth* in Qabalah, attributed to the Divine. The *Sambhoga* body is considered the fruit of Buddhahood, being the manifestation of the Buddha in the Pure Realms—lands of infinite bliss and radiant light in which the Buddha manifests in immense luminescent form with thousands of *Bodhisattvas, Devas* and other beings of light in attendance. This is similar to the World of *Briah* in Qabalah, a realm associated with creative manifestation and Archangelic hosts. The *Nirmana* body is associated with the incarnation of consciousness into physical form, being the historical Buddha who was born, attained enlightenment, and died. This level is associated primarily with the foundation of form and matter, attributable primarily to the World of *Yetzirah*, the astral plane that is the foundation of the physical realm.

Three-in-One

The essential form of the three-in-one divine nature is seen almost universally in religions and mythology around the globe. Images of Father, Mother and Child—or similar symbol sets depicting two opposites that unite to form a third unique thing which is at the same time both, and yet neither, of its parents—abound throughout the mysteries.

The candle on the altar is white, symbolizing spirit and our aspirations toward enlightenment. White light contains all the colors of the visible spectrum, a medium that is the basis for all other colors, and is itself a colorless radiance. In this sense it's a type of carrier signal, which encodes whatever impressions are transferred with it. The candle is associated with the Hebrew letter *shin*, a further representation of spirit or divine fire. As such it is associated with Will, the *Dharma,* the act of speech *(mantra),* activity, the *Dharmakaya,* and the River of Fire.

The bowl of water symbolizes the unity of consciousness, the all-embracing intuitive consciousness associated with enlightenment. Divine consciousness is thus likened to a vast ocean, while individual consciousnesses are the individual drops of water that merge with this great sea. The water in the bowl should be fresh, spring water. Associated with the Hebrew letter *maim,* the water represents Love, the Buddha, the body *(mudra),* passivity, the *Sambhogakaya,* and the River of Water.

The incense may be any sweet-smelling fragrance, preferably red sandalwood, as this scent is particularly evocative of the Great Work. Abramelin incense may also be appropriate due to its associations with the Great Work and the sun. Associated with the Hebrew letter *aleph,* the incense represents Wisdom, the *Sangha,* mind, meditation, equilibrium, the *Nirmanakaya,* and the River of Air.

Three Rivers of Infinite Light

The center (heart) of the triangle contains an image representing the Great Work. This should be a visible image of beauty that evokes the higher aspirations of the participants, and is a reminder of the aspiration toward the Knowledge and Conversation of the Holy Guardian Angel. A statue of the hawk-headed lord Horus, an image of the Buddha, or the image of any other deity or enlightened being is appropriate. This central position in the triangle is the focus (nexus point) for the Three Rivers, from which the central light of the ritual is manifest.

Symbolically, the triangle represents both the source and the meeting point for the Three Rivers of Infinite Light: the River of

Fire, the River of Water, and the River of Air. This forms the central focus for the *Yetziratic* or "astral temple" of the *Diamond Sapphire*. The astral temple is in a region of the Pure Land. This region is within the Heavens of *Chesed* on the *Tree of Life*, a sphere associated with the *Adeptus Exemptus*, and the expression of compassion and mercy. This is the particular region of those who have sworn to undertake the work of liberation for all sentient beings. This is an area populated with myriads of Buddhas, *Bodhisattvas*, *Devas* and other beings of the light. The particular region associated with the Three Rivers and the *Diamond Sapphire* is attributed to *Chesed* of *Tiphareth*. The Temple itself is not a building or enclosure, but rather the wide-open skies, the land and sea, and the radiant gem of light, from which the rivers stream out.

The land is a stretch of fertile peninsula, with the ocean protecting it, and is lush with rich plant-life, fields of lotuses and flowers, trees and green rolling hills. Visible several miles off in the east is the shore of a great, indigo-blue ocean, while in the west the shore is a bit rockier. A rich forest of ancient trees is toward the northwest. Lush green hills, marked with rocks of varying sizes, climb off to the south. A refreshing breeze carries with it the soft scent of the ocean and flowers from the fields. When we enter this region for the ritual, it is at twilight, as sunrise and sunset are the times when the astral tides are strongest. The sun is on the horizon over the ocean in the east, painting the water in rich, golden light, and the sky in brilliant shades of purple and crimson. The full moon hangs opposite the sun in the western sky, radiating its luminous, silvery, spectral glow.

Underneath a rich canopy of stars that forms the stellar body of Nuit, in a sapphire night-sky, a beautiful eleven-petaled lotus rises out of the ground. Upon this, a radiating, silvery-white moon-disc appears. Within this luminous sphere is seen a large, brilliantly clear and radiating double-*vajra,* diamond-like in appearance and radiating intense light. Streaks of electric-blue fire can be seen dancing within the *Diamond Vajra,* and streams of coruscating white light flash out in all directions. A brilliant luminescent river of crimson fire streams out of the *Diamond Vajra* toward the northeast, consecrating and invigorating all things. A similarly radiant river of lapis-blue water flows toward the southeast, purifying and cleansing. And a brilliant, luminous river of yellow air streams toward the west, breathing life and vitality, and renewing all of creation. The *Diamond Vajra* rotates slowly clockwise as it breathes in the stellar fire from the cosmos, then sends the currents back out again into the universe via the *Three Rivers of Infinite Light.*

Opening

Once the *adytum* is prepared—with lit incense and candles, a fresh bowl of water, and any other offerings—the room should be emptied to allow it to be in silence for a brief time. When the Officiant and participants enter the *adytum,* imagine that the entire room is filled with radiant light that emanates from an infinite number of Buddhas and *Bodhisattvas.* As you enter the room, focus on the work at hand, and imagine that beautiful lotus flowers rise from the ground to meet each of your footsteps as you enter the region of the Three Rivers. If participants have *malas,* they should be held in the left hand while entering the *adytum,* symbolic of the passive or receptive act of opening up to the intuition and compassion of the Divine Light. Quietly take a seat, and allow yourself to focus on the radiance of light that surrounds you, and take a few deep, cleansing breaths.

The first ritual act to be performed is the preparation of the space. In a temple dedicated to the light, no preparatory banishings may be necessary. If the space is used for any other activities, however, some form of cleansing should be performed. In general, the *Lesser Banishing Ritual of the Pentagram* is suitable. More experienced Officiants may wish to use another method. Adepti of the Rosy Cross may prefer a completely different formula, such as an Invoking Pentagram or Star Ruby. Many other options are available, and this is left to the discretion of the Officiant.

After the preliminaries, the Officiant silently invokes the presence of the Divine Light and the blessings of the Crowned and Conquering Child of the Aeon.

Next, consciously attune to the Thelemic current while assuming the protective magical armor *(kavacha)* with *"Nu is my refuge, as Hadit my light, and Heru-ra-ha is the Strength, force, vigour of my arms."*

As you say the words, visualize the sun slowly rising above the ocean, its rays of light streaming toward you in brilliant, golden, solar fire. Simultaneously with this, as the glowing light from the dawning sun spreads, see myriads of lotuses growing out of the ground, petals opening to drink in the solar radiance as the *adytum* is transformed into the realm of the Three Rivers.

After this preliminary invocation, the Officiant turns west to face the assembly. Visualize a great light emanating from the east, filling the room with its radiant, warm glow, as though the sun were shining brilliantly from the east.

The gong is now struck once as an audible representation of that limitless light that streams out from the east and spreads into every part of the universe. As this fiery, spiritual essence bathes the world in its glow, the Officiant proclaims the *Law of Thelema* audibly. The response comes not only from the participants present, but from the universe itself, acknowledging and confirming the Aeon of the Crowned and Conquering Child. Countless Buddhas, *Bodhisattvas*, *Devas*, Archangels, Angels and hidden Adepti also acknowledge the Law at this juncture, adding their Will to ours for the attainment of all sentient beings.

All participants are seated in meditative postures. When ready, the *adytum* should be opened by whatever ritual methods the Officiant sees fit. At a minimum, banishing by fiat should be performed:

BAHLASTI! OMPEHDA! *(AL, III:54)*

Pause. Then assume the *kavacha* with the formula of Thelemic Refuge:

> *Officiant: Nu is your refuge as Hadit your Light; and I am the strength, force, vigour, of your arms.*[70]

Turn to face the assembly:

> *[Officiant strikes gong once.] Do what thou wilt shall be the whole of the Law.*
>
> *All: Love is the law, love under will.*

The Voice of Divine Fire

Bathed in this stellar glow of healing light, all participants now chant the sacred *mantra* of the Lord of the Universe. This opens and stimulates the *anahatta chakra* in all present, acknowledging the interior or "midnight" sun within every person—an acknowledgment and call for the Holy Guardian Angel.

The *mantra* is taken from the ancient Egyptian words of the *Stele of Revealing*, which were rendered poetically by Aleister Crowley from the translation from the Boulaq Museum in Cairo, Egypt.

---

[70] Adapted from *Liber AL vel Legis*, III:17.

Parts of this paraphrasing were then inserted into *The Book of the Law* at the instruction of Aiwass. This *mantra* appears in Chapter III, verse 37, of *Liber AL vel Legis* as:

> *Unity uttermost showed!*
> *I adore the might of Thy breath,*
> *Supreme and terrible God,*
> *Who makest the gods and death*
> *To tremble before Thee:—*
> *I, I adore thee!*

The *mantra* is recited three times as an acknowledgment of the three-in-one nature of reality, symbolized in the Three Rivers, the Triple Gem, and the Thelemic trinity of Nuit, Hadit and Heru-ra-ha.

Then chant three times:

A ka dua
Tuf ur biu
Bi a'a chefu
Dudu ner af an nuteru

Refuge and Dedication

The group now takes refuge in the Triple Gem of Nuit, Hadit and Heru-ra-ha. In Buddhism, the act of taking refuge in the Triple Gem is the first and central act of every Buddhist. The Buddha is a representation of enlightenment and liberation, and we take refuge or protection in him as the embodiment of our aspirations toward illumination. The *Dharma* is the collection of sacred writings of the Buddha, which teach the methods of attainment. The *Sangha* is the global society of Buddhists, in particular those who have taken monk's vows. In addition to the meanings attributed to the Three

Jewels in Buddhism, it should also be noted that the Buddha may be seen as a representation of the Holy Guardian Angel, the *Dharma* as the sacred writings of the Law of Thelema, and the *Sangha* as the community of initiates.

The Thelemic Refuge acknowledges the spirit of this practice and imports them into the cosmology of the New Aeon. The particular formula is adapted from *Liber Legis, III:17*:

> *"Fear not at all; fear neither men nor Fates, nor gods, nor anything. Money fear not, nor laughter of the folk folly, nor any other power in heaven or upon the earth or under the earth. Nu is your refuge as Hadit your light; and I am the strength, force, vigour, of your arms."*

While taking refuge, we also aspire to three common goals that are central to the Diamond Sapphire. First, to *"embody the Great Work, consecrating our lives unto the blue-lidded daughter of Sunset, the naked brilliance of the voluptuous night sky."* This is identified as the Knowledge and Conversation of the Holy Guardian Angel, the sole worthy goal from which all others must depend. Second, *"with all sentient beings embrace the Law of Thelema, and come to know and fulfill our True Will, making our Wisdom wide and deep as the sea."* Here the Bodhisattva path is implicit, as our attainment is not possible unless all are on the path toward attainment. This also implies the spread of the Law of Thelema, the embracing of the Law, and an aspiration to the knowledge of the True Will. Third, *"with all sentient beings attain the supreme realization, that we may truly lead the multitude to freedom from all hindrances, that the Aeon of the Crowned and Conquering Child may be manifest here on earth."*

Shakyamuni Buddha taught that you should only seek refuge in yourself, and the path to liberation was within yourself. This is the one true refuge, the secret center within the heart of the Triple Gem.

In the New Aeon, refuge is taken in none other than the Lord of the Universe, the Crowned and Conquering Child, the infinite expansion of contraction of the One Life and Light. It should be noted that these archetypes are not external deities, but rather representations of the One Reality that is hidden in the formula Will and Love.

Central doctrines of the new dispensation are then spoken by the Officiant, affirming the Word of the Law and the true nature of all humanity. Next are spoken words adapted from Shakyamuni Buddha's final teaching, words that are important enough that they are quoted in full here:

> *"Be to yourselves your own Light. Be to yourselves your own refuge. Thou shalt not go looking about for any other light or refuge. Whoever follows, when I am gone, shall be to themselves their own light, their own refuge—whoever shall take the Truth I have taught as their light and their refuge—they now and always will be my true disciples, will be walking in the Universal path. They will see and know the Supreme Bliss."*[71]

This is an important admonition that, at its core, is identical to the Word of the Law of Thelema: find your True Will, and do it, and nothing else. The adaptation in the Diamond Sapphire emphasizes the stellar nature of every sentient being, and is a silent invocation of the Lord of the Universe, represented by the image of our physical sun.

---

[71] *Mahaparinibbana Sutra*, DN 16.

The dedication is a form of Transfer of Merit: taking the benefits accumulated by the performance of the ritual and dedicating them to all sentient beings for their benefit and evolution. The benefits expressed are those that result naturally from the full embracing of the teachings of the Buddha as expressed in the Fourfold Noble Truths and the practice of the Eightfold Noble Path.[72] As the Buddha taught:

> *"Advancing from this Fourfold Noble Truth, the disciples of Buddha will attain all other precious truths; they will gain the wisdom and insight to understand all meanings [...]"*[73]

This act is encoded in the fourfold manifestation of the Law as Light, Life, Liberty and Love, the four secret gates to the Heart of the Master. These Four Gates give entrance to the Fifth, or Quintessence, that secret center of Invisible Light that should guide our every thought, word and deed:

> *"There are four gates to one palace; the floor of that palace is of silver and gold; lapis lazuli & jasper are there; and all rare scents; jasmine & rose, and the emblems of death. Let him enter in turn or at once the four gates; let him stand on the floor of the palace. Will he not sink? Amn. Ho! warrior, if thy servant sink? But there are means and means. Be goodly therefore: dress ye all in fine apparel; eat rich foods and drink sweet wines and wines that foam! Also, take your fill and will of love as ye will, when, where and with whom ye will! But always unto me." (AL, I:51)*

And again, in *Liber Legis*, II:49:

---

[72] For a further discussion, see Crowley's "The Doctrines of Buddhism" (from *The Temple of Solomon the King* in *The Equinox I:4*, p. 125).
[73] *Sri Maladevisimhanada Sutra.*

> "I am unique & conqueror. I am not of the slaves that perish. Be they damned & dead! Amen. [This is of the 4: there is a fifth who is invisible, & therein am I as a babe in an egg.]"

All of this is sealed by the verses of the Officiant taken from Crowley's "The Four Virtues of the Heart of the Master." In all four expressions is the secret fifth element invoked as the very seal (or *mudra*) of the Law, from which the other four rays may emanate.

Following the Transfer of Merit, the Officiant recites passages from the fire and spirit chapters of *Liber LXV*, fire being the active component of aspiration and desire toward the divine, and spirit the answering kiss from on high, which descends as a dove of light into our hearts, raining stellar currents of fire into our being. Of these passages Crowley writes in his Commentary to *Liber LXV*:

> "[...] The coral is the karma produced by the accumulation of our acts. This construction has taken place in time and its need is to be covered by the rhythm of Eternal Delight. The Knowledge and Conversation of the Holy Guardian Angel act as a point of contact between two continua. Neither is comprehensible without the other."

In essence, after we have taken refuge and brought the intent of our aspirations toward the benefit of all sentient beings, our Holy Guardian Angel is once again silently invoked as witness to, and guardian of, this work. Our act of attracting the light and spreading its healing rays outward for the benefit of all beings brings us yet closer, and more open to the love and voice of our Holy Guardian Angel, guaranteeing that we will inhabit the Pure Land that is none other than the world transformed by the influx of radiant, solar light into the consciousness of the Adept.

The ritual continues:

Officiant: We take refuge in Nuit.

All: May we with all sentient beings embody the Great Work, consecrating our lives unto the blue-lidded daughter of Sunset, the naked brilliance of the voluptuous night sky.[74]

Officiant: We take refuge in Hadit.

All: May we with all sentient beings embrace the Law of Thelema, and come to know and fulfill our True Will, making our Wisdom wide and deep as the sea.

Officiant: We take refuge in Heru-ra-ha.

All: May we with all sentient beings attain the supreme realization, that we may truly lead the multitude to freedom from all hindrances, that the Aeon of the Crowned and Conquering Child may be manifest here on earth.

Officiant: The Word of the Law is Thelema.[75] *Every man and every woman is a star.*[76] *Make of yourself a Light. Let all be a Lamp unto oneself, spreading Light in the Darkness even as the rays of the sun shine brilliantly and indiscriminately on all.*

All: In Light, may all sentient beings, boundless as the sky, come to know and fulfill their True Will.
  *In **Life**, may they have happiness and the causes of happiness.*
  *In **Liberty**, may they be liberated from suffering and the causes of suffering.*

---

[74] *Liber AL vel Legis.*, I:64.
[75] Ibid., I:39.
[76] Ibid., I:3.

*In **Love**, may they never be separated from the happiness which is free from sorrow.*
*With **the Law** which informs these all, may they rest in equanimity, free from attachment and aversion.*

Formulation of the Light

The actions that now take place build the combined energy of all participants, and open them up to the divine radiance that floods into the *adytum* and the individual psyches of all present. The regeneration of the world spoken of by the Officiant is none other than the illumination of the individual disciples by virtue of their work and aspirations.

The first part of the vow is to aspire toward the Knowledge and Conversation of the Holy Guardian Angel. All other acts are done in the power of this one aspiration, and by virtue of its intent. In a purely Buddhist ceremony, this section would be the development of the *Bodhicitta* mind, or the opening of the heart to the aspiration of the *Bodhisattva,* usually by means of a *mantra* specific to the lineage.

Next, the aspiration of the *Bodhisattva* itself is recited. The wording used in the Diamond Sapphire is an adaptation from several Mahayana Buddhist lineages, with the emphasis being on practical and effective change and service in the world.

The gong is struck once to seal the vows and intermingle the vibrations from the combined voices with the light that permeates the *adytum*. The entire room should be visualized as growing brighter, with the light wave moving outward to expand the sphere of radiant light that fills the room.

Officiant: This shall regenerate the world, the little world my sister, my heart & my tongue, unto whom I send this kiss.[77]

All: Within the embrace of Light, Life, Love and Liberty that is the Law of Thelema, beneath the Starry Canopy of Heaven that is Nuit, we aspire toward the accomplishment of the Great Work.

For the benefit of all sentient beings, we strive to perfect ourselves that we may live life according to Will, and come to the Knowledge and Conversation of the Holy Guardian Angel.

We strive to embody the One Law of Thelema, establishing the New Aeon of the Crowned and Conquering Child. For as long as Space exists, and sentient beings endure, may we too remain, to dispel the darkness of the world.

Officiant: Come forth, o children, under the stars, & take your fill of love! I am above you and in you. My ecstasy is in yours. My joy is to see your joy.[78] *[Strikes gong once.]*

Optional: Led by the Officiant, all perform the *Lantern of Thebes* (see Chapter 8).

The heart of the ritual now commences. All of the previous ceremonial actions were designed to prepare the participants for this stage of the ritual, in which the actual current will be intensified, consecrated via chanting of the Holy Books, and then directed toward healing and spiritual liberation. The chanting of the words

---

[77] *Liber AL vel Legis*, I:53.
[78] Ibid., I:12–13.

serves as both a *mantra* and an invocation of the spiritual forces being worked with.

The gong is sounded once to establish a current of sound vibration that both acts as an auditory indication of the next step of the rite, and provides a simple form of cleansing and focusing of the psyches of all present. It is important that all participants be in a calm and focused state, with a sense of confident expectancy.

The verses from *Liber VIII* are indicative of the *LVX* or *Light of Tiphareth*, which when fully invoked, calls forth the answering supernal light, or NOX, the Night of Pan. This is the radiating stellar light of the Rosy Cross, *"the light higher than eyesight" (AL, II:51)*, which is manifested by the Third Order in written form in the words of *The Book of the Law*.

The next words spoken by the Officiant are traditional, and refer to the holy nature of the words which are about to be chanted. The intent of both the gong and this preliminary speech by the Officiant is to notify all present, both visible and invisible, that we are about to enter the *Sanctum Sanctorum* of the very *adytum* of our hearts. What follows are the works of Sacred Magick, the Great Work in word and deed, by means of willed creative visualization, conscious recitation, and ritual action. *"Put off thy shoes from off thy feet, for the place whereon thou standest is holy ground." (Exodus 3:5)*

The *dharma* reading is announced, usually a selection of *Liber AL vel Legis*. The chanting is best done monotone, as this provides a type of containment field for the combined energy of all participants. When reading the Holy Books in a ritual setting, there can be an upwelling of emotions as the various *chakras* are stimulated, and the tendency when reading these out loud is for the emotions to be expressed in the reading. In solitary workings this is desirable, as it is a viable means of *"enflaming oneself with prayer."* In a directed group ritual, however, the results are quite different. Disparate voices, inflections and intonations produce a dispersing effect, allowing the energy to dissipate much more rapidly. The discipline of reading monotone actually serves to hold the energy within the place of working, and tie it in closer to each individual's sphere of sensation. Each participant becomes a virtual *athanor* of light, allowing the energy to build up and radiate outward in an extremely dense and slowly expanding ovoid of brilliant, coruscating, white radiance. It is as though the expanding, living, dynamic cells of stellar light from each participant coalesce to form the sphere of light that surrounds the entire group. The end result is a vast increase in the amount of accumulated current that is then *answered* from "on High" by the "kisses of the stars," or *kalas*, (essence) streaming into the combined current of all participants. In effect, a new star is given birth in the place of working, radiating its healing rays outward in all directions, even as the sun of our solar system shines its light on all of the earth.

The Diamond Sapphire Gem of Radiant Light

The Officiant will need to set the pace and tone of the chanting. Chanting evenly, with a medium-level voice, has been found to be the most efficacious method. If keeping the pace and rhythm is difficult for the Officiant, several methods are available, and you are encouraged to experiment with various approaches such as chanting with a drum or other rhythmic music. Experience is the best teacher in this regard, and the Officiant will soon learn to find a natural pace and flow for the readings.

During the reading, those participating should be visualizing their bodies surrounded by a thin, bluish-white, ovoid light. Above the crown of the head is visualized the *sahasrara chakra* ablaze in brilliant, pure white radiance. An azure current of light, flecked with scarlet, is visualized at the *muladhara chakra* at the base of the spine. As the reading progresses, the bluish-red current should be seen to gradually rise up *shushumna,* the central column of subtle channels located within the spine. At the conclusion of the chanting, the current of light should be seen to complete its connection with the top of the spine, at which point the light in the body radiates even more brilliantly, and connects directly with the sphere above the head. At this point all is dissolved into the Silence.

The meditation in Silence that follows is directed toward the healing and spiritual evolution of all sentient beings who have chosen to align themselves with the Great Work. In addition to the instructions in the ritual text itself, it should be noted that a portion of the light should be offered to your Holy Guardian Angel as a token of love and dedication to this work. When conducted by true Adepti, the rose-gold visualizations of light that emanate from the *anahatta chakra* (heart center) of all participants radiate a Tipharic solar current[79], so the white star of the group now transforms into a brilliant, rose-gold fire, enlivening and transforming, consecrating and empowering, quickening the spiritual selves, and burning away the dross. Even when conducted by those who have not attained initiation into *Tiphareth,* the ritual empowers and radiates a Tipharic quality that, when performed repeatedly, will help open the participants to their own spiritual maturity and growth toward the sacred wedding with the Angel, and allow them to become living channels for that fiery Voice of the Angel that is the True Will.

The meditation period should be no less than eleven minutes. In most situations this should be the maximum duration as well, as it is a comfortable amount of time for the average participant.

---

[79] *Tiphareth* of *Briah,* the awakened consciousness of the 5=6 (Adeptus Minor).

New Aeon Tantra

The number eleven is well known within Thelemic circles as the number of Nuit, the Goddess of Infinite Space and Infinite Stars. It is also the number of AVD, the "magick of Light." As the sum of five (human consciousness, the pentagram, the natural order) and six (divinity, the hexagram, the realm of noesis), it is an expression of the Great Work and the Adeptus who has achieved the Knowledge and Conversation of the Holy Guardian Angel. Much more is contained within this significant number that is left to your own discovery.

The end of the period of meditation is signaled by the words of the Officiant. These two sentences from the second chapter of *The Book of the Law* sum up the divinity of humanity and our role in the universe, and act as a powerful key to unlocking the mysteries of Self that form the core teachings of Thelema. They may also function as a powerful catalyst to self-discovery when used as a *mantra*.

The *mantra* from the Stele is chanted again by all participants; however, with this final invocation and equilibration of the current, there are significant changes. The *mantra* is chanted eleven times, as opposed to the previous instruction of three repetitions. Additionally, the gong is sounded at the beginning of every repetition. This functions as a catalyst to channel all of the radiations of current into the center of the stellar sphere at the altar. The Officiants should visualize the altar ablaze with brilliant, coruscating, rose-gold flame.

The ritual continues:

> *Officiant: [Strikes gong once.] The light is come to the darkness, and the darkness is made light. Then is light married with light, and the child of their love is that other darkness, wherein they abide that have lost name and form. Therefore did I kindle him that had not understanding, and in The*

> *Book of the Law did I write the secrets of truth that are like unto a star and a snake and a sword.*[80]
>
> *And unto him that understandeth at last do I deliver the secrets of truth in such wise that the least of the little children of the light may run to the knees of the mother and be brought to understand.*[81]

The Officiant announces the *dharma* reading. This is a selection from any of the canon of the Thelemic Holy Books. In most cases *Liber AL vel Legis*, Chapter I, is most suitable. *Liber VII* and *Liber LXV* are also favorable. At the discretion of the Officiant, any of the Holy Books may be used.

All chant the *dharma* reading in a monotone, following the lead of the Officiant. The silent meditation is directed toward healing. On each inhalation, participants visualize streams of radiant, white light pouring into their bodies, cleansing and empowering them. On each exhalation, the light is transformed into white radiance at the heart center, and then projected back into the universe in all directions, cleansing, healing and inspiring all sentient beings. The meditation should be for no less than eleven minutes. When done:

> Officiant: *There is no law beyond Do what thou wilt.*

> All: Chant the following eleven times, the gong being struck at the beginning of each repetition:

A ka dua
Tuf ur biu
Bi a'a chefu
Dudu ner af an nuteru

---

[80] *Liber VIII.*
[81] Ibid.

Final Dedication and Closing

The final invocation of the Officiant over the elements is adapted from the *Ananda Lahari* ("Ocean of Bliss"), a medieval Hindu tantrik text devoted to the worship of the Goddess.

The inner essence of the eucharist is threefold, composed of the raw elements of existence: fire, water and air—the three primordial *shaktis* or currents. If they are offered, the Cakes of Light and the Grail of Wine are also taken. The Officiant makes any final prayers, invocations, blessings and so on at this juncture.

Each participant is then invited by the Officiant to partake of the eucharist (hold the hands over the fire, smell the incense, and mark the forehead with the water), and to perform any personal ablutions, prayers, offerings and so forth that they feel inspired to do. At a minimum, everyone should be encouraged to partake of the eucharistic elements, and offer a silent invocation to their Holy Guardian Angel.

Some groups may wish to add other eucharistic elements to the altar—fruit, sweets and bread all work well; really anything pleasing to you. If so, these will have been placed on the altar during the initial setup of the *adytum* so they may benefit from the rays of light that were produced during the rite. They may then be consumed by all present as part of the eucharistic stage of the ritual. In all cases, however, the original threefold elemental eucharist should not be changed, and should serve as the primary formula.

The final dedication and transfer of merit occurs, and the Officiant gives a final blessing to all present.

The rite is sealed by vibration of the eleven-fold formula **ABRAHADABRA** by all present, and then closed with the single knock of the Officiant.

The Officiant should visualize that all of the current is now focused above the altar. As the candle is blown out, the current of stellar light should be transferred to the Officiant's heart, where it remains a forever-burning Lamp of Wisdom and Love, a living star beckoning to all who are ready to enter into conscious participation with the Aeon of Horus.

The ritual continues:

> *Officiant: Remember all ye that existence is pure joy; that all the sorrows are but as shadows; they pass & are done; but there is that which remains.[82] [Pause.]*

The Officiant goes to the east of the altar, faces west over the altar elements, and invokes:

> *Oh Goddess of Infinite Space and Infinite Stars, may all my speech, howsoever idle, be recitation of Your mantra; may all the actions with my hand be the making of ritual gesture toward You; may all my walking be the pacing around Thy image in worship; may all my eating and my very living be Homa rites in Your honor; may the act of my lying down be prostration before Thee; may all my pleasures be an offering to Thee! Whatsoever I do may it be counted for the worship of Thee—always to Thee![83]*

The Officiant partakes of the eucharist by first holding hands over the candle flame, then dipping the right forefinger in the water and anointing the forehead, and then smelling the incense while making a silent dedication and prayer.

---

[82] Ibid., II:9.
[83] Adapted from verse 27 of the *Anandalahari*.

If Cakes of Light are employed[84], the eucharist proceeds with the following. The Officiant raises the Grail on high with both hands while saying:

> Thou shalt drain out thy blood that is thy life into the golden cup of her fornication.[85]

The Officiant lowers the Grail to the level of the heart, and holds it with the left hand. The Officiant then raises a Cake of Light, holding it over the Grail on high, while saying:

> Thou shalt mingle thy life with the universal life. Thou shalt not keep back one drop.[86]

The Officiant brings Cake down to heart level, above the opening of the Grail, then silently consumes the Cake of Light and drains the Grail. When done, the Officiant says:

> There is success. (AL, III:69)

> All: Each person in turn is invited to say a prayer or give offerings at the altar, and partake of the eucharist. When done:

> Officiant: I am uplifted in thine heart; and the kisses of the stars rain hard upon thy body. (AL, III:69)
> May Light, Life, Love, and Liberty be extended universally to all, under the regency of the One Law of Thelema.
> All: **ABRAHADABRA.** [Vibrate once. Knock once.]

---

[84] Generally, the Cake and Wine are partaken by the Officiant alone. However, if preferred, the entire congregation may partake. If so, a Cake of Light and goblet of wine should be prepared for each participant ahead of time.
[85] *Liber Cheth*, v. 2.
[86] Ibid., v. 3.

Additional Notes on Performance

The *Diamond Sapphire* ritual has many levels of working, both outer and inner. As you go deeper, the significance and inner mystery of the rite takes on increasingly profound meaning. What follows are some rough notes on impressions in working with this rite.

The Three-Fold Altar

The three-fold altar symbolically represents the *yantra* of the Goddess, which is the reflection into elements of Her *yoni*. In addition to all the dialogue in this chapter, it is significant that this *yoni tattva* is the combined essence of the *Shaktis* (female powers) of the human organism: *iccha* (will), *jnana* (knowledge), and *kriya* (action). These three *Shaktis* form the momentum that is True Will: *svecchacara*, the Sovereign.

The *yoni* is the "Wisdom" essence of the *Tantras*, while the *vajra* is the "Means." As the stellar gateway, the *yoni* is equivalent to *sunyata*, the Void, Nuit.

Resumed in this one symbol of the altar is the entirety of our work, showing both the source and object of all outer and inner devotion, the essence of *samaya*, the source of stellar gnosis, the means of tantrik magick.

The altar then is literally the source of Life, Light, Love and Liberty emanating from the Law.

Iconographically, the red triangle represents Ra-Hoor-Khuit, the Lord of the Aeon. This is really the *heart* of Ra-Hoor-Khuit—and His heart is the Goddess, Nuit. The center of the Lord of the Aeon is *sunyata*. We have a clear indication of the mixing of the male and female currents in the deeper sense that each person contains both essences within. The Lord of the Universe and the Goddess of Infinite Space and Infinite Stars are ONE, and this ONE is NONE (cf. the Mars chapter of *Liber VII*).

Note that this void is not empty, nor is it a place of negative passivity. The void—Nuit—is the source of everything. She expresses every quality, every condition, every permutation. She transcends our world, and is imminent in it. Her body makes up every aspect of our reality, and is the source of absolute bliss.

The Right View

Throughout the ritual, awareness is key. Every action should be done with presence, not dwelling on the past or planning for what's next. Take each moment as it comes, and experience it fully. This is especially important during the readings of the Holy Books. As one of our sister traditions emphasizes, the key of everything is to be Awake and Aware.

A Ka Dua

This *mantra* is another indication of the male-female polarity. As an invocation of the Lord of the Aeon, it works with the current of fire, yet its very words point toward the unity of nothingness that is Nuit. "Unity uttermost showed!"

Bodhicitta in Liber Legis

Relative Bodhicitta is the "mind of awakening," generally taught to be the aspiration of compassion for all sentient beings. The deeper teaching is the *Absolute Bodhicitta*, which is the realization of *sunyata*. The nature of the emptiness is compassion, *"the vice of kings" (AL, II:21).*

This is shown in *Liber Legis* with Nuit, who is the embodiment of *sunyata*. We are directed to dedicate everything to Her. This act is the awakening of the mind to enlightenment—*Relative Bodhicitta*. By giving our all to Nuit, we are inflamed in Love, and it radiates out in all directions. Our realization of Nuit is the realization of *sunyata*—the Void. By giving our all to Her in Love, we come to the experience of Her as pure, immediate, intrinsic Awareness—*Absolute Bodhicitta* embodied in the teachings of our Western tantra, in the Cult of the Star Goddess. *Liber AL* also expressly describes the detrimental effects of not having the Right View, as do the traditional Buddhist teachings on Relative and Absolute *Bodhicitta*.

The Pure Land

Though the land is at first purely Qabalistic, you begin to experience a reification of the land that seems to be based on the *mandala* of the *Stele of Revealing*. The night sky filled with stars is the body of Nuit. The aspirant is Ankh-af-na-Khonsu. The *Vajra*, radiating streams of light, is the Hadit *(bindu* or seed) at the center of Ra-Hoor-Khuit, who is enthroned in the *vajra* throne.

There are retinues of Angels, *Dakinis, Dakas, Dharmapalas, Dikpalas* and higher spirits, in addition to the host of attendant and natural elementals. All are celebrating in this great rite of awakening.

The Dharma Reading

The reading is the work embodied in vibrational form, utilizing the breath *(prana)* and sound *(mantra)*. This energetically blends the subtle channels of the sun/fire *(pingala)* and moon/water *(ida)*, where they will be conjoined in lucid clarity and rise up the central channel *(shushumna)*. The combined essences of Shakti and Shiva, of Nuit and Hadit, of the Red and White fluids, have been mixed by all that came before it (cf. *Atu XIV: Art,* Figure 23). Now comes the heat. Let it build slowly, rising up the central channel with agonizing slowness and buildup of intensity. Do not be distracted. This is the *Kalignarudra*—the great flames at the end of time that burn up all of existence—*"for I have crushed an Universe & naught remains"* (AL, III:72).

The Silence

The exoteric instruction is in the ritual. Esoterically, those that are ripe now enter into the experience of the Void. This is the climax, the consummation of the act, union with Nuit. The cry is that of **HRILIU**, the orgasm of radiant bliss, and it is a profound, luminous Silence.

Eventually you come back from the Void, the first indication being the raining streams of *kalas* (the nectar of the stars from the *yoni* of Nuit) falling gently down from space— *"the kisses of the stars"* (cf. *AL, II:62*).

The Eucharist

The rest of the rite is a rebuilding from emptiness, or an awakening to that which is relative, but with a difference. This is the creation of the universe after *mahapralaya*, the conscious stepping into the New Aeon of the Crowned and Conquering Child. The rite as written is "outer," i.e., for the public.

For the inner rite, let it be done in private, or in circles of dedicated initiates only. And it is best if Cakes of Light are shared, and foaming wines. Let the devotion to the Goddess be celebrated as the celebrants see fit, with offerings of all good things: food, drink, light, incense, flowers, prayer, music, song, dance and eros. All to Nuit.

And let the accumulated merit be distributed in the eight directions of space for all beings!

Visualizations Employed in the Eucharist of the Diamond Sapphire

The Officiant partakes of the eucharist by first holding her hands over the candle flame.

While doing so, the Officiant visualizes radiant streams of cleansing, consecrating, starry fire flowing from the candle into the hands, and with one beat of the heart, filling the entire body with this flaming essence of desire and Love.

The Officiant then dips the right forefinger in the water and anoints the forehead, tracing a circle with an X inside of it, and seeing it in brilliant silvery-blue light. One may also silently intone "Nuit" while tracing the circle, "Hadit" while making a dot in the center, and "Ra-Hoor-Khuit" while tracing the lines of the X.

Next, the Officiant smells the incense while making a silent dedication and prayer. The incense may be seen as airy, golden light suffusing the aura and wafting up into the starry night sky.

If Cakes of Light are employed, the Officiant raises the Grail on high with both hands while saying:

Thou shalt drain out thy blood that is thy life into the golden cup of her fornication.

As the Grail is raised, it should be seen as composed of brilliance, diamond-like, with a flood of effulgent light flowing into it, which is the combination of the Three Rivers.

The Officiant then lowers the Grail to the level of the heart, and holds it with the left hand. As the Grail is lowered, it transforms into a radiant, full moon.

The Officiant then raises a Cake of Light, holding it over the Grail on high:

Thou shalt mingle thy life with the universal life. Thou shalt not keep back one drop.

As the Cake of Light is held up, it is seen in the form of a brilliant, radiating star of white light.

The Officiant brings the Cake down to heart level, above the opening of the Grail.

As the Cake is brought to hover over the Grail opening, it is transformed into the image of the sun, a brilliant, golden-yellow fire. With the cup in the form of the moon beneath it, briefly see a glorious image of the sun and moon conjoined.

Silently consume the Cake of Light, and drain the Grail.

At this point, the Eye in the Triangle is seen on the Officiant's forehead, radiating out streams of light. At the heart center of the Officiant, a four-rayed *vajra* appears, shooting out coruscating flames of light; at the center of the *vajra* appears the conjunction of the sun and moon; and at the region of the genitals, an eleven-petaled lotus of light opens its petals and radiates light upward and outward. Surrounding the now-luminous Officiant is a dark ouroboros serpent. Pause to see this before continuing.

When done, the Officiant says: *There is success.*

Chapter 10
ADVANCED RITUALS & MEDITATIONS

In 2011 I found myself at the apex of several currents that all came together during a trekking journey in the Himalayas from Nepal[87]. My work with the Typhonian Order involved intense *sadhanas* and Dzogchen practices, and these blended with tantrik *vamamarga* (left-hand path) currents from the Uttara Kaula and Kaula Shakta traditions; in particular a deep Kali practice was taking on a life of its own. I was integrating this into my overall work, with the result that the floodgates of consciousness opened, and during a magical retirement in December of the same year, most of the new material and groundwork was received.

The material has come to be known as the *Ananda Arghya (Vehicle of Bliss)*, and consists of tantrik *sadhanas*, guided meditations, and inner yogic alchemical practices. Where the rituals of the *Adamantine Void* have a group focus around the *Diamond Sapphire Gem of Radiant Light* and supporting practices, in the *Vehicle of Bliss* the practitioner fully embraces the Western tantra of *The Book of the Law*, and engages directly with the energies of the Aeon of Horus. The often-opaque quality of this material comes from the fact that much of it erupted into my consciousness abruptly, over intense periods of inspiration. Through doing the rituals, yoga and meditations, you come into a sense of accord with the material in a way that is not easy to translate into words. *Do what*

---

[87] For more on this deeply magical period, see my book *Yogini Magic: The Sorcery, Enchantment and Witchcraft of the Divine Feminine*, Falcon Press.

thou wilt shall be the whole of the Law! The first word, *Do,* is essential in this phase of the work. Only by *Doing* the work actively, and not just reading about it, will the sense of accord develop, and integration with these finer states of consciousness flower.

The tantrik work explores the relationship between the practitioner and power—*shakti*—as it manifests within the framework of the New Aeon. The Egyptian-Thelemic pantheon of Nuit, Hadit and Ra-Hoor-Khuit are engaged in a dynamic and magical weaving of energy. Through these practices, the tantrika is brought into closer realization of their own True Will, and how that Will manifests in the world. As a part of this work, the *tantrika* enters in the *mandala,* the magical world of the New Aeon, and experiences the wonder and bliss of integrating all the levels of consciousness. This is liberation while living, as opposed to a promise of some sort of post-mortem illumination. The consciousness is established in the bliss of nondual awakening, while cognizant all the time of the magical display of reality of the seemingly mundane, material world.

As mentioned above, the material of these chapters is collected together as the *Ananda Arghya (Vehicle of Bliss; Ark of Bliss).* It is represented by the initials **A∴ A∴** with the *trikona* (marks forming an equilateral triangle, single-point down) a representation of the Goddess.

Ananda is Bliss—the cosmic, divine Bliss that is the true nature of the Void. It is the reward of Buddhas, *Bodhisattvas, Kaulas, Naths,* winners of the Ordeal X[88]; all great Truths are expressions of this radiating, all-permeating, all-manifesting, all-embracing Bliss.

---

[88] *"The other images group around me to support me: let all be worshipped, for they shall cluster to exalt me. I am the visible object of worship; the others are secret; for the Beast & his Bride are they: and for the winners of the Ordeal X. What is this? Thou shalt know." (AL, III:22)*

"Remember all ye that existence is pure joy; that all the sorrows[89] are but as shadows, they pass & are done; but there is that which remains." (AL, II:9)

Arghya is traditionally the sacred water used in worship, as well as the vesical (bladder)-shaped container which holds these waters. In *Aleister Crowley & the Hidden God*, Kenneth Grant writes:

> "The one place in Crowley's writings where he gives the meaning of the initials A∴A∴ is in his Magical Record (Cefalu, 1921) where it appears as ACTHP APTOC. This is a corrupt Graeco-Coptic form of Argenteum Astrum (the Silver Star), yet it is the true occult key to the nature of the Order, which is not expressed by the correct Latin version of the name. Argos derives from Arg or Arca, the female generative power symbolized by the moon, the womb-shaped Argha used in the Mysteries, synonymous with the Queen of Heaven. Arghya (Sanskrit) is the libation-cup; Aster Argos is the lunar or 'silver' star."

Some meanings of *argha* are "worthy," "having great value," and "respectful reception of an esteemed guest." It has been connected to *arghya*, "the libation cup, the navi-form, the boat-shaped vessel in which flowers and fruit are offered to the gods, and libations of water are made."[90] Grant has noted the connection between *argha* and the *Argo* of the Greek myths (possibly through *Arka* = the female principle) which were alluded to in the works of Mme. Blavatsky, Hargrave Jennings, and in depth by Gerald Massey.

Arghya (Sanskrit): Variant of *argha* (from the verbal root *arh*, to be worthy, deserve).

---

[89] *Dukka*.
[90] Kenneth Grant.

As an *adjective*, venerable, deserving; as a *noun*, an oblation reverently offered to Gods or exceptionally worthy human beings, and consisting of flowers, water, rice and *durva* (Bermuda) grass; also, the container or vessel in which the libation is made. In short, an offering worthy enough to be given to the God.

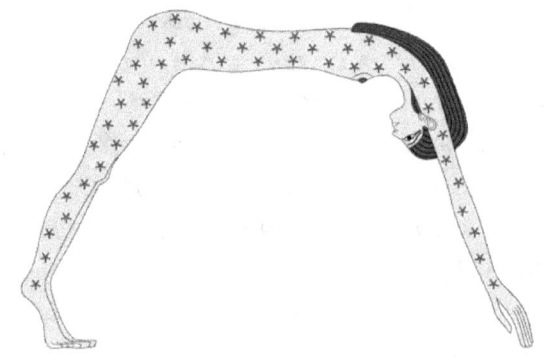

Figure 19
Nuit
(commons.wikimedia.org)

A representation of the *Arghya* is the arch, symbolic of the womb. This is seen most clearly in the arched body of the Star Goddess *Nuit* (Figure 19) as pictured on the *Stele of Revealing* (Figure 1). Nuit is a glyph of the *Graal* (Magical Cup) in which the Great Magical Power *(mahashakti)* resides. This position is the *Kailasa Prastara*, where *"the Goddess towers over her worshippers like Mount Kailas, from which the healing coolness of her snows flows down."*[91]

The *Ananda Arghya* is thus the Ark or receptacle of Divine Bliss, as well as a suitable vehicle and offering of all that one is to the creative power of the Goddess and the radiant cosmic Bliss of such an

---

[91] *Aleister Crowley & the Hidden God*, Kenneth Grant.

offering of Union. It is, in fact, a visible symbol of that Bliss, and the creative womb-matrix of the Great Goddess.

As the *vehicle* of Her Bliss, it is the symbol of Her creative powers, the receptacle of the *Bija* and the all-embracing matrix of creation from which the oceans of all time and space originate. The Devotee puts the entirety of who they are into this ark, that it may carry them across the ocean of space to the Great Mother of the Universe.

As such, the symbol of the *Ananda Arghya* is the 7-rayed star, the Heptagram of BABALON, within a *vesica piscis* (oval figure, symbolic of the *yoni*). In the center of the Heptagram is the *Bindu*.

The *Ananda Arghya* expresses the tantra at the core of *Liber AL vel Legis*. Its Devotees are *sadhakas* of Babalon, residing in the cosmic Bliss atop Mount Kailash with Shiva and Shakti. They celebrate the Mysteries of the Great Goddess, giving and receiving all on Her behalf, and manifesting the Joy and Beauty of Her Mystery to the World. This dynamic of energy is fully experienced as the interplay of Hadit (the One) and Nuit (the All, or Nothing) in the body of the practitioner, and in their expanding consciousness. On another level, these rituals are an embodiment of the dynamic energy of Babalon and the Beast conjoined. By fully utilizing the senses and awareness to become awake and aware to the ever-present play of the cosmic energies which encompass all of existence, the *sadhaka* experiences the union of Babalon and the Beast in their own body and consciousness.

Meditation on *Atu VII: The Chariot* (Figure 4), and *Atu XII: The Hanged Man* (Figure 20), may prove fruitful for a deeper understanding of the *Ananda Arghya*. These are symbolic representations of the *vehicle* and the *bliss*. Similarly, *Atu XIV: Art* (Figure 23) gives indications on the Way of this ritual practice; and *Atu XVII: The Star* (Figure 21), shows the radiance of the Great Star of the Goddess which informs all of this Work.

Figure 20
'The Hanged Man' Card of the Thoth Tarot
(© Ordo Templi Orientis)

Figure 21
'The Star' Card of the Thoth Tarot
(© Ordo Templi Orientis)

The Armor of the Great Goddess
The Battle of Alkapuri

In the *Devimahatmyam,* the battle of Alkapuri is the epic war between the goddess Durga and the demon Mahasasura. This setting is an apt meditation on the practice of this ritual of banishing. Adepts of the Western Mysteries are familiar with the Banishing Rituals of the Pentagram, which are used (among other things) to prepare a space (inner and outer) for ritual.

In Shingon Esoteric Buddhism, there are similar methods of securing the space before entering the *Mandala* known as the *hogu-kongo-sho ("vajra* fence of the sides and corners"), or the *shihoketsu* ("securing the four directions"). With *mudra, mantra* and visualization, a protective barrier (fence) of fiery *Vajras* (Figure 6) is seen around the perimeter of the *mandala.*

The *Kaula Tantras* have another technique involving the *kavacha* (armor) of the great warrior goddess, and the *bija mantras* (seed syllables) of destruction and protection to set up a perimeter.

The *Diamond Sapphire Gem of Radiant Light* indicates a ritual sequence for opening the temple:

> *"The first ritual act performed is the preparation of the space. In a Temple dedicated to the Light, no preparatory banishings may even be necessary. If the space is used for any other activities however, some form of cleansing should be performed. In general, the Lesser Banishing Ritual of the Pentagram is suitable. More experienced Officiants may wish to use another method. Adepti of the Rosy Cross may prefer a completely different formula, such as an Invoking Pentagram or Star Ruby. Many other options are available, and this is left to the discretion of the Officiant.*

After the preliminaries, the Officiant silently invokes the presence of the Divine Light, and the blessings of the Crowned and Conquering Child of the Aeon.

Next occurs the simple formula of opening and attuning to the Thelemic current by taking refuge in the Three Great Lights of Thelema. Stand with the arms side by side, while reciting:

Nu is my Refuge [raise your arms slightly]
As Hadit my Light [continue to raise your arms]
And Heru-Ra-Ha is the Strength, Force, Vigour of my arms.[92]"

[Your arms are now raised and outstretched. Cross your arms over your chest, right over left.]

"While the arms are moving up and the words are being said, visualize the Sun slowly rising above the Ocean, its rays of light streaming out towards you in brilliant solar gold fire. Simultaneously with this, as the glowing light from the dawning sun spreads, see myriads of lotuses growing up out of the ground, petals opening up to drink in the solar radiance, as the Adytum is transformed into the realm of the Three Rivers."

Aspirants of the *Ananda Arghya* may find within this seemingly simple opening from the central ritual of the *Diamond Sapphire* a potent and effective means of preparing a sacred space and banishing. This is the *Armor of the Great Goddess*.

For this ritual, a combination of techniques is employed to produce a remarkably effective and potent banishing. Combining Will

---

[92] After *Liber Legis* III:17

(iccha), Knowledge *(jnana)*, and Action *(kriya)*, the irresistible WORD of the Adept flames forth unimpeded; the *Bodhicitta* may then arise, diamond-like and shining victoriously throughout the Universe.

The ritual act of Thelemic Refuge is also the *Armor of Nuit*, forming an impenetrable shield around your sphere of sensation. Next comes the clearing of the space, and the setting up of a flaming barrier around the perimeter.

Two *bija mantras* (seed syllables) are employed—**HUM** and **PHAT**. These appear in combination with many other *mantras* in both Buddhist and *Kaula Tantra*, often as a means of protecting the *sadhaka*, clearing away obscurations, and allowing the radiant essence within to arise.

> **HUM:** *Bija mantra* of the warrior goddess and Her *kavacha*. It is uttered by Kali during the great battles against the demons, as well as forming the battle cry of Durga during her triumph against the demon Mahishasura. HUM is the seed syllable of "terror" and also of *Bodhicitta*.[93]
>
> **PHAT:** The *sphota* (explosive) or *astra* (weapon) *bija*. Often used at the conclusion of longer *mantras*, as well as in combination with clapping the hands or snapping the fingers to produce a loud, cracking sound. PHAT is the seed syllable of "crushing and destroying."[94]

---

[93] *The Matrix and Diamond World Mandalas of Shingon Buddhism.* Adrian Snodgrass.
[94] Ibid.

The *bijas*, in combination with the visualizations employed, serve a two-fold purpose of both "burning" and "destroying" *everything* antagonistic to the Work, and also generating a protective shield around the perimeter of the working area—a magick circle There is thus a threefold protection of the Armor, the fence or wall around the perimeter, and the burning away and destroying of everything that is not in alignment with the Will, so that *Bodhicitta* may arise clearly and spontaneously, and radiate outwards into the Universe.[95]

Refuge and Armament

1. Say:
   Nu is my Refuge [raise your arms slightly]
   As Hadit my Light [continue to raise your arms]
   And Heru-Ra-Ha is the Strength, Force, Vigour of my arms.

Your arms are now raised and outstretched. Cross your arms over your chest, right over left.

2. While holding this position, see your sphere of sensation radiant with impenetrable, golden armor. Hold this position, and see a field of crimson light, iridescent and glittering, as though composed of millions of ruby crystals, emanating from the armor. Each pulsates with energy as though alive.

3. Quietly vibrate the *bija* **HUM.** Draw out the sound, increasing in intensity, while at the same time see the crimson light react to the vibration by becoming more alive with color and intensity and contracting closer to your body.

---

[95] See also *Ephesians* 6:10–18.

Figure 22
Vajra Mudra
(Kat Lunoe)

4. Now, in one swift movement, dash both hands down and out while giving the *Vajra mudra* with both hands, and explode the energy outwards with the *bija* **PHAT!**[96] Immediately, the crimson light transforms into millions of blazing, crimson *vajras* of light which fly out into all the directions of space, burning everything in their path which is not in alignment with the Will. Extended out into the depths of space, they form into an impenetrable *vajra* fence of fire which completely surrounds and protects you.

5. Pause to feel the protective Armor surrounding your body, and the radiant magick circle of fiery *vajras*.

6. Allow the Awakened mind of *Bodhicitta* to Arise, diamond-like.

---

[96] If desired, the *bijas* may be replaced with **BAHLASTI** and **OMPEHDA** for a different effect.

The Arrow of Arjuna

In Zen Buddhism, *koans* are paradoxical statements, stories or questions used to challenge the student's intellect, and push them towards enlightenment. *Koans* often involve a profound truth or insight that cannot be expressed through language or logical reasoning. The student is encouraged to meditate on the *koan*, and attempt to reach a deep understanding beyond the limitations of the rational mind. The goal is to experience a moment of *satori*, a sudden flash of insight, that can lead to a profound transformation of the student's perception of reality. *Koans* are an important part of Zen practice, and are often used by teachers to guide students on the path towards awakening.

The verses of *The Book of the Law* readily lend themselves to this type of intense concentration, and can be used as meditative subjects in the same way that *koans* are used in Zen settings. The book has many layers of meaning which open up and reveal themselves upon deep contemplation. Additionally, the effects on consciousness itself can be profound. This practice is an excellent, powerful meditation on the verses of *The Book of the Law* to expand consciousness, come to a deeper understanding of Thelema, and to ultimately transcend the words and mental constructs that you have taken for granted. The result of breakthrough can give insight and first-hand experience of gnosis.

With this type of meditative practice, the first obstacle is the untrained and unwieldly mind. Thoughts will flood consciousness with incessant chatter. The desire to understand a word or phrase that is being focused on can become almost maddening, with a feverish intensity. The instinct will be to do anything *but* sit and focus on the passage at hand. In this sense, at this moment, you will be very much at battle—a battle with your Self.

The Practice

Take *The Book of the Law*, and give active *dharana* (concentration) on one passage weekly, in order.

During these meditations, your mind should be focused intently, exclusively, on the passage. This is not a passive, relaxing contemplation. Rather, you should attack the verse with your concentration, attempting with all of your Will to pierce the barrier of the words. As in the *Bhagavad Gita*, you are the warrior-prince Arjuna on the battlefield of Kurukshetra; your mind is the Chariot on the Battlefield; the errant thoughts are your cousins on the Battlefield that have become your mortal enemy; the verse you must penetrate is Krishna, and the Great Reward which lies beyond the veil of the words. You shall pursue your prey relentlessly, mercilessly. This is the warrior meditation, the path of the *Vira* (hero).

At the beginning, dedicate at least 11 minutes to the *dharana*. If you have the time and Will, sit with the verse longer. A traditional measure of time from the Patriarchs of our brethren in the Zen schools is to light a stick of incense, and meditate until it has burned down. However, regular and dedicated practice is far more important than duration.

It is best if these meditations are conducted in a consecrated environment, at the same time and place every day. Ideally, they may be done after the practice of your *sadhana*, so that all the vehicles have already been energized and experienced in sequence.

Have a journal nearby, so that after your time has concluded you may write down any impressions that may have occurred during your practice.

Awakening the Interior Stars

"From the Akasa emanated the Air, from the Air came the Fire; from the Fire—Water; and from the Water came Earth. This is the order of subtle emanation.

The earth becomes subtle and is dissolved in water; water is resolved into fire; fire similarly merges into air, air gets absorption in ether, and ether is resolved in Avidya (ignorance), which merges into the Great Brahma."

— *Shiva Samhita*

"One mounteth unto the Crown by the moon and by the Sun, and by the arrow, and by the Foundation, and by the dark home of the stars from the black earth."

— *Liber LXV, I:9*

This practice is preliminary to many of the more involved *sadhanas*, as well as preparation for meditation or ritual work. The traditional name of this practice is *bhutta shuddhi*: the analysis, purification and synthesis of the elements. Traditionally *bhutta shuddi* is performed near the beginning of tantrik *sadhana* as a means of stimulating and purifying the body. The elements which compose the more subtle aspects of the physical body, and the *chakras* associated with them, are each activated and analysed in turn, before combining them all to produce a unified and energized mind and body for further ritual.

In the current form of the practice, this yogic exercise is an adaptation of the alchemical formula of *solve et coagula*—dissolve and put together. You will be working with the primary *chakras* to extract and purify each of the elements as they appear in the body and mind; after analysis and refinement, the elements are re-assembled, all the while experiencing the underlying foundation of primordial awareness that is both the source and expression of the elements.

The following chart shows the relationship of the *chakras* with the elements, their *bija mantra*, their alchemical quality, and their position in the body. It will be useful to keep this chart in mind, and reference it during the ritual exercise:

Name	Region	Tattva	Bija	Alchemy
Muladhara	Prostatic ganglion	Earth (Prithivi)	LAM	Lead
Svadhisthana	Genitals	Water (Apas)	VAM	Iron
Manipura	Solar Plexus	Fire (Tejas)	RAM	Tin
Anahata	Cardiac Plexus	Air (Vayu)	YAM	Gold
Vishuddha	Thoracic Ganglion	Spirit (Akasa)	HAM	Copper
Ajna	Pituitary body	Consciousness	AUM	Silver
Sahasrara	Pineal gland	The Abyss	—	Quicksilver

The elemental tattvas manifest as a function of the 7 *chakras*. This is a nexus between the material realms and the more subtle, yet fundamental levels of reality that are the "higher realms" and ultimately the base or point of origin for everything—the Void. Regarding the nature of the connection between the elements and the Void, or *samsara* and *nirvana*, the esoteric Buddhism of Shingon states:

> "The distinguishing characteristic of the Esoteric Doctrine is radical non-dualism (advaita, funi li. 'not two'). The exoteric schools of Buddhism perceive that the dharmas of the phenomenal world are in continual flux, changing from one instant to the next, and deduce from this that they are Void (sunyata, koku), lacking in self-nature, and in some sense illusory or unreal. Esoteric Buddhism accepts that the dharmas are transitory and fleeting, but totally rejects the view that they are in any way unreal. Even though the things of the sensible world are ephemeral and every-changing, they are real, just as they are. They physical world and its Voidness are two aspects of a single Reality; there is no Void without phenomenal forms and no phenomenal forms without their Voidness. Forms and the Void are indissolubly merged, and they are both equally real. Unenlightened men, however, see only one aspect of this Reality, whereas the Awakened Buddhas see both aspects in their instantaneous union."[97]

Kobo Daishi, the founder of Shingon, wrote:

> "The six elements produce all things. They produce the four Dharma Bodies and everything in the three worlds. They produce all the dharmas, from the uppermost limits of the Dharma Body down to the lowest of the six realms. Even though the dharmas are differentiated into subtle and gross and distinguished as large and small, they all come out from the six Elements and therefore the Buddha teaches that the six Elements are the essential nature of the Dharma Worlds."

---

[97] *The Matrix and Diamond World Mandalas of Shingon Buddhism*, Adrian Snodgrass.

EARTH — Muladhara — LAM

Located at the region of the prostatic ganglion, the root center is associated with the element of earth as the consolidation of all the other elements. Kabbalistically it is associated with Alchemical lead and the planet Saturn.

Within *Muladhara* is the secret serpent power, the firesnake of *Kundalini*, the cosmic phallus. From the *Shiva Sanhita* we learn of *Muladhara*, that it is,

> "called the root; there dwells the goddess Kundalini. It surrounds all the nadis, and has three coils and a half; and catching its tail in its own mouth, it rests in the hole of the Shushumna."

Again, from the *Shiva Sanhita*:

> "Of the kundalini, it is called the goddess of speech, and the bija (seed). It is endowed with the powers of action and sensation, and circulates throughout the body. It is subtle, and has a flame of fire; sometimes it rises up, and at other times it falls down into the water. This is the great energy which rests in the perineum, and is called the svayambhulinga (the self-born)."

The *Shiva Sanhita* describes the benefits as:

> "It destroys old age, death and troubles innumerable. [...] Whatever the mind desires, he gets. [...] He conquers the mind, and can restrain his breath and his semen; then he gets success in this as well as the other world, without doubt."

The *Sat-Cakra-Nirupana* ("Description of the Six Centers") gives the following benefits to activating this center:

> "By meditating thus on Her who shines within the Mula-Cakra, with the luster of ten million Suns, a man becomes Lord of speech and King among men, and Adept in all kinds

of learning. He becomes ever free from all diseases, and his inmost Spirit becomes full of great gladness."

WATER — Svadhisthana — VAM

The *Svadhisthana* is located at the genital region, and is associated in the Hindu *Tantras* with the element of water. It is colored blood-red. According to the *Siva Samhita*, one in whom this *chakra* is activated,

> "becomes an object of love and adoration to all beautiful goddesses. He fearlessly recites the various Sastras and sciences unknown to him before; becomes free from all diseases, and moves throughout the universe freely. Death is eaten by him, he is eaten by none; he obtains the highest psychic powers [...]."

From the *Sat-Cakra-Nirupana* we are told that:

> "Within [Svadhisthana] is the white, shining watery region of Varuna, of the shape of a half moon, and therein, seated on a Makara, is the Bija VAM, stainless as the autumnal moon. [...] He who meditates upon this stainless Lotus [...] becomes a Lord among Yogis, and is like the Sun illuminating the dense darkness of ignorance. The wealth of his nectar-like words flows in prose and verse in well-reasoned discourse."

FIRE — Manipura — RAM

From the *Shiva Sanhita*:

> "In the abdomen there burns the fire—the digester of food [...] This fire increases life, and gives strength and nourishment, makes the body full of energy, destroys diseases, and gives health.

> When the yogi contemplates on the manipura lotus, he gets the power called pital-siddhi—the giver of constant happiness. He becomes lord of desires, destroys sorrows and diseases, cheats death, and can enter the body of another."

The *Sat-Cakra-Nirupana* states that by meditating on this lotus, you obtain the power to "destroy and create the world."

AIR — Anahatta — YAM

The *Shiva Sanhita* gives the following:

> "In the heart, is the fourth Chakra [...] Its color is deep blood-red [...] and is a very pleasant spot. In this lotus is a flame called vanlinga; by contemplating on this, one gets objects of the seen and unseen universe. [...] He who always contemplates on this lotus of the heart is eagerly desired by celestial maidens. He gets immeasurable knowledge, knows the past, present and future time; has clairaudience, clairvoyance and can walk in the air, whenever he likes. He sees the adepts, and the goddesses known as Yoginis; obtains the power known as Khechari (ability to move in the air), and conquers all who move in the air."

And from the *Sat-Cakra-Nirupana* we learn that the activation of this center makes one,

> "pre-eminently wise and full of noble deeds. His senses are completely under control. His mind in its intense concentration is engrossed in the thoughts of Brahman. His inspired speech flows like a stream of (clear) water [...] and he is able at will to enter another's body."

ETHER/SPIRIT — Vishuddha — HAM

Located at the pharyngeal plexus, the *Vishuddha chakra* is associated with the element of Air. Kabbalistically, it is referred to Venus and the Alchemical element of copper. Associated in the *Tantras* with spirit, the *chakra* is described as a smoky, purple color.

The *Shiva Sanhita* attributes the following *siddhis* to this center:

> "When the Yogi, fixing his mind on this secret spot, feels angry, then undoubtedly all three worlds begins to tremble. [...] he becomes unconscious of the external world, and enjoys certainly the inner world. [...] His body never grows weak, and he retains full strength for a thousand years, it becomes harder than adamant."

And from the *Sat-Cakra-Nirupana*:

> "He [becomes] eloquent and wise, and enjoys uninterrupted peace of mind. He sees the three periods (past, present & future), and becomes the benefactor of all, free from disease and sorrow and long-lived [...] the destroyer of endless dangers."

Further the yogi is able to move freely in the three worlds, and none of the Gods are able to control or resist him.

CONSCIOUSNESS — Ajna — AUM

Located at the center of the brow, *Ajna* is associated with the pituitary body, is often referred to as the "Third Eye", and is associated with Shiva, whose eyes are closed in eternal bliss in union with Shakti. It is said that if Shiva's eye opens, the universe is destroyed in the *kalagnirudra*, the great fire at the end of time.

According to the *Sat-Cakra-Nirupana*, within *Ajna* is the *Shivalingam*, which resembles "continuous streaks of lightning flashes." The *pranava*, AUM, is situated within the *lingam*.

Kabbalistically *Ajna* is associated with Luna and alchemical quicksilver. In the Hindu *Tantras* it is associated with the element of Spirit. According to the *Shiva Sanhita*:

> "The two-petalled Chakra [...] is situated between the two eyebrows. This is the great light held secret in all the Tantras; by contemplating on this, one obtains the highest success."

And from the *Sat-Cakra-Nirupana* we learn that the power of this Lotus gives the ability to,

> "quickly enter another's body at will, and becomes [...] all-knowing and all-seeing. He becomes the benefactor of all [...] and acquires excellent and unknown powers. Full of fame and long-lived, he ever becomes the Creator, Destroyer and Preserver of the three worlds."

SUNYATA — Sahasrara — Silence

As individual consciousness melts away, like a drop in the ocean, this is the opening to the Void.

While not one of the traditional elements, some esoteric schools have attributed alchemical quicksilver to *Sahasrara*. The thousand-petaled lotus marks the connection between the macrocosm and the microcosm in the spiritual constitution of the initiate. The opening of this *chakra* is described with such poetic, mystic terminology as "absorption in the infinite," "union with Nuit," "cosmic consciousness," and many other phrases.

The activation of *Sahasrara* is equated with the opening of the Eye of Shiva, the immolation of the universe in the cosmic fire which precedes the *pralaya* (breath between manifestations of the universe). This is the ejaculation of the *Shivalingam*, the great phallus of light that the initiate has become by virtue of their successive interior workings with the *chakras*. The full ascent of the *kundalini* results in this union with the infinite, where subject and object are united in infinity which, to the ego, appears as annihilation of the all.

According to the *Shiva Samhita*, from the thousand-petaled lotus the *"[...] elixir is continually flowing. This moon-fluid of immortality unceasingly flows [...] in a stream—a continuous stream."* It is said that within *sahasrara* is a *yoni* throne, seen as a red, equilateral triangle with the single point facing downwards. To simply contemplate this is said to destroy all sins, *"and one is never born again as man."* *Sahasrara* is described as,

> *"outside the microcosm of the body, it is the giver of salvation. Its name is verily the Kailas mount, where dwells the great Lord Shiva, who is called Nakula and is without destruction, and without increase or decrease. Men, as soon as they discover this most secret place, become free from re-births in this universe. By the practice of this yoga he gets the power of creating or destroying the creation, the aggregate of elements. When the mind is steadily fixed at this place [...] then that yogi, devoid of all diseases and subduing all accidents, lives for a great age, free from death. [The] fullness of the Samadhi is attained [...] one forgets the world, then in sooth the yogi obtains wonderful power. Let the yogi continually drink the nectar which flows out of it."*

Figure 23
The 'Art' Card of the Thoth Tarot
(© Ordo Templi Orientis)

A cognate magical image of both the *analysis* and *synthesis* of the elements *(solve et coagula)* is resumed in the image of Atu XIV: Art. From *The Book of Thoth*:

> "This state of the great Work therefore consisted in the mingling of the contradictory elements in a cauldron. This is here represented as golden or solar, because the Sun is the Father of all Life, and (in particular) presides over distillation. The fertility of the Earth is maintained by rain and sun; the rain is formed by a slow and gentle process, and is rendered effective by the co-operation of air, which is itself alchemically the result of the Marriage of Fire and Water. So also the formula of continued life is death, or putrefaction. Here it is symbolized by the caput mortuum on the cauldron, a raven perched upon a skull. In agricultural terms, this is the fallow earth.
> [...]

> *Rising from the cauldron, as the result of the operation performed is a stream of light which becomes two rainbows; they form the cape of the androgyne figure. In the centre, an arrow shoots upwards. This is connected with the general symbolism previously explained, the spiritualization of the result of the Great Work.*
>
> *The rainbow is moreover symbolical of another stage in the alchemical process. At a certain period, as a result of putrefaction, there is observed a phenomenon of many-coloured lights."*

Also, the Vision of the Arrow from the 5th Aethyr of *The Vision and the Voice*:

> *"I shudder and tremble at the vision, for all about it are whorls, and torrents of tempestuous fire. The stars of heaven are caught in the ashes of the flame. And they are all dark. That which was a blazing sun is like a speck of ash. And in the midst the Arrow burns! Then I see that the crown of the Arrow is the Father of all Light, and shaft of the Arrow is the Father of all Life, and the barb of the Arrow is the Father of all Love. For that silver wedge is like a lotus flower, and the Eye within the Ateph Crown crieth: I watch. And the Shaft crieth: I work. And the Barb crieth: I wait. And the voice of the Aethyr echoeth: It beams. It burns. It blooms.*
>
> *And now there cometh a strange thought; this Arrow is the source of all motion; it is infinite motion, yet it moveth not, so that there is no motion. And therefore there is no matter. This Arrow is the glance of the Eye of Shiva. But because it moveth not, the universe is not destroyed. The universe is put forth and swallowed up in the quivering of the plumes of Maat, that are the plumes of the Arrow; but those plumes quiver not."*

The Practice

1. Vibrate the *bija mantras* of each element from the bottom *(Muladhara)* up the spine to *Ajna* (and thence out to *Sahasrara)* 11 times each:

Chakra	Tattva	Bija
Muladhara	Earth (Prithivi)	LAM
Svadhisthana	Water (Apas)	VAM
Manipura	Fire (Tejas)	RAM
Anahatta	Air (Vayu)	YAM
Vishuddha	Spirit (Akasa)	HAM
Ajna	Consciousness	AUM

2. Focus on the *muladhara chakra* and the element Earth. Visualize Prithivi as a yellow square in the center of the *chakra*, and vibrate **LAM**. Bring a current of light up from this region to the next.

3. Focus on the *svadhisthana chakra* and the element Water. Visualize Apas as a silver crescent (points up) in the *chakra*, and vibrate **VAM**. Bring a current of light up from this region to the next.

4. Focus on the *manipura chakra* and the element Fire. Visualize Tejas as a red equilateral triangle in the *chakra*, and vibrate **RAM**. Bring a current of light up from this region to the next.

5. Focus on the *anahatta chakra* and the element Air. Visualize Vayu as a blue circle in the *chakra*, and vibrate **YAM**. Bring a current of light up from this region to the next.

6. Focus on the *vishuddha chakra* and the element Ether. Visualize Akasha as a black oval in the *chakra,* and vibrate **HAM**. Bring a current of light up from this region to the next.

7. Focus on the *ajna chakra* and consciousness itself, and vibrate **AUM**. Bring the light up out of the crown of the head *(sahasrara).*

8. Repeat the process, vibrating the *bija* and bringing the light down through the centers from *sahasrara* to *muladhara* where the light rests.

9. Repeat the entire process twice.

10. Bring the light up through the centers again, but this time see it formulate itself as a great snake of light. As it advances up and out of the crown of the head, it merges into the images of Babalon and the Beast in union. Each holds a *kapala*—a bowl made from the cranium of a human skull. Babalon holds a *kapala* filled with menstrual blood, and the Beast holds a *kapala* filled with semen. These together are the tantric "red and white nectars."

11. Babalon and the Beast pour the red and white nectar from the *kapalas* into your skull, and down through all of the centers, until reaching *muladhara.*

12. Vibrate AUM.

The Adamantine Star of Horus

This practice is, at its most essential aspect, a ritual of protection and defense. The ritual also serves to reify the Will of the magician, building up a powerful *karma* united with the Egyptian god Horus. It can be used in place of the more traditional *Ritual of the Pentagram*, a ceremonial practice used in various magical traditions, including the Hermetic Order of the Golden Dawn and its offshoots.

The frequency with which to perform this ritual varies depending on your practice and goals; generally, once a day is good for banishing and cleansing the aura. It can also be done as needed, such as before a magical working or when feeling spiritually unbalanced.

A deeper aspect of the ritual, one which goes well beyond protection and defense, is the evocation of the four Set-beasts. You may interact with the beasts more directly and learn their names, at which point they become your *familiars* that will come when called. If you choose to cultivate the connection with the four beasts, be prepared for the responsibility of having powerful companions, and provide for them accordingly with offerings.

The Practice

1. Stand or sit facing East. Take a few deep breaths. Exhale each breath slowly, allowing yourself to relax and be aware in the present moment.

2. Visualize yourself as the Hawk-Headed Lord Horus in full regalia, with the Double-Crown of Egypt upon your head.

3. To the East, South, West and North are large black beasts seated around you, facing outwards. At first, they appear to be large black dogs, but upon closer examination they are Set-beasts. See their long,

pointed ears; protruding snouts; lithe, muscular, quadruped bodies, and long, forked tails. They sit at attention looking outward, poised, aware and guarding your perimeter.

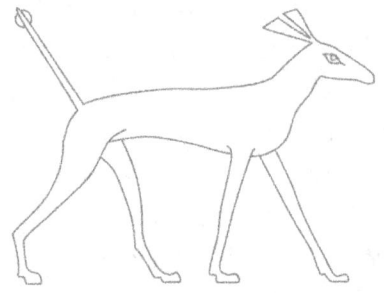

**Figure 24
Set-Beast**
(commons.wikimedia.org)

4. With the perimeter intact, focus again on yourself as the Lord Horus, and become aware of the pulsating star in your heart.

5. Now, with one swift movement, transform yourself into the radiant Hawk of Horus. See your left eye as the Moon, and your right eye as the Sun. Your massive wings create the sky, and your feathered breast is composed all of stars. The Universe reverberates with your cosmic scream.

6. With this visualization, give the **A Ka Dua** *mantra* for at least one round of the *mala* (rosary).

7. Transform yourself back into Horus in human form, as Lord of the Two Kingdoms.

8. Allow the entire scene, including the Set-beasts, to merge with the light in your heart.

9. Remain aware of this Interior Light, the Lord of the Universe enthroned in your Heart.

10. Give *The Sign of Silence* (Figure 10), then open your eyes and rise from meditation, saying **AOM. HA.**

The Sevenfold Palace of the Goddess

This practice works with the secret serpent-fire—*kundalini*—to produce a strong current of energy in the body and consciousness. This build-up of energy can then be directed towards various aims, such as consecrating a talisman or a sigil, performing a magical ritual, or dissolving consciousness into bliss. The practice is complete in itself, and can form the basis of your entire yoga practice. It encompasses several techniques that are brought together to form a synthesis of body, breath and mind. It includes visualization, breath work, and the use of physical yogic techniques: *mudra* (which in this case is a type of mental form or state that is assumed); and *banda* (locks), which are a way of constricting muscles to both hold the breath in certain positions, as well as to push the breath "up" through the central channel of the spine, in order to work with the *kundalini*.

When first learning the practice, it is best to break it into a few sections. First, become familiar with the overall structure and the visualizations. Then you can start to incorporate breath manipulation and the different locks. Go gently, especially if you are not accustomed to yoga or breathwork such as *pranayama*. Ease into the full practice so it can be effective, and you will be more likely to stick with it.

Once you have the mechanics of the exercise down, it can be executed in one sitting. Rather than struggling against it, the entire process should flow easily through the different locks and stages.

The result is an overall sense of warmth and energy, with an expansion of consciousness. In the beginning, set aside an hour each week. Then, as you become more adept, daily practice will build up a strong momentum. This yoga practice, along with the natural meditation that comes from it, is one of the most effective means for energizing the body and mind, a spiritual tonic that will have lasting effects throughout your days.

The Practice

To begin, wear comfortable clothes, and sit in a comfortable position. This can be done in a chair with the back straight and feet flat on the floor, or in the more traditional seated positions like lotus, half-lotus or the Burmese sitting pose (crossed legs). You can even do it lying down, which is great for letting the spine be extended straight without over stretching.

1. Visualize the spine as a thin column of light, snake-like, extending upward from the base of the spine to the base of the brain where it bends forward in an arc extending through the cerebrum and ending at *Ajna* between the eyebrows. This is the Goddess Kundalini.

2. With your eyes gently closed, fix your gaze at the point between the eyebrows. This is the *apanga* (glance) of desire, or adoration towards the Throne of Her Lord.

3. Hold *kecharimudra* (space seal) by expanding the inner opening of the throat, and rolling the tongue back toward the soft palate as far as possible. Do not strain. This *mudra* allows the *amrita*, which descends from on high, to collect and descend through the spine rather than be absorbed by the stomach and destroyed by the digestive process.

4. Inhalation (Ascending Blue Current). Perform *mahabandha,* the "great lock." The great lock is performed by a sequence of three other locks: hold *moolabandha* (root lock) by tightening the sphincter muscles; *uddiyanabandha* (diaphragm lock) by contracting the lower abdomen; and *jalandharabanda* (chin lock*)* by lowering the chin. This three-fold sequence, taken as a whole, is *mahabandha* which prevents the ascending Fire Snake from escaping back down the spine. Inhale calmly and slowly through the mouth and nose simultaneously, making the barely audible sound of "AHHHH" deep in the expanded throat. The breath and sound should be continuous, slow, deep and cool as the breath slowly drifts up the spine like a cool wind. One inhalation should be for a count of 11 or more. See a cool, deep-blue, liquid light flowing up with the inhalation and sound. Pause briefly, hold the breath and feel the blue coolness centered in the forehead *(Ajna chakra,* or "third eye"). Hold the breath for a count of 3 at the beginning; as you become proficient this could be extended. Remember not to strain.

5. Exhalation (Descending Red Current). Relax the muscles, thus releasing the lock (while maintaining *kecharimudra* throughout). Slowly exhale through both the mouth and nose for a count of 11 or more, while making the barely audible sound of "EEEEEE" high in the expanded throat. Feel the breath as a warm, honey-like trickle of crimson liquid flowing back through the hollow tube from *Ajna,* through the cerebellum, to the medulla oblongata, then down slowly and soothingly

through the spine to the coccyx. Feel the warmth of the honey-like trickle while concentrating on the sound "EEEEEE" and the crimson color, mentally transferring all of this to the spine. This completes one cycle.

6. Repeat steps 4–5 for a total of 11 times.

7. *Jyoti Mudra* Meditation. At the conclusion of your cycles, rest in meditation while performing *jyotimudra*: Place the palms of your hands gently over your closed eyes. In this position, hold *mahabandha* and *kecharimudra*, and inhale with the sound of "AHHHH," drawing the cool current upward and seeing the serpentine light move slowly up the spine. Release the Great Seal and the pressure of the fingers (without removing them from their positions) and exhale, sending the current of warm liquid *amrita* down through the spine with the sound of the breath hissing "EEEEEE."

This completes one cycle of *jyotimudra*. Initially, one should be enough. As your practice deepens, you may add more cycles.

The precedent for this yogic exercise lies with the *Shiva Samhita*. In the 4th chapter of the *Shiva Samhita*, a curious description of a yogic practice (the *Yoni Mudra/Mudra of Union*, Figure 16) is given. The practice is said to have miraculous powers, encompassing the entire gamut of *siddhis* (magical powers) and attainments. It is a spiritual tonic, a way to clear *karma*, to have power over others, and to achieve whatever you desire. The full *Yoni Mudra* is a technique that consists of putting the hands into a specific position, breathing *(pranayama)*, body locks *(bandas)*, and visualization that directly stimulates the sleeping *kundalini* at the base of the spine, and directs its ascent to the crown *chakra*. Unlike *Awakening the Interior Stars* which stimulates and purifies the *chakras*, the *Yoni Mudra* assumes that the preliminary purifications have been done. The practice is similar to the *Sevenfold Palace of the Goddess*, but with a different regimen of visualizations to accompany the yoga.

> *"Therefore, those who wish for emancipation should practice this mudra daily. Through practice, success is obtained; through practice, one gains liberation.*
>
> *Perfect consciousness is gained through practice. Yoga is attained through practice; success in Mudras comes by practice; through practice is gained success in pranayama. Death can be cheated of its prey through practice, and man becomes the conqueror of death by practice." (Yoga Sutras of Patanjali)*

As a supplement to this exercise, there is also a "seal" or *mudra* that can be made with the hands, the *Mudra of Union* (Figure 16). Folding the hands into the *Mudra of Union* is symbolically identical to the results of performing the actual yoga and visualization of the *Sevenfold Palace of the Goddess*. By putting the hands into the position of the *mudra*, the mind and body also move into the form of the cosmic *Yoni*, the source and destination of all, the very womb-matrix of creation.

§ § §

Sit comfortably, and compose the mind and body into quiet contemplation by giving the *Mudra of Union*. As the outer world melts away into dream-like imagery, the body and mind take on the form of the *mudra*. The true yoga, that of consciousness itself, awakens.

Notes on Practice

Food should not be taken for at least an hour before this practice; it is important to not work with a full stomach. If the *sadhaka* has a cold, this practice should be done in visualization only; do not attempt to control the breath with *pranayama*, particularly if the lungs or nostrils are not clear due to cold.

Keep the inhalation and exhalation equal and slow. Do not allow any break in the breath. The sound should be steady: "AHHHH... EEEEEE..." The sound is made *with the breath*, not the voice. This is the sound of the cosmic Fire Snake, the Goddess Kundalini.

Pay no attention to whether the breath is coming and going through the mouth or the nose or both. The important point is to draw the breath in from deep inside the throat, and to expel it from high in the throat.

Steps 4 and 5 complete one circulation of practice. Eleven cycles should be completed in one sitting, with two sittings a day (at the two twilights). Do not exceed these 22 cycles until you are very solid in the practice.

Until you are proficient, the *bandhas* may be activated at the start of inhalation, but then immediately released instead of holding for the duration. As your ability to maintain the locks strengthens, they should be held for the duration of the Ascent. Regardless, *kecharimudra* and the *apanga* should be maintained.

The *jyotimudra* is also a subtle, inner version of the *Death Posture*, a type of contemplative *mudra* and inner yoga that Austin Osman Spare utilized.

An outer parallel of this ritual is the ancient *Homa oblatios* that are still conducted in Hindu and Buddhist tantrik rites. In these rituals, a fire pit or hearth is created, often in the shape of a triangle, representing the *yoni*. Offerings are thrown into the fire while *mantras* are recited, and as they are transformed by the flame, so is the consciousness and body of the tantrika conducting the ritual.

With the inner *Homa*, the fire is the *kundalini* in the base of the spine, and the offering is the very consciousness of the *sadhaka*, along with the breath, which is transformed by the various locks and *mudras* as the current of energy moves up and down the spine.

In this practice, surrender yourself completely to Her, giving yourself entirely.

The Boat of Millions of Years

This practice is a type of guided meditation or pathworking. It can be done in isolation as a practice in itself, or during a meditation session before or after one of the more energetic *sadhanas*.

In this pathworking, the small self—the ego—goes through death. What remains? How am I still aware after death? If I am dead, who is experiencing? Who am I? These are some of the questions that may come up in this experience. Something that is always present, awake and aware remains—Pure Awareness itself—experiencing the fantastical and magical display of its own luminous nature.

This meditation works well lying flat on your back—corpse pose. Wear comfortable clothing, get into a relaxed position, and read through the text. You might try recording the words, and playing them back while you listen in a meditative state of awareness.

§ § §

Let the Devotee enter *The Boat of Millions of Years* at Sunset, or in the hours just before Dawn.

1. With your eyes on the last rays of the Sun as it drops below the horizon, plunging the Earth into darkness, exhale your last breath and Die. Fall completely into the arms of death. Let the sensation be real, complete, final. There is no turning back from this gate which we all are promised to enter. After some time—it may be millennia—a gentle breath flows into you.

2. From the Darkness, a point of light appears. Exhale.

3. The point of light expands, until everything is red light. Inhale.

4. The red light solidifies and condenses into white light. Exhale.

5. The white light begins to darken and flicker, turning into sparkling red flames like millions of fireflies. Inhale.

6. The millions of flickering red fires condense into a mist or fog. Exhale.

7. The fog fades into transparency. Inhale.

8. Pause.

9. Exhale.

You are on the Solar Bark, making your way through the Darkness of Night. You are seated at the helm as Horus in the form of Khephra. At the front of the Barge is Tahuti.

As you sail—silently, majestically—through the empyrean, entire galaxies, nebulae, black holes—the host of the Universe—are passed by. You may be approached by demons of the night, or ripening *karmas* may manifest. The Gods and Goddesses themselves may approach you. Pay them no heed. No matter what may come or manifest itself, be it seemingly bad or good, remember: *"they pass & are done, but there is that which remains." (AL, II:9)*

After Aeons of time, the Bark approaches the outer boundaries of Night. With the Dawning rays of the Sun radiating out across the Ocean of Space, you are transformed into the triumphant Hawk-

Headed Lord of Silence and of Strength. Give the Hawk's screem[98] of resurrection and eternal Life with the Dawning Sun.

Having come through the Great Night, with Victory, say:

I am the flame that burns in every heart of man, and in the core of every star. I am Life, and the giver of Life, yet therefore is the knowledge of me the knowledge of death. (AL, II:6)

Allow the vision to fade as the True Sun continues to radiate its Light, Life, Love and Liberty throughout your body, rejuvenating and invigorating every cell with effulgent L.V.X.

Dedicate the merit of this practice to the enlightenment of all sentient beings:

May the combined merit accumulated by this rite be dedicated to the enlightenment and well-being of all sentient beings!

If desired, complete by reading *Liber Tzaddi vel Hamus Hermeticus sub figura XC*.

---

[98] This word is reminiscent of the cry of a hawk.

Chapter 11
CAKES OF LIGHT & THE GRAIL OF WINE

Throughout the rituals of this book, and indeed holding a central status in Crowley's magnum opus *Magick*, is the importance of a regular eucharistic practice. We have seen how the trinity of primary elements are incorporated for the eucharist: fire, water and air (see, for example, *Preparation: Trinity of Elements* in Chapter 9). This is the default practice, and can be expanded significantly using your own ingenium.

However, there is another eucharist, tied in directly with the canon of Thelema: the Cakes of Light, and the Grail of Wine. In this chapter I will take a closer look at this eucharistic offering, exploring some of the esoteric elaborations and considerations in working with the multifaceted nature of the ritual.

The Cakes of Light

Thelemites will generally be aware of the cakes from Aleister Crowley's writings. Anyone that has attended a Gnostic Mass will likely have encountered the cakes and partaken of them in celebratory fashion. The recipe for making the cakes was taken from *The Book of the Law* in Chapter III, vv 23–25:

> *"For perfume mix meal & honey & thick leavings of red wine: then oil of Abramelin and olive oil, and afterward soften & smooth down with rich fresh blood. The best blood is of the moon, monthly: then the fresh blood of a child, or dropping from the host of heaven: then of enemies; then of the priest or of the worshippers: last of some beast, no matter what.*

This burn: of this make cakes & eat unto me. This hath also another use; let it be laid before me, and kept thick with perfumes of your orison: it shall become full of beetles as it were and creeping things sacred unto me."

Kenneth Grant elaborates on the substance of the Cakes:

"The four elements from which the magician conjures the fifth, viz: spirit, or a spirit (for the sorcerer is primarily a conjuror of spirits), are explicable only with reference to the biochemistry of the Draconian Tradition. Water, the mystical fluid of life, symbolizes blood; not arterial blood—no spirit ever took body that way—but menstrual blood: the primal menstruum of manifestation whereby spirit is made flesh.

The element earth was ascribed to flesh, as blood congealed, a liquid transformed into solid by caking and becoming the living embodiment of spirit. Hence the symbolic cakes of light of which one ingredient is menstrual blood. (Note: The mother-cake was a name for the placenta, a symbol of manifestation.)"[99]

And:

"To the spirit that energized the primal water with the principle of Life, the Egyptians of the Solar cult ascribed the element air. But originally, that is before the role of the male in the process of reproduction was understood and generally acknowledged, air typified the second phase of the feminine formula, as water (i.e. blood) characterized the first. Water represented the pubescent virgin, bleeding and wet; air char-

---

[99] Kenneth Grant, *Cults of the Shadow*, p. 56. Starfire Publications.

acterized the gestator, the mother, dry and puffed up or bellying with wind. The element fire was the symbol of the Will and an adumbration of the energy of the Fire Snake, invoked and bound into the other elements by the spell of the sorcerer. The fusion of water, air, earth and fire resulted therefore in the production or manifestation of spirit, or a spirit."[100]

The Grail of Wine

At the most basic level, a glass of red wine is taken as the liquid component of the eucharist, to complement the "bread" component of the Cakes of Light. Looking into what the wine represents opens the door to the tantrik, left-hand offerings of many older traditions.

The wine is the *vinum sabbati* (wine of the sabbath). "The Vinum Sabbati (Wine of the Sabbath) was the mystical effusion of the Scarlet Woman, the ever-virgin Whore of the Stars."[101] This is none other than the Great Goddess Babalon, the universal *shakti* that is both transcendent and imminent in the universe, the very womb of creation and the fabric of all that is. (See Chapter 3: *Babalon* for more on Her).

Embodying Babalon is one of the roles of the sacred Priestess, the *suvasini* ("scented woman") in the *Tantras*, the *Scarlet Woman* in the Western mysteries of Thelema. Through the stimulation of her erogenous zones, the lunar *kalas* are produced and released, generating the alchemical elixirs which are used in the tantrik magick rites. In this role of the Priestess embodying Babalon, she is also referred to as the "Goddess 15":

---

[100] Kenneth Grant, *Hecate's Fountain*, pp. 103–104. Starfire Publications.
[101] Kenneth Grant, *Aleister Crowley & The Hidden God*. p. 114. Starfire Publications.

"In the lesser lunar cycle of twenty-eight days, fourteen are dark with diminishing light, fourteen wax bright. The fifteenth day thus became the day of the Goddess. The moon takes twenty-eight days to traverse the twelve zodiacal stations and the number twenty-eight consequently became a glyph of the female, as did thirty of the male.

As thirty-one is the highest aliquot component of ninety-three, so five is the highest aliquot component of fifteen. Five was the primal number of woman as the genetrix long before the stellar seven and the lunar twenty-eight. For five days woman was engulfed in darkness and eclipsed; from her issued the deluge that primitive man rightly identified as the substance which would later congeal and flesh forth progeny. Blood was recognized as liquid flesh and the female expressed (through the number five) her nubility, which was the archetypal nobility because the only known lineage was of the blood of the mother alone.

The male's role in the procreative process was at that time unknown. The five-day eclipse was the seal of woman's nobility, the nobility that wears the scarlet mantle of nature herself, the one unimpeachable rubric of her sovereignty.

And because she was seen to renew life upon earth, woman was likened to the goddess in the sky, who renewed herself through celestial cycles, as a type of resurrection, a return to unity and ultimate perfection in the heavens and the hells. The number five thus became the seal of authority in the world of spirits; it was represented by the pentagram or five-pointed star, still used by magicians for establishing contact with and controlling transmundane entities. The origin of the magical pentagram can thus be traced to the first observed facts of elemental nature.

> *Five was the number of the female; six, or sex, that of the male, in so far as sexual activity again became 'lawful' after the cessation of the deluge. In AL (I, 24), Nuit proclaims: 'I am Nuit, and my word is six and fifty,' which is her manner of saying 56, or the 5 and the 6, 33 indicating that she is the virgin and the mother combined, thus identifying herself with the Whore of the Stars (i.e. the moon), the breeder who brings forth independently of the individualized father. In other words her cult—whether stellar or lunar—is pre-solar. This is important because it implies that Horus, her child, the Crowned and Conquering Child of the Therionic Cult, is the 'child' or essence of the mother alone. This is borne out by AL, II, 4: 'Yet she shall be known & I never.' 'She' is the Goddess Fifteen [...]"*[102]

This Goddess 15 also refers directly to the aspect of the goddess as revealed in the *Ananda Lahari*, the medieval text which plays a central role in the Typhonian Gnosis, and her 15-syllable *mantra* (called the *panchadasi*):

Ka E I La Hrim
Ha Sa Ka Ha La Hrim
Sa Ka La Hrim

Each syllable is attuned to one of the *kalas*, with a final 16th *bija*:

> "*The final bija, Krim, is the bija-mantra of Goddess Kalika, the hidden Principle of Creation described in the Ratrisukta as 'Night'. She it is who reveals the universe as a shadow (chaya). She is the reflex of all colours (kalas), Herself 'without colour'; black. Yet is She the background of light, and the*

---

[102] *Aleister Crowley & The Hidden God*, Kenneth Grant. pp. 115–116.

crescent (sashi-kala) on Her brow denotes that She is the originator of nada-bindu-kala, the trikona at the centre of the Sri Chakra. When fully self-expressed She appears as Uma, with the glamour of the full moon, and is then known as Sri Vidya. Her essence, however, is always Ama (darkness). Uma (light) and Ama (darkness) are the twin poles between which flashes the vibration AUM. As japa of the bija-mantras leads the Fire Snake progressively higher, so do the energies released in the lower chakras, bordering the subconsciousness, become increasingly active."[103]

A simple ritual meditation to stimulate the *kundalini* while vibrating the *bija mantras* is outlined as:

"The specific root-mantras utilized in the evolution or uncoiling of the Fire Snake are:

1) OM-kara, which concentrates the trikona Bindu-Nada-Kala and which is represented zoömorphically by the elephant-god Ganesh.

2) Hrim, which awakens and releases the Fire Snake.

3) Aim, which causes it to ascend.

4) Srim, which maintains its creative surge.

5) Krim, which consummates the entire process."[104]

We have then one means of stimulating the "fire snake" to produce the nectar which is then incorporated into the Wine, or imbibed directly.

To understand the Cakes of Light is to look back towards history. In ancient Egypt, the ritual of offering bread and beer to the gods dates back to prehistoric times, and formed an integral part of

---

[103] *Beyond the Mauve Zone*, Kenneth Grant. p. 88. Starfire Publications.
[104] Ibid.

religious practice. These offerings symbolized sustenance for both the living and the dead, facilitating communication between the earthly and divine realms. In medieval Europe, alchemists and mystics imbued food and drink with symbolic significance, viewing them as vehicles for spiritual transformation and enlightenment. In at least one interpretation, the process of transmuting base metals into gold served as an allegory for the soul's journey towards perfection. The practices of ancient Egypt and medieval alchemy exerted a significant influence on Western esoteric traditions, including the development of ceremonial magic and occult philosophy. The concept of sacred food offerings persisted throughout the ages, evolving to suit the needs and beliefs of different cultures and spiritual movements.

In Hindu Tantric traditions, the food and drink offerings (*prasad*) are consecrated and distributed to devotees as a form of divine blessing. These offerings often consist of simple foods such as fruits, sweets and grains, symbolizing the abundance and benevolence of the divine. In the *vamamarga* or "left-hand path" of tantra, the *prasad* took the form of *bali*—meat offerings, along with alcohol and mixed sexual fluids.[105]

In Tibetan Buddhism, offerings known as *tormas* are meticulously crafted and offered to deities as part of tantric ceremonies. These ritual objects serve as representations of enlightened consciousness and are imbued with symbolic significance.

Tantric offerings in both Hinduism and Buddhism are imbued with profound symbolism and serve as a means of invoking divine

---

[105] A discussion of the tantrik offerings in this context is in Chapter 13: *The Five-Fold Worship of the Goddess*. For a thorough discussion of the historical aspects in left-handed tantra, see my book *Yogini Magic*, Chapter 16: Offerings.

blessings, purifying the mind and body, and fostering spiritual growth. More critically, the very act of offering represents a reciprocal relationship between the practitioner and the divine, establishing and emphasizing the interconnectedness between the practitioner and the divine. As the *Book of the Law* indicates: "There is no difference." By participating in these eucharist and offering practices, the magician acknowledges and embodies the non-dual reality expressed throughout the *Book of the Law*.

In commenting on verse 23 of Chapter III of *The Book of the Law*, Kenneth Grant gives details on the inner ingredients and their production with Western techniques of the sexual gnosis:

"The verse gives a recipe for making the cakes of light which can be cooked only by a priestess in her scarlet phase. 'The best blood is of the moon, monthly: then the fresh blood of a child, or dropping from the host of heaven: then of enemies; then of the priest or of the worshipper: last of some beast, no matter what.' These ingredients are particularized in verse 24 as: 1) the blood of the full moon, 2) the first flowering of the pubescent female, or kalas of the stars,34 3) 'enemies' = thoughts; which implies the need for control of the mind and the direction of thoughts to magical ends, 4) semen produced by IX°+, 5) semen produced by XI°+. The resulting hell-broth is to be burnt (cooked) and made into cakes of light. The cakes are to be magically masticated. This is the secret rite of the Wine of the Sangraal, and of the Vinum Sabbati which is not swallowed but retained beneath the tongue until absorbed into the system. Or, alternatively, the cakes may be placed before the image of Set and 'kept thick with perfumes of your orison,' i.e., constantly greased, anointed, or nourished, by

means of the rite of the VIII°+. The substance will then become full of beetles as it were and creeping things sacred to me. These slay, naming your enemies; & they shall fall before you.

Also these shall breed lust & power of lust in you at the eating thereof.

Also ye shall be strong in war. Moreover, be they long kept, it is better; for they swell with my force. All before me.

The beetle is one of the zoötypes of the Holy Graal, the vessel of that supreme excrement which is the blood of Babalon, the Scarlet Woman of Whoredom in whose vulva seethes the sperm of Saints. Creeping things are emblematic of the Ophidian Current. They manifest in the aura of the priestess and appear to swarm like vermin over her body, which represents the cakes of light. If the vermin are magically slain, the 'enemies' (i.e. the distracting thoughts of the magician) are destroyed, and pure bliss remains over."[106]

The eucharistic practices within Thelema, embodied by the Cakes of Light and the Grail of Wine, are profound expressions of the union between the mundane and the divine. These rituals, rooted in ancient traditions and enriched by a deep occult symbolism, serve as potent tools for spiritual transformation. By partaking in these sacred rites, we engage in a timeless act of communion with the higher aspects of existence.

Through the careful preparation and consumption of the Cakes of Light and the Grail of Wine, we enact a ritual that transcends the boundaries of the physical world, inviting the divine presence into our lives, and aligning ourselves with the universal flow of energy. This sacred practice is a reminder of our interconnectedness with

---

[106] *Hecate's Fountain*, Kenneth Grant. pp. 103–104. Starfire Publishing.

the cosmos and our potential to attain higher states of consciousness.

As we continue to explore and refine these rituals, we deepen our understanding of the mysteries of Thelema and our own spiritual journeys. The eucharist becomes a beacon of light, guiding us toward the realization of our True Will and the fulfillment of our highest potential. By embracing these sacred traditions, we open ourselves to the infinite possibilities of spiritual growth and enlightenment, ultimately achieving a harmonious balance between our earthly existence and our divine essence.

Both the Thelemic Cakes of Light and tantric offerings share common themes of transformation, communion, and spiritual nourishment. The act of consuming sacred substances serves as a means of uniting with higher states of consciousness and accessing divine energies. Through the transformation of mundane substances into sacred offerings, we physically enact the alchemical process of spiritual evolution and enlightenment. Through ritualized consumption, practitioners aim to transcend the apparent limitations of the material world and commune with higher realms of existence. Through repeated acts of such communion, the mind becomes more sensitized to seeing between worlds, and seeing through the illusory nature of materialism. By engaging in these practices, we seek to deepen the spiritual connection with everyday life, gain insight into the nature of reality, and attain a sense of inner peace and fulfillment. In short, to know and do our True Will.

Chapter 12
TANTRIK SADHANAS

The Great Seal of the Goddess

The *Great Seal of the Goddess* is a tantrik *sadhana*—essentially a meditation and ritual, that focuses on the union and dissolution of the self with the divine feminine energy as expressed by the Egyptian Goddess, Nuit. The ritual is performed to attain a state of heightened awareness, connection and union with the divine. Through mastery of the *sadhana*, the boundaries between "self" and "other" are dissolved, opening up to the pristine cosmic radiance of awakened consciousness.

The overall approach involves preparing the space, centering the mind, and establishing a connection with the Goddess through visualization, *mantra* chanting, and *mudras* (hand gestures). The ritual can be performed at night, under a canopy of stars, to enhance the sense of cosmic connection. Or, through visualization, the cosmic landscape can be brought into any situation—be it outside in the wilderness or inside a building.

This, as well as the following *sadhanas,* all follow a similar pattern that derives from older tantrik rituals. The many practices throughout this book have served as both preparations and as part of the magical and tantrik toolkit that will be used throughout the *sadhanas.* The ritual consists of several steps:

Outline of the Sadhana

0. Preliminary: Prepare the ritual space and perform any necessary banishing rituals. Light a candle and incense, and establish rhythmic breathing.

1. Opening: Invoke the *Refuge and Armor of the Great Goddess,* and raise the arms in a gesture of union. Recite the Law of Thelema, and perform an awakening of the interior stars through visualization.

2. Dissolution: Enter a state of deep meditation. Visualize yourself in a vast desert of black sand, under a canopy of stars. Surrender yourself to the Goddess, offering all that you are to her in a state of complete union and ecstasy.

3. Creation: After experiencing the dissolution, focus on the inner light, representing the inmost essence of creation. Generate *Bodhicitta* (enlightened mind), and send blessings to all of creation while reciting the *Mantra of Revealing* (see Chapter 14). Visualize the creation of the universe and the birth of a new cycle of time.

4. Light in Extension: Extend your light to the four directions of space, affirming the qualities of light, life, liberty and love. Recognize yourself as Ra-Hoor-Khuit, the divine self, enthroned at the center of the universe.

5. Manifestation: Take on the form of Ra-Hoor-Khuit, and affirm your divine nature and power. Merge your inner vision with the external world, perceiving the world as regenerated and composed of starlight.

6. Eucharist (optional): Consume a symbolic elixir and food, offering them to the Goddess, and affirming the mingling of your life with the universal life.

7. Transfer of Merit and Close: Extend your blessings and positive qualities to all beings. Close the ritual with the word "**ABRAHADABRA**".

The *Great Seal of the Goddess* ritual is performed to deepen your connection with the divine feminine energy, experience union with the Goddess, and expand your consciousness and awareness. It is a transformative practice that aims to bring about a sense of oneness, divine love, and spiritual realization.

The Sadhana

0. Preliminary

Prepare the *Adytum* as for the performance of the *Diamond Sapphire*. At the simplest, have a bowl or cup of fresh water, a white candle, incense,[107] a *mala* and a bell. Perform any preparatory banishings as needed. (All of this *may* be omitted, and the *sadhana* performed completely on the astral.) In any case, this practice is best done at night, underneath a canopy of stars.

Be seated in *asana*. Light the candle and incense. Center and focus your mind, and take three cleansing breaths. See your sphere of sensation filling with radiant, pure, white light, surrounded by a thin, blue shell. Allow awareness of this to fade as the light and your breath become one. Establish rhythmic breathing.

1. Opening
Refuge and Armor of The Great Goddess

Say:

Nu is my Refuge [as you raise your arms slightly]

---

[107] Red sandalwood or rose is preferred, but any "sweet smelling" incense is suitable.

As Hadit my Light [continue to raise your arms]
And Heru-Ra-Ha is the Strength, Force, Vigour of my arms.[108]

Your arms are now raised and outstretched. Cross your arms over your chest, right over left. Hold this position for a moment to allow the interior union symbolized by the outer gestures to seal. Strike the bell, and say:

Do what thou wilt shall be the whole of the Law.
Love is the law, love under will.

Awakening the Interior Stars

Focus on the base of the spine and become aware of the coiled energy. With a slow, deep inhalation, bring the current of light up the spine and out through the opening at the crown of the head, where it rests at the pulsating sphere of brilliance. Exhale, bringing the light back down to the base. Repeat three times. On the third ascent, the light at the crown becomes even brighter, erupting in *"ultimate sparks of the intimate fire," (AL, III:67)* and this fiery starlight rains down upon your sphere of sensation and body, immersing you in the warmth and coruscating brilliance of stellar nectar.

Establishing the Light

Perform *pranayama* with *kumbhaka* (holding the breath) to stabilize the light. Close the right nostril, and inhale with the left to a count of 4. Close both nostrils, and hold the breath for a count of 16. Exhale through the right nostril for a count of 8. Immediately inhale through the right nostril to a count of 4. Close both nostrils, and hold the breath for a count of 16. Exhale through the left nostril

---

[108] After *Liber AL vel Legis*, III:17

for a count of 8. This makes one cycle. Repeat for a minimum of 3 cycles.

Circulation of the Light

Chant three times while circulating the light:

A ka dua
Tuf ur biu
Bi a'a chefu
Dudu ner af an nuteru

Establishing the Guru

Give the *Mudra of Union* (Figure 16) while silently invoking the Name of the Holy Guardian Angel.[109] When complete, release the *mudra*.

2. The Great Seal of The Goddess (Dissolution)
Offering of Self

Allow the outer world to fade as you see yourself in a vast desert of black sand at night, underneath a canopy of stars. The desert sand is cool and refreshing underneath you. There is nothing else in sight as far as you can see, just a sea of black sand in all directions, and the vast canopy of stars. There is no light save for the brilliant stellar ocean. You can clearly see the band of the Milky Way stretching its luminous river of light across the night sky, and an infinite sea of stars fills the expanse of night. The sky has never been so clear and luminous. Feel the complete awe and vastness of the depths of this infinite sea of stars dancing radiantly in the darkness of space. As

---

[109] If this Name is not known, give the *mudra,* and aspire intently to union with the Angel, opening up to the reciprocal descent of the Light.

you become aware of the immensity of the night sky, it may feel as though you are at the edge of a great precipice, and at any moment you could fall up into the night sky.

Inflame Thyself with Prayer

Recite the following, with increasing intensity and emotion:

> *"Come forth, o children, under the stars, & take your fill of love!*
> *I am above you and in you. My ecstasy is in yours. My joy is to see your joy.*
> *Above the gemmed azure is*
> *The Naked splendour of Nuit;*
> *She bends in ecstasy to kiss*
> *The secret ardours of Hadit.*
> *The winged globe, the starry blue,*
> *Are mine, O Ankh-af-na-khonsu!*
> *Then saith the prophet and slave of the beauteous one: Who am I, and what shall be the sign? So she answered him, bending down, a lambent flame of blue, all-touching, all penetrant, her lovely hands upon the black earth, & her lithe body arched for love, and her soft feet not hurting the little flowers: Thou knowest! And the sign shall be my ecstasy, the consciousness of the continuity of existence, the omnipresence of my body." (AL, I:12–14 & 26)*

The feeling of the sky pulling you in becomes increasingly powerful. Willingly offer all that you are to Nuit, while continuing to yearn towards the starry sky saying:

> *"Then the priest answered & said unto the Queen of Space, kissing her lovely brows, and the dew of her light bathing his*

whole body in a sweet-smelling perfume of sweat: O Nuit, continuous one of Heaven, let it be ever thus; that men speak not of Thee as One but as None; and let them speak not of thee at all, since thou art continuous!

But to love me is better than all things; if under the night-stars in the desert thou presently burnest mine incense before me, invoking me with a pure heart, and the serpent flame therein, thou shalt come a little to lie in my bosom. For one kiss wilt thou then be willing to give all; but whoso gives one particle of dust shall lose all in that hour. Ye shall gather goods and store of women and spices; ye shall wear rich jewels; ye shall exceed the nations of the earth in splendour and pride; but always in the love of me, and so shall ye come to my joy. I charge you earnestly to come before me in a single robe, and covered with a rich head-dress. I love you! I yearn to you! Pale or purple, veiled or voluptuous, I who am all pleasure and purple and drunkenness of the innermost sense, desire you. Put on the wings, and arouse the coiled splendour within you: come unto me! To me! To me! Sing the rapturous love-song unto me! Burn to me perfumes! Wear to me jewels! Drink to me, for I love you! I love you. I am the blue-lidded daughter of sunset; I am the naked brilliance of the voluptuous night-sky. To me! To me!"

Establishing the Great Seal

The pull of the starry sky becomes even more potent; it takes every ounce of restraint within you to resist and continue building the tension between self and other, one and all; all the while wanting to completely surrender every fiber of your Self to Her. You are acutely aware of the intense love and longing from Her as well, her desire and love for you are infinite as she opens up to you and speaks softly. See the goddess almost whispering these words in your ear:

> "None, breathed the light, faint & faery, of the stars, and two.
> For I am divided for love's sake, for the chance of union.
> This is the creation of the world, that the pain of division is as nothing, and the joy of dissolution all.
> I give unimaginable joys on earth: certainty, not faith, while in life, upon death; peace unutterable, rest, ecstasy; nor do I demand aught in sacrifice.
> This shall regenerate the world, the little world my sister, my heart & my tongue, unto whom I send this kiss."

At this, the pull is unbearable. Release all your restraint, and completely surrender yourself to Her, falling into the sky. As you fall up, the black desert, the stars, the night sky, all fade into the brilliant light of ecstasy as you become one with Her body, dissolving into the ecstasy of union. Remain in the Bliss of Union, in the complete pristine primordial Awareness that is the Void.

3. 0=2 (Creation)

After some time, you become aware that something wishes to express itself. Become aware of a single, radiant point of light. Understand that this is the Khabs, the inmost light of Hadit, and the seed point *(bindu)* of all manifest creation. You are that.

Recite the *Mantra of Revealing* (Chapter 14) for one or more rounds of the *mala* while focusing on the Light that is radiating out in all directions:

om hrung bhagavati vri vhru hru aha

During the recitation of the Light *mantra,* a cloud of stellar nebulae forms a faint nimbus around the core star. This continues to take form, eventually revealing itself as a vast ouroboros serpent circling widdershins about the *bindu*.

As your consciousness focuses on this *bindu*, it suddenly contracts and becomes a million times brighter, and then explodes outwards. This is the Creation of the Universe and the beginning of a new cycle of time. In a flash, see all of the universe created anew, as you are acutely aware of the starry light which infuses and penetrates all of manifest creation. The world reappears, but is somehow different—filled with radiance.

4. Light in Extension

Having identified yourself as the Khabs, extend your light to the Four Directions of Space in an act of Creation. Focus Awareness towards the East, and say these words, adapted from *The Heart of the Master*:

LIGHT is throned in the Heart of the Master, so that he thinks no evil. For in that Light all is Truth.

Focus Awareness towards the West, and say:

LIFE wells in the Heart of the Master; Death is but the Systole of that marvelous pulse.

Focus Awareness towards the South, and say:

LIBERTY leaps in the Heart of the Master, for every man and every woman is a star.

Focus Awareness towards the North, and say:

LOVE burns in the Heart of the Master: he, seeing only God in every thing, with the white flame of worship purges it of all its fancied imperfection.

Now return Awareness to the Center of All, the Khabs, and say:

By virtue of his LAW he floods each thought with love, and marries it in turn to every other thought; and of each bridal night the fruits are twin, the Rapture of Silence, and some new World unguessed of Phantasy; of these behold one grim and grotesque, this lyric and that lordly, the grievous and the gracious equal in His sight, for they know neither limit nor let in the infinite variety of their Beauty, making new Harmonies with every hour, beyond belief or Joy.

5. Manifestation

Allow the Light of the Khabs to solidify such that you take on the form of Ra-Hoor-Khuit enthroned at the Center of the Universe as on the *Stele of Revealing*. The Stellar Temple is vast, extending to all the directions of space:

I am in a secret fourfold word, the blasphemy against all gods of men.
I am the Lord of Thebes, and I
    The inspired forth-speaker of Mentu;
For me unveils the veiled sky,
    The self-slain Ankh-af-na-Khonsu
Whose words are truth, I invoke, I greet
    Thy presence, O Ra-Hoor-Khuit!
Unity uttermost showed!
    I adore the might of Thy breath,
Supreme and terrible God,
    Who makest the gods and death
To tremble before Thee—
    I, I adore thee!
Appear on the throne of Ra!

> *Open the ways of the Khu!*
> *Lighten the ways of the Ka!*
> *The ways of the Khabs run through*
> *To stir me or still me!*
> *Aum! let it fill me!*
>
> *The light is mine; its rays consume*
> *Me: I have made a secret door*
> *Into the House of Ra and Tum,*
> *Of Khephra and of Ahathoor.*
> *I am thy Theban, O Mentu,*
> *The prophet Ankh-af-na-Khonsu!*
>
> *By Bes-na-Maut my breast I beat;*
> *By wise Ta-Nech I weave my spell.*
> *Show thy star-splendour, O Nuit!*
> *Bid me within thine House to dwell,*
> *O winged snake of light, Hadit!*
> *Abide with me, Ra-Hoor-Khuit!*

om hrung heru aha

Give the *Mudra of Union*. See the Inner temple become brighter, and then transform into radiant, starry light. Open your eyes, merging the interior vision with the exterior, and see that the world is new, regenerated, and composed of starlight, *"ultimate sparks of the infinite fire."*

[Ring the bell] There is no law beyond: Do what thou wilt.

6. Eucharist (optional)

This section is optional. If done, a suitable elixir and a plate of food should be placed near the shrine. For indications see *Liber AL vel Legis,* I:51. Alternately, have a Cake of Light and a Chalice of wine as in the *Diamond Sapphire.*

Hold your hands over candle flame. Then dip your right forefinger into the water, and anoint your forehead. Smell the incense. Give the *Mudra of Union.*

Hold the chalice on high with both hands while saying:

> *Thou shalt drain out thy blood that is thy life into the golden cup of her fornication.*

Lower the chalice to heart level, and hold it with the left hand. Raise the Cake of Light, holding it over the chalice on high saying:

> *Thou shalt mingle thy life with the universal life. Thou shalt not keep back one drop.*

Bring the Cake of Light to heart level, above the opening of the chalice. Then silently consume the Cake of Light, and drain the chalice while mentally offering everything to Nuit. When done, say:

> *There is success.*

7. Transfer of Merit and Close

As you see a warm glow in the heart center, with radiance gently flowing out in all directions of space, say:

> *I am uplifted in thine heart; and the kisses of the stars rain hard upon thy body.*
> *May Light, Life, Love and Liberty be extended universally to all, under the regency of the One Law of Thelema.*
> *May all attain the Stone of the Wise, the Summum Bonum, True Wisdom and Perfect Happiness.*
> **ABRAHADABRA**

The Commentary

The meditations from Crowley's *Liber V vel Reguli* form a concise meditation in itself, suitable for contemplating the profound depths of awareness that are opened up with this *sadhana*. You might read through these words either after conclusion of the *sadhana*, or on days when you are not actively doing the ritual. The words are an inspiring and thrilling exploration of nondual awakening. The second section, from *De Lege Libellum*, is a meditation on the reformulation of the Universe as an expression of the Four Rays of the Light of the Master—the inner, hidden light of the Holy Guardian Angel.

> *"I also am a Star in Space, unique and self-existent, an individual essence incorruptible; I also am one Soul; I am identical with All and None. I am in All and all in me; I am, apart from all and lord of all, and one with all.*
>
> *I am God, I very God of very God; I go upon my way to work my Will; I have made Matter and Motion for my mirror; I have decreed for my delight that Nothingness should figure itself as twain, that I might dream a dance of names and natures, and enjoy the substance of simplicity by watching the wanderings of my shadows. I am not that which is not; I know not that which knows not; I love not that which loves not. For I am Love, whereby division dies in delight; I am Knowledge, whereby all parts, plunged in the whole, perish and pass into perfection; and I am that I am, the being wherein Being is lost in Nothing, nor designs to be but its Will to unfold its nature, its need to express its perfection in all possibilities, each phase a partial phantasm, and yet inevitable and absolute.*

I am Omniscient, for naught exists for me unless I know it. I am Omnipotent, for naught occurs save by Necessity, my soul's expression through my Will to be, to do, to suffer the symbols of itself. I am Omnipresent, for naught exists where I am not, who fashioned Space as a condition of my consciousness of myself, who am the centre of all, and my circumference the frame of mine own fancy.

I am the All, for all that exists for me is a necessary expression in thought of some tendency of my nature, and all my thoughts are only the letters of my Name.

I am the One, for all that I am is not the absolute All, and all my all is mine and not another's; mine, who conceive of others like myself in essence and truth, yet unlike in expression and illusion.

I am the None, for all that I am is the imperfect image of the perfect; each partial phantom must perish in the clasp of its counterpart, each form fulfill itself by finding its equated opposite, and satisfying its need to be the Absolute by the attainment of annihilation."

From *De Lege Libellum*:

"Know first, that from the Law spring four Rays or Emanations: so that if the Law be the centre of your own being, they must needs fill you with their secret goodness. And these four are Light, Life, Love, and Liberty.

By Light shall ye look upon yourselves, and behold All Things that are in Truth One Thing only, whose name hath been called No Thing for a cause which later shall be declared unto you. But the substance of Light is Life, since without Existence and Energy it were naught. By Life therefore are you made yourselves, eternal and incorruptible, flaming forth as suns, self-created and self-supported, each the sole centre of the Universe.

Now as by Light ye beheld, by Love ye feel. There is an ecstasy of pure Knowledge, and another of pure Love. And this Love is the force that uniteth things diverse, for the contemplation in Light of their Oneness. Know that the Universe is not at rest, but in extreme motion whose sum is Rest. And this understanding that Stability is Change, and Change Stability, that Being is Becoming, and Becoming Being, is the Key to the Golden Palace of this Law.

Lastly, by Liberty is the power to direct your course according to your Will. For the extent of the Universe is without bounds, and ye are free to make your pleasure as ye will, seeing that the diversity of being is infinite also. For this also is the Joy of the Law, that no two stars are alike, and ye must understand also that this Multiplicity is itself Unity, and without it Unity could not be. And this is an hard saying against Reason: ye shall comprehend, when, rising above Reason, which is but a manipulation of the Mind, ye come to pure Knowledge by direct perception of the Truth.

Know also that these four Emanations of the Law flame forth upon all paths: ye shall use them not only in these Highways of the Universe whereof I have written, but in every Bypath of your daily life."

The Heart of the Master

This practice is the complement to *The Great Seal of the Goddess*. As such, it *may* be viewed as the inner *sadhana* of Hadit. Where the previous ritual opens consciousness to the expansiveness of the cosmos, this *sadhana* emphasizes the Hadit aspect of awareness or singularity. This is the cosmic "I", the individuated self, before its immersion in the totality of awareness. It is designed to cultivate a deep sense of self-individuation before immersing yourself in the totality of awareness. The meditation consists of several stages:

Outline of the Sadhana

1. **Opening:** Establish a centered and focused mind through three cleansing breaths. Visualize a sphere of radiant white light surrounded by a thin, blue shell; allow it to merge with your breath. Perform rhythmic breathing while raising your arms and reciting the *Refuge and Armor of the Great Goddess,* followed by the invocation of the *Law of Thelema.*
2. **Awakening the Interior Stars:** Direct your attention to the base of the spine and visualize coiled energy. Inhale deeply, guiding the current of light up the spine and out through the crown of the head, creating a pulsating sphere of brilliance. Exhale and bring the light back down to the base, repeating this process three times. On the third ascent, envision the light at the crown becoming brighter, and erupting in "ultimate sparks of the intimate fire," which then showers down upon your body and sphere of sensation.
3. **Establishing the Light:** Use *pranayama* with breath retention to stabilize the light. Perform a cycle of alternate nostril breathing while chanting a specific *mantra* to circulate the light.
4. **Pralaya (Dissolution):** Focus on each *chakra* and its corresponding element; visualize their dissolution and the world transforming accordingly. Begin with the

base chakra (muladhara) and the earth element, gradually progressing through the *chakras* and elements. Ultimately, focus on the *crown chakra (sahasrara)*, and allow individual awareness to dissolve, entering a state of primordial awareness.

5. **The Heart of the Master (Creation):** Shift your attention to a single radiant point of light, representing the inmost light of Hadit (Khabs) and the seed of all creation. Merge your consciousness with the Khabs; experience its intensification into a brilliant orb of fire. Extend your light to the four directions of space; reflect on the qualities of Truth, Life, Liberty and Love.

6. **Realization of the Adamantine Body:** Recite the Deva *mantra* of Heru-Ra-Ha, symbolizing the unification of divine forces. Open your eyes. Integrate your interior vision with the external world, perceiving it as regenerated and composed of starlight.

7. **Eucharist (optional):** This section involves partaking in a ritual meal of symbolic offerings. Anoint your forehead with water, smell the incense, and give the *Mudra of Union*. Hold a chalice and a Cake of Light, reciting verses from *Liber AL vel Legis*. Consume the Cake of Light, drink from the chalice, and mentally offer everything to Nuit.

8. **Transfer of Merit & Close:** Express gratitude for the experience and extend the blessings of Light, Life, Love and Liberty universally under the Law of Thelema. Aspire for all beings to attain wisdom, happiness and the ultimate goal symbolized by the "Stone of the Wise." Conclude with **"ABRAHADABRA"**, representing the integration and manifestation of divine forces.

The Sadhana

1. Opening

Sit in *asana*. Center and focus your mind as you take three cleansing breaths. See your sphere of sensation filling with radiant, pure, white light, surrounded by a thin, blue shell. Allow awareness of this to fade as the light and your breath become one. Establish rhythmic breathing.

Refuge and Armor of the Great Goddess

Say:

Nu is my Refuge [as you raise your arms slightly]
As Hadit my Light [continue to raise your arms]
And Heru-Ra-Ha is the Strength, Force, Vigour of my arms.

Your arms are now raised and outstretched. Cross your arms over your chest, right over left. Hold this position for a moment to allow the interior union symbolized by the outer gestures to seal. Strike the bell, and say:

Do what thou wilt shall be the whole of the Law.
Love is the law, love under will.

2. Awakening the Interior Stars

Focus on the base of the spine; become aware of the coiled energy. With a slow, deep inhalation, bring the current of light up the spine and out through the opening of the crown of the head where it rests at the pulsating sphere of brilliance. Exhale, bringing the light back down to the base. Repeat three times. On the third ascent, the light at the crown becomes even brighter, finally erupting in *"ultimate sparks of the intimate fire,"* (AL, III:67). This fiery starlight rains down upon your sphere of sensation and body, immersing you in the warmth and coruscating brilliance of stellar nectar.

3. Establishing the Light

Perform simple *pranayama* with *kumbhaka* (holding the breath) to stabilize the light. Close the right nostril, inhale with the left to a count of 4. Close both nostrils, and hold the breath for a count of 16. Exhale through the right nostril for a count of 8. Immediately inhale through the right nostril to a count of 4. Close both nostrils, and hold the breath for a count of 16. Exhale through the left nostril for a count of 8. This makes one cycle. Repeat for a minimum of 3 cycles.

Circulation of the Light

Chant three times while circulating the light:

A ka dua
Tuf ur biu
Bi a'a chefu
Dudu ner af an nuteru

Establishing the Guru

Give the *Mudra of Union* (Figure 16) while silently invoking the Name of the Holy Guardian Angel.[110] When ready, release the *mudra*.

4. Pralaya (Dissolution)

Focus on *muladhara* and *Prithivi* as a Yellow square in the base chakra *(The Tattvas,* Figure 7). As the earth element dissolves, see the world becoming transparent.

---

[110] If this Name is not known, give the *mudra* and aspire intently to union with the Angel, opening up to the reciprocal descent of the Light.

Focus on *svadhisthana* and *Apas* as a silver crescent (points up) in the genital *chakra*. As the Water element dissolves, see the world as through a thick mist or fog.

Focus on *manipura* and *Tejas* as a red, equilateral triangle in the stomach *chakra*. As the Fire element dissolves, see flashing sparkles of red light permeating the world like fireflies.

Focus on *anahata* and *Vayu* as a blue circle within the heart *chakra*. As the Air element dissolves, see the world as composed of brilliant white light.

Focus on *vishuddha* and *Akasha* as a black oval in the throat *chakra*. As the element of Spirit dissolves, see the world as composed entirely of red light.

Focus on *ajna* as a brilliant point of light in the center of your forehead. As consciousness itself dissolves, see the world go entirely black.

Focus on *sahasrara* above the head. Allow individual awareness to completely drop away.

Awaken to the Self-Arising, Primordial Awareness of the Void.

Remain in awareness of this condition for some time before moving on.

5. The Heart of the Master (Creation)

After some time, you become aware that something wishes to express itself. Become aware of a single radiant point of light. Understand that this is the Khabs, the inmost light of Hadit. This is the seed point or *bindu* of all manifest creation.[111]

---

[111] See *Liber NV*.

Identify all that you are with the Khabs, which grows in intensity until it is a brilliant, penetrating, lustrous orb of fire radiating in space. Now extend your Light to the four directions of space. Say:

LIGHT *is throned in the Heart of the Master, so that he thinks no evil. For in that Light all is Truth.*
Falsehood is but a function of the conditions of Time and Space, and the idea of evil comes only from perceiving the oppositions which are transcended by Truth. So each thing that hath its root in Necessity; were the least of these lost, the whole Work should be marred.

LIFE *wells in the Heart of the Master; Death is but the Systole of that marvelous pulse.*
Faint are the phantoms of Illusion; these, seized on by that vivid stream, thrill and throb with the glow of his reality; he leaves no possible form inane or inert; in him do all partake the sacrament of birth to Truth.

LIBERTY *leaps in the Heart of the Master; for every man and every woman is a star. Each follows, free and joyful, its own Will; for every Will alike has its essential function in the rhythm of the Heart of the Master. No star can stray from its self-chosen course: for in the infinite soul of space all ways are endless, all-embracing: perfect.*

LOVE *burns in the Heart of the Master: he, seeing only God in every thing, with the white flame of worship purges it of all its fancied imperfection. His boundless adoration kindles space itself, leaving no void that is not compassed by his passion.*
By virtue of his LAW he floods each thought with love, and marries it in turn to every other thought; and of each bridal night the fruits are twin, the Rapture of Silence,

> *and some new World unguessed of Phantasy; of these behold one grim and one grotesque, this lyric and that lordly, the grievous and the gracious equal in His sight, for they know neither limit nor let in the infinite variety of their Beauty, making new Harmonies with every hour, beyond belief or Joy.*

As your consciousness focuses on this *bindu*, it suddenly contracts, becomes a million times brighter, and then explodes outwards. This is the Creation of the Universe, and the beginning of a new cycle of time. In a flash, see all of the universe created anew, but you are acutely aware of the starry light which infuses and penetrates all of manifest creation. There is no difference between the radiant Void and the Universe.

6. Realization of the Adamantine Body

Recite the *mantra* of Heru-Ra-Ha for at least one round of the *mala*:

om hrung heru aha

Open your eyes, merge the interior vision with the exterior, and see that the world is new, regenerated and composed of starlight. Say:

There is no law beyond 'Do what thou wilt.'

7. Eucharist (optional)

This section is optional. If done, there should be a suitable elixir and plate of food previously placed near the shrine. For indications see *Liber AL vel Legis*, I:51. Alternately, have a Cake of Light and chalice of wine as in the *Diamond Sapphire*.

Hold your hands over the candle flame, then dip your right forefinger into the water and anoint your forehead; then smell the incense. Give the *Mudra of Union*. Hold the chalice on high with both hands while saying:

> Thou shalt drain out thy blood that is thy life into the golden
> cup of her fornication.

Lower the chalice to heart level, and hold it with your left hand. Raise the Cake of Light, holding it over the chalice on high. Say:

> Thou shalt mingle thy life with the universal life. Thou
> shalt not keep back one drop.

Bring the Cake of Light to heart level, above the opening of the chalice. Then silently consume the Cake of Light, and drain the chalice while mentally offering everything to Nuit. When done, say:

> There is success.

8. Transfer of Merit & Close

See a warm glow in the heart center, with radiance gently flowing out in all directions of space. Say:

> I am uplifted in thine heart; and the kisses of the stars rain
> hard upon thy body.
> May Light, Life, Love and Liberty be extended universally
> to all, under the regency of the One Law of Thelema.
> May all attain the Stone of the Wise, the Summum Bonum,
> True Wisdom and Perfect Happiness.

ABRAHADABRA

The Sadhana of Lalita-Babalon

Lalita-Babalon is a tremendous figure, a composite of both tantrik and Thelemic lore, embodying a multifaceted symbolism that merges elements from Eastern traditions with the Western esoteric system. In tantrik philosophy, Lalita is associated with the concept of the divine feminine, representing the dynamic and creative aspects of the universe. Her name, Lalita, translates to "playful" or "charming," highlighting her joyful and exuberant nature. Babalon, on the other hand, finds her roots in Thelemic philosophy, where she is considered the scarlet woman and the embodiment of liberated feminine sexuality.

Within the realm of New Aeon Tantra, Lalita-Babalon symbolizes the union of Shakti, the cosmic feminine energy, and Shiva, the divine masculine consciousness. She represents the creative force that brings about the manifestation of the universe. Lalita's playful nature signifies the joy and ecstasy that can be found in the act of creation and the dance of life. Her image often includes multiple arms, each holding different attributes such as weapons, musical instruments, or symbols of power, representing her ability to embrace and express various aspects of existence. At the same time, the symbolism of Babalon riding the Great Beast in the throes of ecstasy, points towards the deeper blissful nature of this Goddess.

In Thelemic symbolism, Babalon is the goddess who initiates transformative experiences and liberates individuals from the constraints of societal norms. She is seen as a powerful force of change, pushing humanity toward its true potential. Babalon is depicted as a seductive and alluring figure, embodying raw sexuality and passion. She challenges traditional morality, and encourages individuals to embrace their desires and explore the depths of their being.

The imagery surrounding Lalita-Babalon often includes elements such as the Scarlet Woman, the Cup of Babalon (symbolizing the womb and the vessel of life), and the serpent (representing the primal life force and Kundalini energy). The union of these symbols creates a potent and transformative energy, inviting you to embrace your own desires, explore your sexuality, and fully engage with life's experiences.

Overall, Lalita-Babalon symbolizes the union of opposites, the dance of creation and destruction, and the liberation of the self. She embodies the power of the divine feminine, urging you to embrace your passions, break free from societal constraints, and actively participate in the act of creation. Through her symbolism, she serves as a guide and inspiration for those seeking to explore their own inner depths, and unlock their true potential.

§ § §

Throughout this ritual, there are repeated actions such as offerings of incense and light, giving the *Mudra of Union*, and visualizing the forms of the Goddess. The ritual combines visualization, meditation, chanting and symbolic gestures to invoke and connect with the energy and presence of Lalita-Babalon.

The *sadhana* of Lalita-Babalon follows a similar outline to the previous two rituals. Here is a summary and outline of the ritual:

Outline of the Sadhana

0. **Preliminary:** Prepare the space with necessary tools and perform any banishing rituals. Sit comfortably, and light a candle and incense. Center your mind, take cleansing breaths, and establish rhythmic breathing.
1. **Opening:** Raise your arms and recite the *Refuge and Armor of the Great Goddess*. Cross your arms over your chest, strike the bell, and recite the Law and Love. Awaken the interior stars by visualizing energy rising up the spine and resting at the crown.

2. **Establishing the Light:** Perform pranayama with breath-holding to stabilize the light. Chant the given mantra while circulating the light.
3. **The Dhyana of Lalita Babalon:** Meditate on the form of the Goddess as described, imagining her beauty and radiance. Offer incense and light while holding the *Mudra of Union* (Figure 16). Allow the image to crystallize into radiance and form a Mystic Lotus at your *Anahatta* center.
4. **The Dhyana of the Victorious Queen Babalon:** Meditate on the form of the Goddess as the Queen of the Apocalypse, visualizing her in flames and surrounded by celestial beauty. Offer incense and light while holding the *Mudra of Union*.
5. **Chanting the Song of Her Victory:** Chant the *Song of Her Victory* with a *mala*; recite the *mantra* while meditating on the Goddess' form. Give the *Mudra of Union* and receive the crown of stars and roses from her right hand.
6. **Great Seal:** Inhale deeply, visualizing a 49-petal rose of flame at your *Anahatta* center. Hold the breath, perform the three locks of *mahabandha*, and then release locks, relaxing the muscles.[112] Exhale slowly, give the *Mudra of Union*, and recite the 1st Enochian Key.
7. **Daughter of Fortitude and the Thunder: Perfect Mind:** Inflame yourself with prayer; recite the words of the Daughter of Fortitude. Give the *Mudra of Union* and recite the *Thunder: Perfect Mind* passage.

---

[112] See Chapter 10 *(The Sevenfold Palace of the Goddess)* for more details on performing these locks.

8. **Bodhicitta:** Generate *Bodhicitta* and the mind of enlightenment, sending out blessings to all of creation with the *Mantra of Revealing* (see Chapter 14).
9. **Eucharist (optional):** If desired, partake in the Eucharist by consuming a suitable elixir and offering Cakes of Light.
10. **Transfer of Merit and Close:** The ritual concludes by transforming all merit that was generated from the ritual out in all directions, and closing the circle.

The Sadhana

0. Preliminary

Prepare the *Adytum* as for the performance of the *Diamond Sapphire*. At the simplest, have a bowl or cup of fresh water, a white candle, incense[113], a *mala,* and a bell. Perform any preparatory banishings as needed. (All of this *may* be omitted, and the *sadhana* performed completely on the astral.)

Be seated in *asana*. Light the candle and incense. Center and focus your mind, taking three cleansing breaths. See your sphere of sensation filling with radiant, pure, white light, surrounded by a thin, blue shell. Allow awareness of this to fade as the light and your breath become one. Establish rhythmic breathing.

1. Opening

Refuge and Armor of the Great Goddess

Say:

Nu is my Refuge [as you raise your arms slightly]

---

[113] Red sandalwood or rose is preferred, but any "sweet smelling" incense will be suitable.

As Hadit my Light [continue to raise your arms]
And Heru-Ra-Ha is the Strength, Force, Vigour of my arms.

Your arms are now raised and outstretched. Cross your arms over your chest, right over left. Hold this position for a moment to allow the interior union symbolized by the outer gestures to seal. Strike the bell, and say:

Do what thou wilt shall be the whole of the Law.
Love is the law, love under will.

Awakening the Interior Stars

Focus on the base of the spine; become aware of the coiled energy. With a slow, deep inhalation, bring the current of light up the spine and out through the opening at the crown of the head, where it rests at the pulsating sphere of brilliance. Exhale, bringing the light back down to the base. Repeat three times. On the third ascent, the light at the crown becomes even brighter, erupting in *"ultimate sparks of the intimate fire" (AL, III:67)*; this fiery starlight rains down upon your sphere of sensation and body, immersing you in the warmth and coruscating brilliance of stellar nectar.

2. Establishing the Light

Perform *pranayama* with *kumbhaka* (holding the breath) to stabilize the light. Close the right nostril, inhale with the left to a count of 4. Close both nostrils, and hold the breath for a count of 16. Exhale through the right nostril for a count of 8. Immediately inhale through the right nostril to a count of 4. Close both nostrils, and hold the breath for a count of 16. Exhale through the left nostril for a count of 8. This makes one cycle. Repeat for a minimum of 3 cycles.

Circulation of the Light

Chant three times while circulating the light:

A ka dua
Tuf ur biu
Bi a'a chefu
Dudu ner af an nuteru

Establishing the Guru

Give the *Mudra of Union* while silently invoking the Name of the Holy Guardian Angel[114]. When ready, release the *mudra*.

3. The Dhyana of Lalita Babalon

Meditate on the form of the Goddess as She Who Plays:

"She is standing glorious upon a field of lilies, on a lake of crystal amidst a sea of glass. She is proud and delicate, and beyond imagination fair. She is like a child of twelve years old. She has very deep eye-lids, and long lashes. Her eyes are closed, or nearly closed. She is naked. Her whole body is covered with fine gold hairs, that are the electric flames that are the spears of mighty and terrible Angels whose breast-plates are the scales of Her skin. And the hair of Her head, that flows down to Her feet, is the very light of God himself. Her hair is bedecked with seven stars, the seven breaths of God that move and thrill its excellence. Her hair is tied with seven combs, whereupon are written the seven secret names of God that are not even known of the Angels, or of the Archangels, or of the Leader of the Armies of the Lord. Holy, Holy, Holy are thou,

---

[114] If this Name is not known, give the *mudra* and aspire intently to union with the Angel, opening up to the reciprocal descent of the Light.

and blessed by Thy name for ever, unto whom the Aeons are but the pulsings of Thy blood."[115]

With this *dhyana* clear, say:

"This is the Daughter of the King. This is the Virgin of Eternity. This is She that the Holy One hath wrested from the Giant Time, and the prize of them that have overcome Space. This is She that is set upon the Throne of Understanding. Holy, Holy, Holy is Her name, not to be spoken among men."[116]

Offer incense and light. Give *Mudra of Union*. Allow the image to crystallize into radiance, deep crimson gems of lights, which stream into your *Anahatta* where they form a Mystic Lotus.

4. The Dhyana of the Victorious Queen Babalon

Meditate on the form of the Goddess as Queen of the Apocalypse[117]:

"She stands triumphant in the Heavens amidst flames of blue, green and violet. Each tongue of flame, each leaf of flame, each flower of flame, is one of the great love stories of the world. And now there is a most marvelous rose formed from the flame, and a perpetual rain of lilies and passion-flowers and violets. And there is gathered out of it all, yet identical with it, the form of a Woman like the woman in the Apocalypse, but her Beauty and Radiance are such that one

---

[115] Adapted from the Vision of the 9th Aethyr, *Liber 418*.
[116] Ibid.
[117] Ibid.

cannot look thereon, save with sidelong glances.[118] *Her head sparkles and coruscates with its own light of gems.*

The vision changes from glory unto glory, for at each glance the vision is changed. And this is because She transmitteth the Word to the Understanding, and therefore She hath many forms, and each goddess of love is but a letter of the alphabet of love. This is She that poureth the Water of Life upon Her head, whence it floweth to fructify the earth. Above Her head the sky is filled with the most wonderful bands of light, a thousand different curves and whorls. Beneath Her feet are vast plains, enormous deserts with great rocks."

Offer incense and light. Give the *Mudra of Union*.

"Now She is seated upon a great throne of turquoise and lapis lazuli, and she is flawless like emerald, and upon the pillars that support the canopy of Her throne are sculptured the ram, and the sparrow, the cat, and the strange fish. Behold! How She shineth! Behold! How Her glances have kindled all these fires that have blown about the heavens!"

5. Chanting the Song of Her Victory

With this *dhyana* clearly in mind, chant the *Song of Her Victory* with the *mala* for 7, 11, or 156 rounds:

Omari tessala marax
Tessala dodi phornepax
Amri radara poliax
Armana piliu
Amri radara piliu son'
Mari narya barbiton

---

[118] Sanskrit *apanga*. The side-long glances of the Devi direct currents of force.

**Madara anaphax sarpedon
Andala hriliu**

Translation:

*"I am the harlot that shaketh Death.
This shaking giveth the Peace of Satiate Lust.
Immortality jetteth from my skull,
And music from my vulva.
Immortality jetteth from my vulva also,
For my Whoredom is a sweet scent like a seven-stringed
 instrument,
Played unto God the Invisible, the all-ruler,
That goeth along giving the shrill screem of orgasm."*

Give the *Mudra of Union*. From Her right hand She casts forth seven stars that form a crown upon your head, and seven roses that rest upon the stars.[119] She speaks:

"Every one that hath seen me forgetteth me never, and I appear oftentimes in the coals of the fire, and upon the smooth white skin of woman, and in the constancy of the waterfall, and in the emptiness of deserts and marshes, and upon great cliffs that look seaward; and in many strange places, where men seek me not. And many thousand times he beholdeth me not. And at last I smite myself into him as a vision smiteth into a stone, and whom I call must follow."[120]

---

[119] Adapted from the Vision of the 7th Aethyr, *Liber 418*.
[120] Adapted from the Vision of the 2nd Aethyr, *Liber 418*.

Offer incense and light. Give the *Mudra of Union*. Allow the vision to become brighter in intensity, then dissolve to pure, brilliant, dark crimson light which crystallizes into a Secret and Holy Fire resting in your *Anahatta* center.

6. Great Seal

Breath in slowly and deeply, bringing the light up the spine as you see a living 49-petal rose of flame at your *Anahatta* center. Hold the breath for a count of 3, giving *mahabandha*[121] Release locks, exhale slowly. Give the *Mudra of Union* and say:

Ad Gloriam Regina Babalon!

Recite the 1st Enochian Key:

Ol sonf vorsg, goho Iad balt, lansh calz vonpho: sobra z-ol ror i ta Nazpad Graa ta Malprg Ds hol-q Qaa nothoa zimz Od commah ta nobloh zien: Soba thil gnonp prge aldi Od vrbs oboleh grsam Casarm ohorela caba pir Od zonrensg cab erm Iadnah Pilah farzm zurza adna Ds gono Iadpil Ds hom Od toh Soba Ipam lu Ipamis Ds loholo vep zomd Poamal Od bogpa aai ta piap piamo-i od vaoan ZACARe c-a od ZAMRAM Odo cicle Qaa Zorge, Lap zirdo Noco MAD Hoath Iaida

Translation:

"I reign over ye, saith the God of Justice, in power exalted above the Firmament of Wrath, in whose hands the Sun is as a sword, and the Moon as a through thrusting Fire: who measureth your Garments in the midst of my Vestures, and trussed you together as the palms of my

---

[121] The combination of the three yogic energy locks—*jalandhara banda*, *uddiyana banda* and *mula banda*—is the great lock, *maha bandha*. See *The Sevenfold Palace of the Goddess* in Chapter 10.

hands. Whose seats I garnished with the Fire of Gathering, and beautified your garments with admiration. To whom I made a law to govern the Holy Ones, and delivered ye a Rod, with the Ark of Knowledge. Moreover you lifted up your voices and sware obedience and faith to him that liveth and triumpheth: whose beginning is not, nor end cannot be: which shineth as a flame in the midst of your palaces, and reigneth amongst you as the balance of righteousness and truth! Move therefore, and show yourselves! Open the mysteries of your creation! Be friendly unto me, for I am the Servant of the same your God: the true worshipper of the Highest!"

7. Daughter of Fortitude[122]

Inflame Thyself with prayer while reciting:

"I am the daughter of Fortitude, and ravished every hour, from my youth. For behold, I am Understanding, and Science dwelleth in me; and the heavens oppress me. They covet and desire me with infinite appetite; few or none that are earthly have embraced me, for I am shadowed with the Circle of the Stone, and covered with the morning Clouds. My feet are swifter than the winds, and my hands are sweeter than the morning dew. My garments are from the beginning, and my dwelling place is in my self. The Lion knoweth not where I walk, neither do the beasts of the field understand me. I am deflowered, and yet a virgin; I sanctify, and am not sanctified. Happy is he that embraceth me: for in the night season I am sweet, and in the day full of pleasure. My company is a

---

[122] Adapted from the spirit visions of John Dee and Edward Kelly from the communication they received on May 23, 1587. For more see en.wikipedia.org/wiki/Babalon

harmony of many Cymbals, and my lips sweeter than health itself. I am a harlot for such as ravish me, and a virgin with such as know me not: For Lo, I am loved of many, and I am a lover to many; and as many as come unto me as they should do, have entertainment. Purge your streets, O ye sons of men, and wash your houses clean; make yourselves holy, and put on righteousness. Cast out your old strumpets, and burn their clothes; abstain from the company of other women that are defiled, that are sluttish, and not so handsome and beautiful as I, and then will I come and dwell amongst you: and behold, I will bring forth children unto you, and they shall be the sons of Comfort. I will open my garments, and stand naked before you, that your love may be more enflamed toward me. As yet, I walk in the clouds; as yet, I am carried with the winds, and cannot descend unto you for the multitude of your abominations, and the filthy loathsomeness of your dwelling places."*

7. The Thunder: Perfect Mind[123]

After a pause, continue, building momentum while becoming increasingly aware of the expansion of consciousness, as you recite:

*"I was sent forth from the power, and I have come to those who reflect upon me, and I have been found among those who seek after me. Look upon me, you who reflect upon me, and you hearers, hear me. You who are waiting for me, take me to yourselves. And do not banish me from your sight. And do not make your voice hate me, nor your hearing. Do not be ignorant of me anywhere or any time. Be on your guard! Do not

---

[123] Adapted from *The Thunder: Perfect Mind*. See, for example, pbs.org/wgbh/pages/frontline/shows/religion/maps/primary/thunder.html

be ignorant of me. For I am the first and the last. I am the honored one and the scorned one. I am the whore and the holy one. I am the wife and the virgin. I am the mother and the daughter. I am the members of my mother. I am the barren one and many are her sons. I am she whose wedding is great, and I have not taken a husband. I am the midwife and she who does not bear. I am the solace of my labor pains. I am the bride and the bridegroom, and it is my husband who begot me. I am the mother of my father and the sister of my husband and he is my offspring. I am the slave of him who prepared me."

8. Bodhicitta

Generate *Bodhicitta,* sending out blessings to all of creation with the *Mantra of Revealing* (one round of the *mala* or more).

om hrung bhagavati vri vhru hru aha

9. Eucharist (optional)

If this section is done, there should be a suitable elixir and plate of food previously placed near the shrine. For indications see *Liber AL vel Legis,* I:51. Alternately, have a Cake of Light and chalice of wine as in the *Diamond Sapphire.*

Hold your hands over the candle flame, then dip your right forefinger into the water and anoint your forehead; then smell the incense. Give the *Mudra of Union.* Hold the chalice on high with both hands while saying:

Thou shalt drain out thy blood that is thy life into the golden cup of her fornication.

Lower the chalice to heart level, and hold it with the left hand. Raise the Cake of Light, holding it over the chalice on high:

Thou shalt mingle thy life with the universal life. Thou shalt not keep back one drop.

Bring the Cake of Light to heart level, above the opening of the chalice. Then silently consume the Cake of Light, and drain the chalice while mentally offering everything to Nuit. When done, say:

There is success.

10. Transfer of Merit & Close

See a warm glow in the heart center, with radiance gently flowing out in all directions of space, as you say:

I am uplifted in thine heart; and the kisses of the stars rain hard upon thy body.
May Light, Life, Love and Liberty be extended universally to all, under the regency of the One Law of Thelema.
May all attain the Stone of the Wise, the Summum Bonum, True Wisdom and Perfect Happiness.
ABRAHADABRA

The Sixteen Jeweled Palace

"*That which is to be denied shall be denied; that which is to be trampled shall be trampled; that which is to be spat upon shall be spat upon. These things shall be burnt in the outer fire.*"

— *Liber Stellae Rubeae sub figura LXVI*

The ritual follows a layout derived from the *Tantraloka*, a tantrik text composed by the Kashmiri philosopher and yogi Abhinavagupta in the 10th century. The *Tantraloka* is considered a significant text in the Tantrik tradition, providing a comprehensive understanding of Tantra, its rituals, spiritual practices, and underlying philosophy. Its teachings have influenced various tantrik lineages, and continue to be studied and practiced by those interested in exploring the esoteric aspects of spirituality.

In keeping with the syncretic nature of Thelema, The *Sixteen Jeweled Palace* incorporates elements from various mystical and occult traditions, along with the tantrik aspects. With its invocation of Yoginis, sacred circles, and offerings, the ritual is a testament to the ongoing evolution and adaptation of esoteric practices as they are embraced and reinterpreted within modern spiritual frameworks like Thelema. This *sadhana* contains elements from different spiritual traditions in a framework that can then be used in transformative ritualistic experiences.

The name itself relates to the goddess in her form as *Sodashi*, the Sanskrit word for "16". She is called the Goddess Sixteen because she contains all the *kalas* (magickal powers emanating from the stars), and is often depicted in the form of a sixteen-year-old girl.

After the preliminary preparations of purifying the elements and *pranayama* (breath control), the participants invoke the Guru lines in the resplendent Void. Then they place an equal-armed cross at the nape of the neck while calling upon Ganesh (the elephant-headed Hindu deity) for protection. The participants are guided through different circles, each representing various divine beings and energies.

It begins by preparing offerings of candles, incense, flowers, lamb and alcohol. The participants are instructed to prepare themselves as they see fit. Starting from the outermost circle, the guardians of the four great ages are invoked. Moving inward, there is a circle with the perfected ones, followed by the great princesses of the lineages. In the innermost circle, a triangle is formed by the three great *shaktis* representing different aspects of divine power. At the center of it all resides Adyashakti, the primal energy.

From the center, the palace with enthroned goddesses rises up, forming a Jeweled Pyramid of Fire. Offerings are given, and then the participants rejoice and sing specific verses. The ritual concludes with giving blessings and thanks with the mind of *Bodhicitta* (awakening mind) and expressing gratitude to the Guardians before allowing all to re-absorb. The closing of the ritual is left to the discretion of the participants.

§ § §

Let offerings of candles, incense, flowers, lamb and alcohol be prepared ahead of time, and be on hand.

Let the *Devotees* prepare themselves as they see fit.

After the usual preparations of purifying the elements and *pranayama,* invoke the Guru lines in the resplendent Void, then place the equal-armed cross at the nape of the neck while calling upon Ganesh to protect. (Alternatively, first give the *Armor of the Great Goddess;* see Chapter 12.)

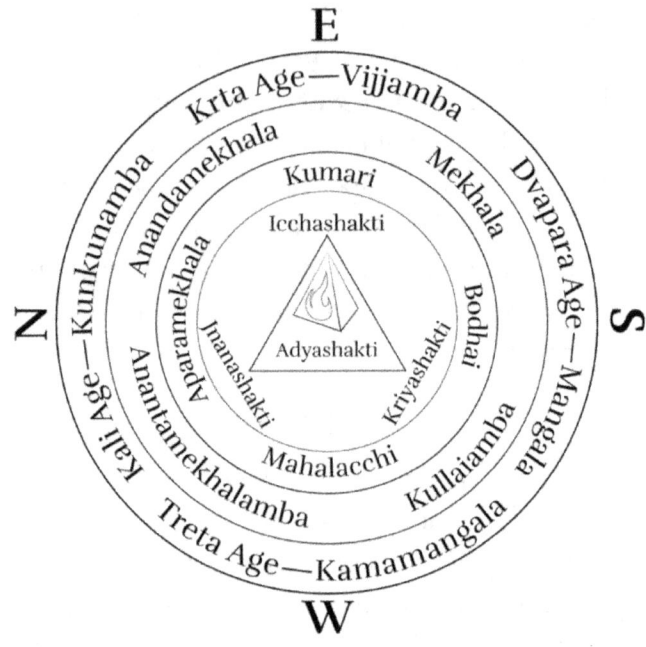

**Figure 25
The Sixteen Jeweled Palace**
(Kat Lunoe)

At the outermost circle, partially veiled in darkness, the guardians of the four great ages:

E—Krta Age—**Vijjamba**
S—Dvapara Age—**Mangala**
W—Treta Age—**Kamamangala**
N—Kali Age—**Kunkunamba**

In the next circle, the perfected ones:

NE—**Anandamekhala**
SE—**Mekhala**
SW—**Kullaiamba**
NW—**Anantamekhalamba**

Within this, a circle with the great princesses of the lineages:

E—**Kumari**
S—**Bodhai**
W—**Mahalacchi**
N—**Aparamekhala**

In the inner most circle, a triangle of the three great *shaktis*:

E—**Icchashakti**
SW—**Kriyashakti**
NW—**Jnanashakti**

At center of All:

Adyashakti

From the Center, the palace with enthroned goddesses rise up, establishing a Jeweled Pyramid of Fire with its base firmly on the earth, and its apex high in the stars.

Give offerings, then rejoice while singing the *Song of the Syrens*:

>**Mu pa telai, O chi balae**
>**Tu wa melai Wa pa malae: —**
>**A, a, a Ut! Ut! Ut!**
>**Tu fu tulu! Ge; fu latrai,**
>**Tu fu Tulu Le fu malai**
>**Pa, Sa, Ga. Kut! — Hut! — Nut.**
>**Qwi Mu telai AI OAI**
>**Ya Pa melai; Rel moai**
>**u, u, u. Ti — Ti — Ti!**
>**Se gu melai; Wa la pelai**
>**Pe fu telai, Tu fu latai**
>**Fu tu lu. Wi, Ni, Bi.**

(See Chapter 1 for the Translation of the Song.)

With the mind of *Bodichitta,* give blessings and thanks:

Olalam! Imal! Tutulu!

Give thanks to the Guardians; allow all to re-absorb.
Let the *Devotees* close as they see fit.

The Starry Yantra

This rite serves as a ritual opening and establishes a circle of art for advanced tantrik work. Also adapted from the *Tantraloka*, the ritual begins with the customary preparations of purifying the elements and practicing *pranayama*. Following this, invoke the Guru lines in the resplendent Void, and place an equal-armed cross at the nape of the neck while invoking the protection of Ganesh, the Hindu elephant-headed deity.

You then visualize a spark of deep, red light in the East, which gradually becomes brighter and extends counterclockwise, establishing a circle of stellar fire. Within this circle, you visualize the *Dakinis* (witches) of the directions. Each *Dakini* is depicted as a young, naked figure with disheveled hair, and adorned with garlands of skulls and rich jewels. They carry a sword and a skull, and display *mudras* of fearlessness and granting boons.

The *Dakinis* of the directions are associated with specific qualities and manifestations. Brahmi represents the East and is depicted with warm, golden-yellow skin, symbolizing the cool breeze, dawn's first light, and the scent of flowers. Maheshwari represents the West, and has deep, electric-blue skin, representing the dark waters of the ocean. Narayani represents the South, and has radiant, crimson skin, emanating passionate warmth and the heat of fire. Chamunda represents the North and has deep, onyx skin, symbolizing space itself, snowcapped mountains, and a dense, dark forest of trees.

In the intermediate spaces between the cardinal directions, additional *Dakinis* are visualized. Kaumari represents the South-East with warm, golden-red skin like a setting Sun. Narasimhi represents the South-West with warm, red skin and dark, blue shadows. Aparajita represents the North-West with cool, greenish-blue skin and flashing white teeth. Varahi represents the North-East with deep, reddish skin and dark, green shadowy flashes.

The *Dakinis* which form such a central part of the ritual are derived from the *Matrikas,* the tantrik mother goddesses in Hindu and Buddhist traditions. The term *"Matrika"* translates to "little mother" or "divine mother," and refers to a group of eight goddesses who are considered the consorts of the eight forms of Bhairava, a fierce manifestation of Shiva.

In the ritual, each *Dakini* embodies unique qualities and symbolism. They are considered powerful forces of energy, and are often associated with transformative aspects of consciousness:

1. **Brahmi (East):** Brahmi is associated with the East and is depicted with warm, golden-yellow skin. She represents the qualities of intellect, wisdom and creativity. Her presence brings a sense of inspiration, new beginnings, and the rising sun. Brahmi is often connected with Saraswathi, the goddess of knowledge, arts and learning.
2. **Maheshwari (West):** Maheshwari embodies the West and is characterized by deep, electric-blue skin. She represents the element of Water, and the power of emotions. Maheshwari is associated with the vastness and depth of the ocean, symbolizing the ebb and flow of life. She can evoke feelings of intuition, introspection and emotional transformation.

3. **Narayani (South):** Narayani is linked to the South and is portrayed with radiant crimson skin. She embodies the fiery qualities of passion, vitality and power. Her presence brings forth the transformative energy of Fire, symbolizing purification, courage and the pursuit of desires. She is associated with the goddess Durga, known for her fierce form and warrior-like attributes.
4. **Chamunda (North):** Chamunda represents the North and is depicted with deep onyx skin, resembling the vastness of space. She embodies the wild and primal aspects of nature. Chamunda is associated with death, destruction and the dissolution of illusions. Her presence invokes liberation, spiritual transformation, and the breaking of boundaries.
5. **Kaumari (South-East):** Kaumari is associated with the South-East, and is characterized by warm, golden-red skin, like a setting sun. She embodies the energy of warriorhood, bravery and protection. She is often depicted as a youthful goddess with a spear, representing the strength and determination needed to face challenges and overcome obstacles.
6. **Narasimhi (South-West):** Narasimhi represents the South-West, and is depicted with warm red skin and dark blue shadows. She symbolizes the merging of opposites, and the integration of fierce and gentle qualities. Narasimhi carries both ferocious and compassionate energies, representing the transformative power of embracing your shadow aspects.
7. **Aparajita (North-West):** Aparajita is associated with the North-West, and is characterized by cool, greenish-blue skin and flashing white teeth. She embodies the

energy of victory, invincibility and fearlessness. She represents the ability to overcome obstacles, conquer challenges, and achieve goals with determination and perseverance.

8. **Varahi (North-East):** Varahi represents the North-East, and is depicted with deep reddish skin and dark green shadowy flashes. She embodies the primal force of the earth and is associated with fertility, abundance and nourishment. Varahi carries the energy of grounding, stability and manifestation. She is often depicted as a boar-headed goddess, symbolizing her connection with the earth's resources.

The *Dakinis* of the directions in *The Starry Yantra* ritual serve as powerful guides, each offering unique qualities and energies for you to invoke and work with. Their presence creates a sacred space, and invites you to connect with their transformative power, ultimately facilitating personal growth, spiritual evolution, and the integration of diverse aspects of consciousness.

Within the center of this circle, the devotee conducts the work "outside of time and dimensions." When the work is complete, the *Dakinis* are reabsorbed into the heart center with gratitude. The circle of fire is visualized winding backward upon itself in a clockwise direction until it vanishes back into the Void.

The closing of the ritual is left to the discretion of the Devotee, allowing for personal expression and individualized completion.

The seeming simplicity of this ritual conceals a depth of ritual exploration. Combining elements of Tantra and Thelema, incorporating tantrik practices and visualizations within the framework of Thelemic spirituality, it offers a transformative experience by engaging with the energies and symbolism of the *Dakinis* and the circle of stellar fire, which is none other than the radiant expanse of consciousness itself.

After the usual preparations of purifying the elements and *pranayama*, invoke the Guru lines in the resplendent Void. Then place the equal-armed cross at the nape of the neck while calling upon Ganesh to protect. (Alternatively, first assume the *Armor of the Great Goddess*; see Chapter 12).

See a spark of deep, red light in the East which becomes brighter, extending widdershins, and establishing a circle of stellar fire.

Visualize the *Dakinis* of the directions—each young, naked, with long disheveled hair; eyes hungry with lust and passion; wearing garlands of skulls, with rich jewels on the ears, wrists, hips and ankles; carrying a sword and a skull; giving the *mudras* of fearlessness, and granting boons.

> **East: Brahmi**, skin glistening warm, golden yellow; with a cool breeze and dawn's first light, the sweet scent of flowers.
> **West: Maheshwari**, with deep, electric-blue skin; dark waters of the ocean flowing around her feet.
> **South: Narayani**, with radiant, crimson skin; passionate warm heat of fire emanating from her presence.
> **North: Chamunda**, with deep, onyx skin like space itself; snowcapped mountains, and a dense dark forest of trees behind her.

In the intermediate spaces,

> **South-East: Kaumari**, warm, golden-red skin like the Sun setting.
> **South-West: Narasimhi**, warm, red skin with dark, blue shadows.

North-West: Aparajita, cool, greenish-blue skin, and flashing white teeth.
North-East: Varahi, deep, reddish skin with dark, green shadowy flashes.

From here let the *Devotee* conduct the work in the Center of the Circle, outside of time and dimensions.

When complete, reabsorb the *Dakinis* in the heart center, giving thanks. See the circle of fire winding backwards upon itself (clockwise), until it again vanishes into the Void.

Let the *Devotee* close as they see fit.

The Feast of the Stars

The Feast of the Stars is a quarterly ritual celebrated during the Equinoxes and Solstices. It involves offerings to the Goddess and Her attendants, the Yoginis, who are seen as emissaries and fierce warriors. The ritual aims to strengthen the connection between the practitioner and these guiding intelligences. It involves various steps such as preliminary preparations, invoking the Great Goddess, awakening the interior stars, establishing light through pranayama, offering oneself to the attendants of the Goddess, invoking the Adamantine Void, and concluding with a dedication of merit.

Outline of the Sadhana

0. Preliminary:
- Sit in *asana*
- Light the candle and incense
- Center and focus the mind
- Establish rhythmic breathing

1. Opening:
- Invoke the Great Goddess

- Recite specific phrases to establish connection and intention

2. Awakening the Interior Stars:
- Focus on the base of the spine
- Guided visualization and breathing to awaken energy centers
- Imagery of ascending light through the spine and out through the crown

3. Establishing the Light:
- *Pranayama* with *kumbhaka* (breath retention)
- Chant to circulate the light within

4. The Feast of the Stars:
- Offer of self through visualization in a vast desert under the starry sky
- Invite the Goddess' attendants to partake in a feast prepared by the practitioner
- Mindful eating and drinking, experiencing sensations amplified on the astral plane

5. The Adamantine Void:
- Invoke *mantras* of the Void
- Gestural invocation

6. Song of the Syrens:
- Rest in the primordial radiance of the *Adamantine Void*
- Recite a song with symbolic verses

7. Dedication of Merit and Close:
- Thank the guardians and dedicating the merit
- Close with a final invocation and affirmation of principles

This quarterly celebration strengthens and maintains the link established between the Devotee at their *diksa* (initiation), and the guiding intelligences that inform the *Ananda Arghya*. These guardians are the *Mes Khut Ukha,* the "children of the radiant night," which act as sentinels at the outposts of the *Adamantine Void,* stars in the night sky that outline the darkness of the Goddess, shining their light in the eternal Night. This practice energizes and empowers the *astroeides*[124] of the Devotee, which helps to develop the depth of their *sadhana,* and their capacity for higher workings.

0. Preliminary

Be seated in *asana*. Light the candle and incense. Center and focus your mind, taking three cleansing breaths. See your sphere of sensation filling with radiant, pure, white light, surrounded by a thin, blue shell. Allow awareness of this to fade as the light and your breath become one. Establish rhythmic breathing.

1. Opening

Refuge and Armor of The Great Goddess

Say:

Nu is my Refuge [as you raise your arms slightly]
As Hadit my Light [continue to raise your arms]
And Heru-Ra-Ha is the Strength, Force, Vigour of my arms.

Your arms are now raised and outstretched. Cross your arms over your chest, right over left. Hold this position for a moment to allow

---

[124] "Star body." This is the adamantine *vajra* body of the Devotee that traverses all the realms of the empyrean in this and future lives. This body is developed through the ritual practices of the *Ananda Arghya*.

the interior union symbolized by the outer gestures to seal. Strike the bell, and say:

Do what thou wilt shall be the whole of the Law.
Love is the law, love under will.

2. Awakening the Interior Stars

Focus on the base of the spine and become aware of the coiled energy. With a slow, deep inhalation, bring the current of light up the spine and out through the opening of the crown of the head, where it rests at the pulsating sphere of brilliance. Exhale, bringing the light back down to the base. Repeat three times. On the third ascent, the light at the crown becomes even brighter, finally erupting in *"ultimate sparks of the intimate fire" (AL, III:67)*. The fiery starlight rains down upon your sphere of sensation and body, immersing you in the warmth and coruscating brilliance of stellar nectar.

3. Establishing the Light

Perform *pranayama* with *kumbhaka* (holding the breath) to stabilize the light. Close the right nostril, inhale with the left to a count of 4. Close both nostrils, and hold the breath for a count of 16. Exhale through the right nostril for a count of 8. Immediately inhale through the right nostril to a count of 4. Close both nostrils, and hold the breath for a count of 16. Exhale through the left nostril for a count of 8. This makes one cycle. Repeat for a minimum of 3 cycles.

Circulation of the Light

Chant three times while circulating the light:

A ka dua

Tuf ur biu
Bi a'a chefu
Dudu ner af an nuteru

Establishing the Guru

Give the *Mudra of Union* (Figure 16) while Silently invoking the Name of the Holy Guardian Angel[125]. When ready, release the *mudra*.

4. The Feast of the Stars
Offering of Self

Allow the outer world to fade as you see yourself in a vast desert of black sand at night, underneath a canopy of stars. The desert sand is cool and refreshing beneath you. There is nothing else in sight as far as you can see, just a sea of black sand in all directions, and the vast canopy of stars. There is no light except the brilliant, stellar ocean. You can clearly see the band of the Milky Way stretching its luminous river of light across the night sky, and an infinite sea of stars fills the expanse of night. The sky has never been so clear and luminous with such light. Feel the complete awe and vastness of the depths of this infinite sea of stars dancing radiantly in the darkness of space. As you become aware of the immensity of the night sky, it may feel as though you are at the edge of great precipice, and that at any moment you could fall up into the night sky.

Now, without preconceptions or visualizations, make a willful offering to the attendants of the Goddess, inviting them into your sanctuary. From all directions they swarm in, coming close to your

---

[125] If this Name is not known, give the *mudra* and aspire intently to union with the Angel, opening up to the reciprocal descent of the Light.

circle. Invite them to take seats and partake of the great Feast you have prepared for them. Open your heart to the host of stars, each one a living, radiant being.

Invite them into yourself, that they may enjoy for a time the senses of the body and physical experience. With every exchange comes a reciprocal transfer of energy—as they feed within you, you also are gifted by them.

Let the star goddesses feast upon your body and within your body. Hold nothing back.

Eat and drink mindfully, each taste amplified on the astral a millionfold. As you eat, they eat within you. As you drink, they drink within you. They are beside you, taking turns experiencing within your body.

When complete, offer with love any leftovers to the goddess that presides in the North-East corner.[126]

5. The Adamantine Void

With a single act of Will, give the *Great Mantras of the Void*:

om hrung bhagavati vri vhru heru aha

Give the *Mudra of Union*.

6. Song of the Syrens

Rest in the primordial radiance of the Adamantine Void with the *Song of the Syrens*:

**Mu pa telai, O chi balae
Tu wa melai Wa pa malae: —
A, a, a Ut! Ut! Ut!**

---

[126] This is *Shoshika (Ucchista Chandalani)*. She is naked, with deep, red skin; long, black, disheveled hair; and is seated on a corpse.

Tu fu tulu! Ge; fu latrai,
Tu fu Tulu Le fu malai
Pa, Sa, Ga. Kut! — Hut! — Nut.
Qwi Mu telai AI OAI
Ya Pa melai; Rel moai
u, u, u. Ti — Ti — Ti!
Se gu melai; Wa la pelai
Pe fu telai, Tu fu latai
Fu tu lu. Wi, Ni, Bi.

(See Chapter 1 for the Translation of the Song.)

7. Dedication of Merit and Close

Thank the guardians for coming to the Feast, and for their continuing guidance and protection. Then dedicate the merit, and close with:

> *"I am uplifted in thine heart; and the kisses of the stars rain hard upon they body.*
> *May Light, Life, Love and Liberty be extended universally to all, under the regency of the One Law of Thelema.*
> *May all sentient beings, through all space and time, have Real Peace, Real Freedom, Real Happiness!*
> **ABRAHADABRA"**

Chapter 13
THE FIVE-FOLD WORSHIP OF THE GODDESS

"I know that awful sound of primal joy; let us follow on the wings of the gale even unto the holy house of Hathor; let us offer the five jewels of the cow upon her altar!"
— *Liber Liber vel Lapidis Lazuili,*
Adumbratio Kabalae Aegyptiorum sub figura VII

"That which produces Bliss should be used in worship, since it ravishes the heart."
— *Tantraloka*

In this chapter we look at some of the underlying symbolism and tantrik principles that blossom in the offerings given in *Great Seal of the Goddess* and related *sadhanas*.

The *panchatattva* is the five-fold tantrik offering of sacred elements to the Goddess: *pancha* (five) plus *tattva* (elements). It is also referred to as the *panchamakara* or "five M's" because the traditional five elements all begin with the letter M: *Madhya* (wine), *Mamsa* (meat/flesh), *Meena* (fish), *Mudra* (parched grain), *Maithuna* (coitus). The Devanagari character is *Ma*. This is also a short form of adoration for the Goddess Herself, who is called by Her Devotees the "Mother of the Universe", and affectionately referred to as *Ma*.

The connection to the Hebrew letter *maim* should not be ignored. As the letter of *the Mother*, it represents the Great Sea, the waters of life, and the deep, oceanic depths of the cosmos—all apt representations of that primordial, all embracing N.O.X., or cosmic night that is *sunyata*. Soror Meral notes that,

> "[In] Alchemy, the tradition is that water is the mother, the seed root of all minerals and of life since life arose from the sea. We all come from water, we are baptised by it into life and our animal bodies are made up of a great deal of water."[127]

Atu XII: The Hanged Man (Figure 20), is a visual representation of some of the symbols associated with this letter, which may be summarized as *"the annihilation of the self in the Beloved."*[128] From *The Book of Thoth*:

> "In Mother-Deeps of Ocean the God-Man
> Hangs, Lamp of the Abyss Aeonian
>
> Let not the waters whereon thou journeyest wet thee. And, being come to shore, plant thou the Vine and rejoice without shame."

Five is a very important number, being the sacred pentagram; not only a representation of the traditional Western elements and the regency of Divine Will, but the very ensign of the Star Goddess Herself: *"The Five-Pointed Star, with a Circle in the Middle, & the Circle is Red." (AL, I:60)*

The *five jewels of the cow* is an example of the "twilight language"[129] of all authentic tantrik writings—the Holy Books of

---

[127] *The Thoth Tarot, Astrology & Other Collected Writings,* Phyllis Seckler.
[128] *The Book of Thoth.*
[129] Sanskrit: *sandhya bhasha.*

Thelema being among these just as much as the initiated writings of the East. Such writings require the light of initiated interpretation to understand them. This is both a protection against their falling into the hands of the profane, as well as a result of the very nature of such writings, which embody timeless and eternal Truth in human language, which at best can only point the way. The cow in ancient Egypt and India was revered as the physical avatar of the Great Goddess; the five jewels are the elements of the *panchatattva*.

The tantrik traditions of the Shakta cult of India, as well as the tantrik Buddhist rites of the *ganachakra*, share the common understanding that the Goddess must be worshipped with these offerings.

The ritual of *Panchatattva* is *rahasyapuja* (secret worship). The actual method of worship is initiated, and is handed down orally, never to be written down. Because of the twilight language found in the *Tantras*, the interpretation of elements and its practice has long been shrouded in mystery. In fact, the number of elements has changed over time; there is evidence in the living traditions of India that the original offerings may have numbered three: liquor, meat and sexual union.

The tantrik traditions which fed into Buddhism transformed the ritual according to the customs and consciousness of *Vajrayana*. The *ganachakra* feast of the elements elaborated upon the core rite. As the wrathful *dakinis, bhairavis, vajrapalas* and other protectors and attendants of the *mandalas* were brought into Buddhism, the need to placate these energies with blood and meat was still present. Buddhism replaced animal meat and blood with ritual cakes made of grains and sugar (called *torma*). to feed the energies while still attending to the need for *ahimsa* (non-violence) against living creatures. Alcohol may still be present in some forms of the *vajrayana*, although rather than being consumed by the *sadhaka*, it may be simply tasted, and then spat out upon the offerings to the *Dakinis*. Similar interpretations found their way into other lineages.

The ritual and the energy released may be understood primarily as an alchemical transformation. Regardless of what god/goddess or tradition is being worked with, the *energies* and *protectors* are manifest and aware. Once accustomed to the taste of the *panchatattva*, they will come to expect it regularly. The Devotee will do well to give this serious consideration, and commit to a regular offering.

Kenneth Grant, in commenting on an initiated reading of the *Ananda Lahari* ("Ocean of Bliss"), gives a deeper interpretation of the five elements:

> *"Mamsa still continues to be flesh; meena still floats like fish in the water by which it is surrounded; mudras are secrets to all but initiates and cannot be communicated except by word of mouth and face to face with the Guru; and maithuna alone can rejuvenate her after the exhaustion of the Puja."*

He continues:

> *"The wine or madhya is the urine of the Suvasini[130] after the Fire Snake has absorbed the amrita or nectar of the ultimate chakra, Sahasrara. This nectar or soma is the 'moon-juice' of ancient Vedic lore. The flesh, mamsa, is the lunar emanation embodied in the menstrual fluid at a certain stage of its flow; and the fish (meena) is a secretion that swims in the waters of the lotus-pool. The maithuna is the mystical congress of Shiva and Shakti—Consciousness and its Power—in the Sahasrara Chakra.*
>
> *[...]*

---

[130] Tantrik priestess.

For the fully initiated Kaula Adept, the universe is a manifestation of perpetual joy, bliss, Amrita (deathlessness), from which he distils the elixir of immortality. Liber AL, today, echoes his paen of rapture:

'Remember all ye that existence is pure joy; that all the sorrows are but as shadows; they pass & are done; but there is that which remains.' "

The *Five-Fold Worship of the Goddess* is a central Mystery of Her Divine Promise of *"unimaginable joys on earth: certainty, not faith, while in life, upon death; peace unutterable, rest ecstasy; nor do I demand aught in sacrifice."* (AL, I:58)

No sacrifice is demanded, as the giving of the entirety of one's Self is a natural expression of the all-encompassing Love of the Goddess, being both the means and reward of Union with Her.

Let the Devotee then remember Her and give All to Her.

Notes on Practice

On a Tuesday, Saturday, New Moon, Full Moon, Lunar or Solar eclipse, Equinox, Solstice or any of the Feast Days of *The Book of the Law*, or any other holy day, let the *Fivefold Worship of the Goddess* be given at Midnight. And the effects are magnified if any of the prescribed times are combined; for example, on a Tuesday during a lunar eclipse of the full moon at midnight.

Let the *Fivefold Worship of the Goddess* be given after *sadhana* at the appointed time. No food should be consumed for at least one hour before this practice. However, this is not to say that you should undertake austerities. *Liber AL vel Legis,* II:24 shall be your guide in this.

Understand that this practice has both an Outer and an Inner essence. Unite these into One. The ancient *Tantras* unanimously say, and we agree: once anything is consciously offered or dedicated to Her, *it belongs to Her forever.* That thing may never be used for personal reasons again. Consider this well before offering or dedicating *any* of the Five Elements.

Let the Devotee prepare an offering of the Five Elements for the Goddess. This shall consist of alcohol, meat, fish, grain and Union. At *minimum* have three elements physically present, being alcohol, either meat or grain, and Union. Understand that it is said in the *Tantras* that the great *Devi* and all the *Shaktis* love above all things the intoxication of liquor, the taste of flesh, and the Bliss of Union, so meat, alcohol and Bliss are always the preferred choice of She whom we Adore. Much evidence exists to show that the oldest form of this practice consisted of these three elements, with the expansion into five coming at a later time.

The Hindus and Buddhists say that alcohol is cursed by the Gods, and require purification and dedication of the elements with *mantras. Liber AL vel Legis,* II:22 shows that with the proper orientation, this curse is negated. We think, therefore, that this is best left to the conscience of the Devotee and their desired method of Work, remembering always the inherent vows of *Thelemic Samaya,* and in particular the injunction of *Liber AL vel Legis,* III:62. That said, as with **this and *any other* offering**, it is necessary to consciously consecrate and dedicate its use to the Great Work.

> *The first cup shall always be given to Nuit as the Goddess of Infinite Space and Infinite Stars.*
> *The second, to your Gurus and Teachers.*
> *The third, to the Holy Guardian Angel.*

The fourth, to the Goddess or God in the rupa[131] of the sadhana, which will include all of the attending Shaktis, Dakinis, Yoginis, Ganas, Lokapalas and other attendants.

The fifth, to the Great Work and the enlightenment of All beings.

These five shall always be given, but others may be added if appropriate, at the discretion and inspiration of the Devotee.

There is no law beyond Do what thou wilt.

Preparing the Wine

Have the alcohol, meat and other offerings laid out before the altar.

Give *Mudra of Union,* while silently offering all that you are and all that you have to the Goddess and Her attendants.

Hold the bottle of alcohol with your left hand, and place the right hand onto the lid. Pause while silently affirming that you hold dominion over the elements.

Open the lid with **BAHLASTI!**

Remove the lid with **OMPEHDA!**

Place the middle finger in the hole of the bottle while saying:

Do what thou wilt shall be the whole of the Law. Love is the law, love under will.

Oh Great Form of the Goddess, infuse great joy into the essence of this offering! May it produce full Bliss!

---

[131] Sanskrit: form.

> *You are the amrita that is infinite and the embodiment of awakened consciousness! Fill this nectar with that essence and awaken within.*
> *May this Amrita contain all the tastes and infinite knowledge.*
> *May this cup of Self which contains the nectar of Self, be sacrificed completely into the fire of the Supreme Self!*

With the *mala*, give one round of **OM HRIM KROM SVAHA** over the bottle. Give *Mudra of Union*. Say:

> *There is no Law beyond: Do what thou wilt.*

With the ring finger, take a drop of the wine and place it on the forehead.

Applying the Sacred Elements in Offerings

> "Here, there is no purity and no impurity, no dualism nor nodualism, no ritual nor its rejection, no renunciation and no possession [...] all observances, rules and regulations are neither enjoined nor prohibited in this way."
> — *Malinivijayottaratantra*

To grasp the significance of the offerings, we must delve into the concept of the *gunas* which serve as an underlying framework governing all aspects of existence.

In the realm of Hindu philosophy, the three *gunas*—*sattva* (lucidity), *rajas* (activity), and *tamas* (inertia)—stand as fundamental qualities or attributes that permeate the entire universe, including the intricate tapestry of human nature and behavior. These *gunas* occupy a pivotal role in elucidating the very essence of reality, and the distinctive characteristics that define individuals.

Within the pages of the *Bhagavad Gita* this concept of the three *gunas* is explored, as Lord Krishna imparts his wisdom to the perplexed warrior, Arjuna. In this text, Krishna expounds upon the triad of *gunas*, and delineates their significance in the context of human conduct and disposition:

Sattva

This facet is intricately entwined with qualities epitomizing purity, wisdom and enlightenment. In the *Bhagavad Gita*, *sattva* is extolled as the embodiment of goodness and equilibrium. Individuals predominantly influenced by *sattva* radiate serenity and composure, dedicated to their spiritual evolution with an unwavering moral compass. Krishna, the divine guide, extols *sattva* as the pathway to liberation and self-realization.

Rajas

Rajas, on the other hand, is aligned with attributes such as desire, passion and attachment. Within the *Bhagavad Gita's* verses, *rajas* is described as the embodiment of restlessness and ceaseless activity. When *rajas* prevails, individuals are driven by insatiable desires, unbridled ambition, and the relentless pursuit of material wealth. Krishna cautions against excessive attachment to *rajas*, which can ensnare one in a web of suffering and bondage.

Tamas

Tamas embodies qualities of darkness, ignorance and inertia. The *Bhagavad Gita* portrays *tamas* as the essence of obscurity and lethargy. Those under the sway of *tamas* often manifest laziness, befuddlement and a profound lack of motivation. Lord Krishna advises against succumbing to *tamas* as it has the potential to obstruct spiritual growth and bind individuals to the unending cycle of birth and death.

Throughout the verses of the *Bhagavad Gita,* Krishna urges Arjuna to transcend the dominion of the three *gunas.* He imparts the wisdom of performing one's duties with selfless devotion *(bhakti),* and a detachment from the outcomes, thus transcending the influence of the *gunas.* This, he emphasizes, is an indispensable step on the path to spiritual enlightenment and the ultimate attainment of liberation *(moksha).*

The three *gunas* can also be mapped to the three types of Tantrik practitioners: *Divya, Vira* and *Pashu.* These correspond with *The Book of the Law*'s Hermit, Lover and Man of Earth.

The Hermit — Divya — Sattva

Divya is the "divine" practitioner, infused with *Sattva.* Their *sadhana* is the highest level of refinement, and the very relationship to *sadhana* and ritual changes from that of the other levels in a dramatic way. The Hermit is a conscious co-creator with the Universe, the master Yogi Magician that fully embodies the principles of *Svecchacara*: Living life in according to Will.

The Lover — Vira — Rajas

Vira is the "hero," so called because this tantrika walks the razor's edge of sensory and energetic transformation. They are actively working on burning away the dross of their personality and all obstacles. They work with the body and senses as well as transformative consciousness. When one thinks of tantra and magick, this is usually the level that comes to mind. This is the warrior magician, striving to achieve the Knowledge and Conversation of the Holy Guardian Angel: the Adept.

The Man of Earth — Pashu — Tamas

The *pashu* is the "beast." This is the unrefined and gross material practitioner. We all start here, and slowly pull ourselves out of the materialistic and illusory qualities of supposed reality in the process of Initiation. The emphasis here is on trying to rise above the mind-dulling and hypnotic sleepiness of *tamas,* to strive to see through materialistic blindness and answer that question: Who am I?

§ § §

In the *Five-Fold Worship of the Goddess* and the accompanying *sadhanas,* we are typically working with the Lovers/Vira/Rajas energy. You touch upon the offerings made and begin to explore the depth of what it means to share energy in this way, incorporating meat, alcohol and the bliss of union through sexual acts. These elements are categorized as *rajasic,* symbolizing fire, heat and agitation. In the alchemical context, they represent sulphur—the agent of dissolution—which cleanses away perceived "impurities" to reveal the metaphorical gold within. The practitioners of this path adopt the archetype of the *Vira,* striving to elevate their consciousness from the confines of a materialistic, neurotic persona to a divine realm—an unbound state of Self-Realization while living.

However, this path is not the sole approach, and may not be the optimal choice depending on individual circumstances and goals. The three *gunas* are not static, and the approaches in tantra may cycle through the different levels of conscious awareness. You may find at different times and circumstances that you approach the rituals and offerings at different levels of awareness, be it the Hermit, the Lover, or the Man of Earth.

For the offerings, meat may be substituted with other elements. For example, the *Kularnava Tantra* indicates the use of ginger and garlic as a substitute for meat. Instead of alcohol, often coconut water or milk is substituted. Sexual energy can be generated through seemingly endless combinations and interactions, including visualization. Arthur Avalon elaborates in his commentary on the *Kularnava Tantra*:

> "In the Tantra, the worshippers are, it is well known, divided into three broad categories of pasu, animal man, vira, the heroic man, divya, the godly man. To each of these classes of seekers, it should be mentioned, the Five ingredients have different connotations: divyatattva, the divine or symbolic meaning for the divya sadhaka; pratyaksa tattva, literal, to the Vira who is constitutionally and temperamentally equipped to ride on the crest of Nature, subjugating and transforming her in the course of his sadhana and fulfils the onerous conditions laid down by the Sastra. To one who is neither a divya nor a vira but is on the lowest rung of the ladder, pasu, Panchatattvas are substitutional [...]. Instead of wine they use coconut water, instead of meat, garlic and so on."

When consciousness is refined to a condition of constant awareness and in accord with the True Will, the elements for offering are transcended along with the Hermit. The nature of the relationship between consciousness and the interaction with the different energies is completely transformed. Wine becomes the nectar of *Amrita* that descends from the *Sahasrara chakra* above the crown of the head, the Elixir of Life and Immortality. Meat—the animal sacrifice—transforms into the sacrifice of the Adept's own animal nature to the Will. Fish becomes the offering of all senses, the constant sea of sensations that endlessly flow through awareness. Grains are the offering of the Adept's own body, the expression of the earth element. Finally, sexual union becomes the ultimate expression of Self-Realization, the ultimate bliss of union with Divine consciousness.

By standing as Awareness—living from the Center—every action manifests spontaneously as True Will. From this perspective, you are not blindly following rules. Learn to adapt and work with your circumstances. Learn to listen to your inner guidance. Find what works for you in any situation. Let your intuition lead you to what is correct for your specific situation as one star in the company of stars.

Svecchacara!

Do what thou wilt shall be the whole of the Law!

Chapter 14
THE MANTRA OF REVEALING

This chapter delves into the *Mantra of Revealing*—also known as the *Mantra of the Void*—and explores its various forms and applications. The *Mantra of Revealing* encompasses the energies of the Aeon and gives rise to eleven primary vibrations. Understanding and working with these *mantras* opens up the potential for invoking and attuning to different aspects of consciousness.

The chapter begins by introducing the Sevenfold (full) form of the *Mantra of Revealing,* which serves as the foundation. From there, derivative forms and *bijas* (seed syllables) are presented, each representing specific aspects of the divine. These forms include the *Devi vidya* of Nuit, the *Deva mantra* of Heru-Ra-Ha, and the *bijas* of Nuit, Hadit and Ra-Hoor-Khuit, among others.

A primary way of approaching the *mantra* is the *Call of the Children of the Stars,* a type of walking meditation or pathworking, where visualization, *mantra* and movement all combine. An almost psychedelic experience can be produced, where the visualized landscape overlays the physical. Conceiving of the universe of experience as a great *mandala,* you are encouraged to seek a secluded place in nature, away from the distractions of human activity. Ideally, this practice takes place during the evening as the sun sets and the shadows lengthen. The Devotee walks mindfully, reciting the call "hu hu" in synchronization with their footsteps and breathing. As you immerse yourself in the natural surroundings, a vision of the Great Mother Tree may appear, with owls perched on its branches. One owl captures your attention and continues to call out "hu hu," drawing you into a profound expansion of consciousness.

The purpose of this ritual is to connect with the cosmic vibrations and the wisdom of the stars. By immersing yourself in nature and aligning with the *Call of the Children of the Stars,* you enter a state of heightened awareness and unity with the cosmos. The resonance of the Call merges with the vibrations of the stars, expanding consciousness and dissolving boundaries into pure awareness.

This is a powerful technique for those seeking to explore the depths of consciousness, align with divine energies, and commune with the cosmic forces symbolized by the stars and the Great Mother Tree. By engaging in this ritual, you can experience a profound sense of connection, transcendence and spiritual awakening.

An Examination of the *Mantra of Revealing*

First is The Sevenfold (full) form **om hrung bhagavati vri vhru heru aha**

From the Sevenfold *mantra,* sparks of stellar flame expressing the primordial essence of the Aeon radiate outward. As the sparks coalesce into beams of light vibrating in the Void, the dew formed thereon gives birth to those that follow.

Second, is the Fivefold form **om hrung bhagavati heru aha**

Third, the *Devi vidya* of Nuit **om bhagavati aha**

Fourth, the *Deva mantra* of Heru-Ra-Ha **om hrung heru aha**

Fifth, the *bija* of Nuit is **vri**

Sixth, the *bija* of Hadit is **vhru**

Seventh, the *bija* of Ra-Hoor-Khuit is **hru**

Eighth, the invoking magick *vidya* of Nuit is **va ru ii**

Ninth, the invoking magick *mantra* of Hadit is **va ha ru uu**

Tenth, the invoking magick *mantra* of Heru-Ra-Ha is **ha ru hu**

Eleventh, the *Call of the Children of the Stars* is **hu hu**

These are the Eleven primary forms. There are countless others which will open to you with the Lamp of the Holy Guardian Angel.

The Call of the Children of the Stars

The experience of awareness—the perception of the world—is conceived of as a great *mandala*. At the center stands the Mother of the Forest, her roots descend deep into the rich, fertile soil of the earth, and her great branches rise up into the heights of the sky. She stands between the Sun and the Moon, with a canopy of stars. In the evening, the starlight coalesces into dewdrops on her pine needles. From the Mother comes the call of the Children of the Stars: *hu hu... hu hu... hu hu...*

Find a secluded place in a forest or in the mountains. Get as far away from the sounds of humankind as possible, and surround yourself with nature. A hiking trail in the wilderness is ideal, as activating the *Call of the Children of the Stars* is best done with movement in nature. And it is best if the Call is activated towards dusk, as the Sun is starting to set and the shadows are lengthening—as the day comes to an end.

Walk mindfully, taking in all of the natural wonder and sounds of the wild that surround you. Mentally recite the call repeatedly: *hu hu, hu hu, hu hu.* Let the repetition match with your footsteps and breathing, but do not force this. Allow the vibrations, the footsteps, the breathing, all to come into sync naturally, of their own accord.

A vision of the Great Mother Tree will appear. You realize the call is coming from owls that are sitting on the branches and soaring through the sky. One owl in particular looks directly at you, and calls out **hu hu, hu hu, hu hu**.

Allow consciousness to expand into the eyes of the owl, as the Call resonates throughout the cosmos. It seems the stars themselves respond, vibrating and twinkling brighter in the night sky, the resonance of their light beams mixing with the vibrations of the Call. All expands and dissolves into pristine awareness.

Chapter 15
THE HIDDEN GOD

"And that which thou hearest is but the dropping of the dew from my limbs, for I dance in the night, naked upon the grass, in shadowy places, by running streams.
And it is the song of the syrens. And whoever heareth it is lost."

— *Liber 418*, Cry of the 2nd Aethyr

This practice explores the concept of the Hidden God—the inner guru within—and incorporates elements from Dzogchen. The focus is on accessing the radiant Awareness of the Void and experiencing the state of awakened consciousness. From Dzogchen, *guruyoga* is considered the highest and most sublime practice. To quote the great *siddha* Namkhai Norbu, *"Guruyoga is the root of all transmissions."* The practice of *guruyoga* is the ultimate practice, as it is the natural condition of awakened consciousness. At its most foundational level, *guruyoga* is the ultimate Self Realization, the experience of the True Guru within—whether conceptualized as the "Holy Guardian Angel", the "Higher Self", or any other manifestation of wisdom and awareness. As has been emphasized repeatedly throughout these practices, the source of Truth—the Guru—lies within, not in some external authority.

Within Dzogchen, *guruyoga* is based on the principle of *rigpa*, which can be thought of as "pure awareness" or "primordial consciousness." *Rigpa* is the fundamental nature of mind, a state of pristine awareness that is ever-present, all-encompassing, and unconditioned. It is described as the innate wisdom and luminosity that underlies all phenomena.

The guru is regarded as a representative or manifestation of *rigpa*. Through the practice of *guruyoga*, practitioners seek to merge their own individual awareness with the awakened state embodied by the guru. This is not a mere intellectual or conceptual understanding, but a direct experiential realization of *rigpa*.

The practice of *guruyoga* involves several aspects:

Outer Guru: Initially, practitioners establish a connection with an external guru. This guru is seen as a source of inspiration, guidance and blessings. You cultivate devotion, trust and reverence towards the guru, recognizing their wisdom and enlightened qualities.

Inner Guru: Through contemplation and meditation, you begin to recognize the guru's qualities as reflections of your own inherent nature. The outer guru becomes an avenue to connect with your own inner guru, the essence of *rigpa* within yourself. This inner guru represents the awakened state that is already present within each individual.

Merging with the Guru: In the advanced stages, you seek to dissolve the dualistic separation between yourself and the guru. Through devotion, visualization and meditation, you merge your awareness with the guru's enlightened mind. This process allows for a direct transmission of wisdom, compassion and awakened presence. At this stage there is no difference between Outer and Inner.

The practice of *guruyoga* is not limited to a specific ritual or technique, but is ultimately about recognizing the inseparability of the guru's awakened state and your own true nature. It is a means of awakening to the non-dual nature of reality, and experiencing the direct recognition of the nature of consciousness.

It is important to note that even in the context of Dzogchen, while *guruyoga* emphasizes the role of the guru, it does not advocate blind faith or dependence on an external authority. Instead, it encourages you to recognize your own innate wisdom, and realize your true nature. The guru serves as a skillful means to facilitate this process of awakening and liberation.

In the tantra of the New Aeon, the primacy of consciousness is also recognized. The practice incorporates the letter **A** (pronounced "Ah") as a symbol of primordial consciousness, representing the state of awakened mind. Various depictions of the letter **A** from different esoteric traditions, including tantrik Buddhism, Hinduism and Egyptian hieroglyphics, are mentioned. The **A Ka Dua** *mantra* is introduced as a powerful tool within the ritual of the *Diamond Sapphire Gem of Radiant Light*. Each line of the *mantra* activates one of the Four Worlds, corresponding to the physical, emotional, devotional and divine bodies.

The state of the Hidden God is described as the unity of all paths, systems and *dharmas*, resolving into the Adamantine Void. It represents the fulfillment of all vows and commitments, and is the essence of all practices and beliefs. You are encouraged to enter this state through the sound of a long and melodious **A**, aligning with your true nature.

The *Song of the Syrens* functions to stabilize the energetic body and consciousness. It involves working with the subtle channels of light in your stellar body. The *Song* is also seen as a way to call upon the guardians of the *Ananda Arghya*, and rest in the primordial awakened consciousness of the Void.

The practice does not require visualizations. Instead, the focus is on the vibrational aspect of the sounds, stimulating your subtle centers, and relaxing the mind into its natural condition. The *Song of the Syrens* contains poetic verses that convey a sense of initiation, triumph and the attainment of will.

The practice concludes with dedicating the merit to Nuit, the Egyptian goddess of the night sky, and to the benefit of all sentient beings. This dedication is a wish for peace, freedom and happiness for all.

Overall, this practice draws on the historical references to Dzogchen, and the practice of *Guru Yoga*, while presenting them within a new Thelemic perspective. It aims to guide you towards the experience of awakened consciousness and unity with the cosmic forces symbolized by the Void and the Hidden God.

§ § §

Within the esoteric traditions of tantrik Buddhism and Hinduism, the state of primordial consciousness is represented by the sound of the letter **A**.

In Sanskrit, the first letter of the so-called *Garland of Letters*[132] is glyphed:

Figure 26
Sanskrit 'A'

---

[132] The characters of the Sanskrit alphabet are written in *devanagari*, the alphabet of the *nagas* (serpent demi-gods). The letters are said to form a garland about the neck of the Great Goddess.

The letter **A** ("Ah") in Tibetan script appears thus:

Figure 27
Tibetan 'A'

In Shingon esoteric Buddhism the letter **A** is represented:

Figure 28
Kanji 'A'

For the Devotee of *Ananda Arghya,* the most direct key to accessing the radiant Awareness of the Void lies hidden in plain sight in the Great Egyptian *mantra*:

A ka dua
Tuf ur biu
Bi a'a chefu
Dudu ner af an nuteru

In the ritual of the *Diamond Sapphire Gem of Radiant Light,* this *mantra* plays a dominant role. As we see in the *Lantern of Thebes,* each line of the *mantra* activates one of the Four Worlds, and the corresponding energetic response in the physical, emotional, devotional and divine bodies.

The first line, **A Ka Dua,** is translated as "Unity uttermost showed." The first word, **A**, is the very root vibration of **Unity**. This is the sound of *sunyata,* the diamond void at the very essence of all reality. The sound of **A** is the vibration of the primordial state of mind, of pure consciousness, the state of primordial awakened consciousness.

The letter **A** in Egyptian Hieroglyphics is glyphed by the Royal Vulture:

Figure 29
Egyptian 'A'

The root vibration of Awakened Consciousness, the pristine clarity of the Adamantine Void, is thus visually glyphed by the Lord of the Universe.

To be in this state is to be in the state of the Guru, the Hidden God. This *is* the unity of all paths, all systems, all *dharmas,* all of *samsara* resolved into the adamantine Void. This is the fulfillment of all vows and commitments. This is the direct result of all practices and beliefs. This is the All and None, the Heart of the Master, and the Womb of the Great Goddess.

The Practice

Relax with cleansing breaths, and then sound a long and melodious **A** ("Ahhhhhhhhh..."), entering the primordial Awake-Aware condition of your true nature.

After this, you may then rest in your natural condition with the *Song of the Syrens*. Where the **A** of **A Ka Dua** is a direct transmission of the ultimate and natural condition of mind, the *Song of the Syrens* stabilizes your energetic body and consciousness by working with the subtle channels of light in your stellar body. The *Song* is also particularly loved by the guardians of the *Ananda Arghya*, and is their favorite "love chant" to call them into your presence. This song may be sung by all Devotees to rest in the primordial awakened consciousness of the Adamantine Void.

No visualizations are required. The sound vibrations both stimulate the subtle centers of the Devotees consecrated *astroeides* ("Star body") and relaxes the mind into its natural condition that resides *"aloof and alone"* atop Mount Kailash in a timeless eternity of Bliss.

Song of the Syrens

Mu pa telai, O chi balae
Tu wa melai Wa pa malae: —
A, a, a Ut! Ut! Ut!
Tu fu tulu! Ge; fu latrai,
Tu fu Tulu Le fu malai
Pa, Sa, Ga. Kut! — Hut! — Nut.
Qwi Mu telai AI OAI
Ya Pa melai; Rel moai
u, u, u. Ti — Ti — Ti!
Se gu melai; Wa la pelai
Pe fu telai, Tu fu latai
Fu tu lu. Wi, Ni, Bi.

(See Chapter 1 for the Translation of the Song.)

When complete, dedicate the merit of your practice to Nuit, and to the benefit of all sentient beings, that they may all experience Real Peace, Real Freedom, and Real Happiness.

Chapter 16
SUPPORTING PRACTICES

The Lunar Adorations

The moon has held a significant role in tantrik rituals throughout history, representing aspects of divinity, and serving as a symbol of feminine power and cosmic forces. In tantrik traditions, the moon is associated with the divine feminine, often embodied by goddesses such as Kali, Lalita or Chinnamasta. It is revered as a source of divine energy and illumination, guiding practitioners towards spiritual awakening and liberation.

In Western paganism and Thelema, the moon also holds a prominent place. Drawing inspiration from ancient mythologies and occult traditions, the moon is seen as a potent symbol of cyclical nature, intuition and the subconscious mind. Lunar phases, such as the moon's waxing and waning, are deeply connected to the ebb and flow of life and spiritual growth.

One aspect of the moon is associated with the goddess Nuit, who represents the infinite expanse of the night sky. The lunar symbolism in Thelema is intertwined with the concept of will, emphasizing the alignment of individual desires and intentions with the cosmic currents.

The moon's importance in these traditions extends beyond its astronomical significance. It serves as a gateway to connect with the spiritual realms, harnessing the intuitive and transformative energies associated with the lunar cycles. Through moon-centered practices, you can access hidden knowledge, enhance your intuition, and navigate your spiritual journeys with a deeper understanding of the interconnectedness of the universe.

Figure 30
'The Moon' Card of the Thoth Tarot
(© Ordo Templi Orientis)

In *The Book of Thoth,* Atu XVIII: The Moon tarot card holds profound symbolism, and represents a pivotal stage in the journey towards self-realization and spiritual enlightenment. The Moon card depicts a moonlit landscape with a path leading into the distance, flanked by two towers or pillars. The moon shines down upon the scene, casting a pale light that illuminates the path ahead.

The card symbolizes the realm of the subconscious mind, intuition and the hidden aspects of your psyche. It represents the deeper layers of the Fool's journey, where illusions, fears and unconscious patterns come to the surface for examination and transformation. It serves as a reminder that self-discovery requires confronting shadows, and delving the depths of your subconscious.

The two towers or pillars on the card are often associated with duality and polarity. They represent the opposing forces and energies within yourself, and the need to find balance and integration. The Moon card signifies a time of uncertainty, where appearances can be deceiving, and the truth may be obscured. It invites us to trust our intuition, and navigate the mysteries of the subconscious with courage and discernment.

The path shown in the card signifies the journey through the depths of the psyche, guided by the moon's astral light. It suggests that embracing the unknown, and exploring the hidden realms of the mind is necessary for personal growth and spiritual evolution. The Moon card also carries an element of mystery and initiation as we face the tests and challenges that arise from the depths of being.

Furthermore, The Moon card in *The Book of Thoth* is associated with the astrological sign of Pisces, highlighting its connection to intuition, dream states, and the fluid nature of consciousness. It encourages us to trust our instincts, and tap into the wisdom of the subconscious mind. Meditation and dreamwork help us to embrace the transformative power of intuition. The moon invites us to delve into the depths of the subconscious and navigate the unknown with inner guidance and self-awareness.

As a powerful symbol of the divine feminine, cyclical nature, and spiritual illumination, working with the Moon allows you to tap into the mystical and transformative energies associated with lunar cycles. Through this inner work, following the fluid and dreamlike qualities of the Moon, the self is guided towards self-discovery and transformative spiritual growth.

The Adorations

Let the Devotee be mindful of the course of the Moon through the heavens, and give worship to the Goddess in Her form of the Moon when seeing Her. This may be done with the Vedic *Gayatri mantra*:

**Om bhur bhuvah svah
tat savitur varenyam
bhargo devasya dhimahi
dhiyo yo nah pracodayat**

*Om we meditate on the effulgent glory of the divine light
May it inspire our understanding*

Alternatively, the many forms of the Goddess in India each have their own *gayatri*, which also may be used. Some examples:

Tripurasundari:

**Om Tripurasundari vidmahe
kameshvari dhimahi
tanno klinne pracodayat**

*Om let us contemplate Tripurasundari
let us think of Kameshvari
may that wetness direct*

Kali:

**om mahakalyai ca vidmahe
smasana vasinyai ca dhimahi
tanno kali prachodayat**

*Om let us contemplate the Great Goddess
who takes away darkness,
let us think of She who resides in the cremation grounds,
may she grant increase*

It is better still if the Devotee has a chosen and preferred form of the Goddess,[133] in which case use the prayer associated with Her, or compose your own verse in celebration of Her. You may find suitable verses in the *Saundarya Lahari,* various tantrik writings, Greek epics, the Holy Books of Thelema, and so on.

These devotions should be particularly emphasized when the Moon is full. At such times, you may wish to give the longer *Song of the Syrens* from the Cry of the 2nd Aethyr, *Liber 418.*

Song of the Syrens

Mu pa telai, O chi balae
Tu wa melai Wa pa malae: —
A, a, a Ut! Ut! Ut!
Tu fu tulu! Ge; fu latrai,
Tu fu Tulu Le fu malai
Pa, Sa, Ga. Kut! — Hut! — Nut.
Qwi Mu telai AI OAI
Ya Pa melai; Rel moai
u, u, u. Ti — Ti — Ti!
Se gu melai; Wa la pelai
Pe fu telai, Tu fu latai
Fu tu lu. Wi, Ni, Bi.

(See Chapter 1 for the Translation of the Song.)

Establishing the Place

This ritual may be used to open a new location or space to the current of energy you are working with, such as installing a new shrine or temple.

---

[133] Sanskrit *Ishtadevita.*

The ritual is also suitable for field work, such as making a connection between the current and a location that you are visiting; e.g., a powerful historic location where a connection is desired.

The ritual is also useful in your personal *sadhana* for establishing a connection with the protectors, in which case it may be used at the end of *sadhana,* but *before* going into the *Fivefold Worship of the Goddess.*

In all cases, some form of food offering should be given for the Guardians and the local spirits.

The ritual involves various steps including purification, invocation of protective forces, circulation of energy, and dedication. Key elements include establishing refuge in the Great Goddess, awakening internal energy centers, invoking guardians, activating the altar, and sealing the space with blessings.

Outline of the Sadhana

0. Preliminary
- Set up the space with necessary items
- Perform any preparatory banishings
- Center and focus the mind

1. Opening
- Invoke refuge in the Great Goddess and the strength of Heru-Ra-Ha
- Affirm the Law of Thelema

2. Awakening the Interior Stars
- Focus on the base of the spine and raise energy up through the crown

3. Establishing the Light
- Stabilize the light through *pranayama* with breath retention

4. Circulation of the Light
- Chant while circulating the light

5. Establishing the Guru
- Invoke the Holy Guardian Angel silently while performing the *Mudra of Union* (Figure 16)

6. Call of the Guardians
- Invoke guardians and protectors, calling upon them to establish presence
- Evoke each guardian with their name and attributes

7. Activating the Altar
- Breathe light into the heart and establish connection with the shrine or altar

8. Establishing Place
- Invoke the presence of resident spirits and protectors, uniting efforts

9. Song of the Syrens
- Recite a mystical chant

10. Declaration and Seal
- Declare the space as a center of light, life, love and liberty
- Dedicate the merit of the practice to the enlightenment of all beings

11. Bodhicitta and Dedication of Merit
- Express dedication to universal well-being and enlightenment
- Conclude with "**ABRAHADABRA**"

0. Preliminary

This practice is best done at night, underneath a canopy of stars. Prepare the *Adytum* as for the performance of the *Diamond Sapphire*. At the simplest, have a bowl or cup of fresh water, a white candle, incense,[134] a *mala,* and a bell. Perform any preparatory banishings as needed.

Be seated in *asana*. Light the candle and incense. Center and focus your mind, taking three cleansing breaths. See your sphere of sensation filling with radiant, pure, white light, surrounded by a thin, blue shell. Allow awareness of this to fade as the light and your breath become one. Establish rhythmic breathing.

1. Opening

Refuge and Armor of the Great Goddess

Say:
Nu is my Refuge [as you raise your arms slightly]
As Hadit my Light [continue to raise your arms]
And Heru-Ra-Ha is the Strength, Force, Vigour of my arms.

Your arms are now raised and outstretched. Cross your arms over your chest, right over left. Hold this position for a moment to allow the interior union symbolized by the outer gestures to seal. Strike the bell, and say:

Do what thou wilt shall be the whole of the Law.
Love is the law, love under will.

2. Awakening the Interior Stars

Focus on the base of the spine and become aware of the coiled energy. With a slow, deep inhalation, bring the current of light up the spine and out through the opening at the crown of the head, where it rests at the pulsating sphere of brilliance. Exhale, bringing the light back down to the base. Repeat three times. On the third

---

[134] Red sandalwood or rose is preferred, but any "sweet smelling" incense will be suitable.

ascent, the light at the crown becomes even brighter, finally erupting in *"ultimate sparks of the intimate fire" (AL, III:67)*; this fiery starlight rains down upon your sphere of sensation and body, immersing you in the warmth and coruscating brilliance of stellar nectar.

3. Establishing the Light

Perform simple *pranayama* with *kumbhaka* (holding the breath) to stabilize the light. Close the right nostril, inhale with the left to a count of 4. Close both nostrils, and hold the breath for a count of 16. Exhale through the right nostril for a count of 8. Immediately inhale through the right nostril to a count of 4. Close both nostrils, and hold the breath for a count of 16. Exhale through the left nostril for a count of 8. This makes one cycle. Repeat for a minimum of 3 cycles.

4. Circulation of the Light

Chant three times while circulating the light:

A ka dua
Tuf ur biu
Bi a'a chefu
Dudu ner af an nuteru

5. Establishing the Guru

Give the *Mudra of Union* while Silently invoking the Name of the Holy Guardian Angel.[135] When ready, release *mudra*.

---

[135] If this Name is not known, give the *mudra* and aspire intently to union with the Angel, opening up to the reciprocal descent of the Light.

6. Call of the Guardians

In a state of calm relaxation, sound a long and resonant "Ahhhh." Then recite:

> *"Oh Daughter of the Snow Capped Mountains! Oh Radiant Night of Bliss and Awakening! Mes Khut Ukha,[136] Guardians and Protectors of the Ananda Arghya, we call you here!*
>
> *Guardians, Protectors and Attendants of the lineage the Great Goddess! Come now and establish your presence in this shrine of Ordo Sunyata Vajra!*
>
> *We call upon you to stir and descend from your celestial palaces of Mount Kailash!"*

Evoke each of the guardians by reciting their Sanskrit or Greek names, as below:

MATRIKA	GREEK	CHAKRA
AOM Chamundayai namaha!	Alcyone	Sahasrara
AOM Varahiyai namaha!	Celaeno	Ajna
AOM Kaumariyai namaha!	Taygeta	Vishuddha
AOM Aindriyai namaha!	Maia	Anahatta
AOM Mahesariyai namaha!	Electra	Manipura
AOM Vaishnaviyai namaha!	Merope	Svadhisthana
AOM Brahmiyai namaha!	Asterope	Muladhara

AOM Vajra Mahasunyatayai namaha!

> *"Awaken and open your dark lustrous eyes, and look upon us with your favour! One glance from your attendant's eyes grants instant enlightenment!*

---

[136] Egyptian, "Children of the Radiant Night." These are the daughters of the Great Void of Nuit.

Cosmic Dawn is Awakening, and the celestial flowers are opening their petals. The morning breeze of enlightenment is bracing. Awaken and bless us, your successors and heirs!

Lotus-hidden bees, having come out into the open with the opening of the starry dew laden petals, are singing hymns to your glory. Awaken and be with us!

The soles of your feet are the most dazzling, Great Goddess! The white nails in your beautiful toes exceed even the full moon splendor! Send your attendants now to receive our gifts of Light and Love!

Let your flood of Beauty wash over us! Let your nectar of Bliss rain down upon us! Let this place always be a suitable center of your radiance!

Great Goddess, may all my speech, howsoever idle, be recitation of Mantra! May all the actions of my hand be Mudra! May all my walking be the pacing of the ground around Thy image in worship! May all my eating be Homa! May the act of lying down be prostrations before Thee! May all my pleasures be an offering to Thee! Whatsoever I do may it be counted for worship of Thee!

Establish this place forever in your honor! Always be present! May your presence and guidance enable us to bring all beings across the oceans of samsara!

Let the teachings of your lineage flow like honey into our hearts, and forever be clear and powerful to enlighten all beings! Protect the teachings and the lineage of Ananda Arghya as your Vehicle of Great Bliss! Inform the lineage holders of the Ordo Sunyata Vajra!

Let your presence guide us and direct us as true successors and heirs of your radiant Bliss!"

Give *Mudra of Union*.

Open to the presence of the retinue of *Dakinis, Bhairavis, Yoginis, Nityas, Lokapalas* and other attendants and protectors of the lineage and the Great Goddess.

With a single act of Will, give the *Great Mantra of the Void*:

Om hrung bhagavata vri vru heru aha

Give *Mudra of Union*.

7. Activating the Altar

Place your palms together and turn your hands in towards your chest so the finger tips are pointing at the *anahatta chakra*. Simultaneously breathe in with one deep breath, seeing a current of light stream in from above your head into your heart. Hold the breath, establishing connection between the stellar stream and your heart. Exhale slowly, turning the fingertips towards the shrine or altar. Separate the hands so that both are extended parallel with open hands, palms upturned towards the shrine.

8. Establishing Place

Say:

May your Vehicle of Bliss take seat here! May the resident spirits and protectors of this place unite with us in this effort!

Seal the current with the *Mudra of Union*. Pause. Release *mudra*.

9. Song of the Syrens

Mu pa telai, O chi balae
Tu wa melai Wa pa malae: —
A, a, a Ut! Ut! Ut!
Tu fu tulu! Ge; fu latrai,

> Tu fu Tulu Le fu malai
> Pa, Sa, Ga. Kut! — Hut! — Nut.
> Qwi Mu telai AI OAI
> Ya Pa melai; Rel moai
> u, u, u. Ti — Ti — Ti!
> Se gu melai; Wa la pelai
> Pe fu telai, Tu fu latai
> Fu tu lu. Wi, Ni, Bi.

(See Chapter 1 for the Translation of the Song.)

10. Declaration and Seal

Say:
May this space be a center of Light, Life, Love and Liberty!
May all sentient beings enjoy happiness!
May they all be freed from pain and suffering!
May they never be separated from the highest happiness!

Give *Mudra of Union*. Silently dedicate merit of this practice to the enlightenment of all sentient beings.

11. Bodhicitta and Dedication of Merit

Say:
I am uplifted in thine heart; and the kisses of the stars rain hard upon they body.
May Light, Life, Love and Liberty be extended universally to all, under the regency of the One Law of Thelema.
May all attain the Stone of the Wise, the Summum Bonum, True Wisdom and Perfect Happiness.
ABRAHADABRA

Chapter 17
THAT WHICH REMAINS

"Remember all ye that existence is pure joy; that all the sorrows are but as shadows; they pass & are done; but there is that which remains."

— *Liber AL vel Legis, II:9*

These words resonate with a timeless wisdom, reminding us of the inherent joy that permeates the fabric of existence itself. Looked at directly, existence is bliss. The very act of Awareness is filled with a spontaneously arising joy.

Within the tapestry of life, sorrows may indeed cast their dark shadows, fleeting and ephemeral as they are. They come and go, transient visitors on the stage of our experience. Yet, amidst the vicissitudes of joy and sorrow, there exists an immutable essence, a luminous core that transcends the transient nature of worldly phenomena.

This verse serves as a poignant reminder that while challenges and hardships may punctuate our journey, they are but temporary illusions, ephemeral veils obscuring the radiant truth that lies beneath. Beyond the fleeting dance of joy and sorrow, there exists a reservoir of enduring bliss, a sublime realization of our inherent connection to the divine.

In the face of adversity, it is imperative to cultivate the awareness that joy is not contingent upon external circumstances, but rather springs forth from the depths of our being. It is the recognition of this eternal truth that empowers us to navigate the ever-changing currents of life with grace and resilience.

To remember that existence is pure joy is to embrace a paradigm shift in our perception, transcending the narrow confines of duality to behold the sublime unity that underpins all creation. It is an invitation to relinquish attachment to fleeting pleasures and transient pains, and to attune ourselves to the radiant essence of pure, unadulterated joy that lies at the heart of existence itself.

As we heed the wisdom contained within these sacred words, let us strive to cultivate a deep and abiding sense of joy that transcends the fluctuations of the external world. Let us remember that amidst the ephemeral shadows of sorrow, there is an eternal light—the light of Gnosis—that guides us on our journey, illuminating the path to profound realization and boundless bliss.

Throughout the journey of this book, one resounding truth echoes like a clarion call: the natural and uninhibited expression of the True Will belongs to every individual as an inalienable right. This foundational principle stands as the bedrock upon which the entire structure of spiritual exploration is erected. To understand and embrace this truth is akin to grasping a master key, capable of unlocking the profound mystery of one's existence.

Embedded within these pages lie a plethora of rituals, meditations, and yogic practices, each meticulously crafted not as mere abstractions or esoteric novelties, but as potent tools honed with precision. These tools serve a singular purpose: to empower individuals to discern and enact their True Will. Through diligent practice and unwavering commitment, you can navigate the intricate pathways of consciousness, untangling the threads of destiny to reveal the resplendent tapestry of their purpose.

The tantra expounded in the *Book of the Law,* like all authentic spiritual teachings, transcends passive contemplation or intellectual digestion. It pulsates with the vitality of direct experience, beckoning earnest seekers to embark upon a journey of radical transformation. The rigid boundaries delineating self from other, mundane from divine, dissolve into the luminous expanse of Gnosis.

These teachings are not relics of a bygone era, nor are they rigid dogmas to be blindly adhered to. They are dynamic and vibrant, resonating with the eternal rhythm of the cosmos. Through their practical application, life itself becomes the crucible of initiation, wherein every moment teems with the potential for awakening.

Crucially, tantra is not a compartmentalized pursuit divorced from the fabric of daily existence. While this book elucidates numerous ritualistic and yogic practices, it is imperative to transcend the illusory dichotomy between spiritual and non-spiritual domains. Your daily interactions, whether mundane tasks or profound rituals, are imbued with equal significance. Whether you are at work, among friends, or navigating the aisles of a grocery store, the essence of spiritual practice permeates every facet of life. Strive to remain anchored in Awareness, recognizing the One Taste of experience that flows seamlessly through all manifestations of existence.

In the poignant verses of Norbu's *Little Song of "Do as You Please,"* we find an exhortation to embrace the spontaneity of the moment and dance freely in the grand theater of existence. The verses encapsulate the quintessence of the tantrik path—a jubilant celebration of the boundless creativity inherent within each soul. "Doing as you please" is not an endorsement of reckless abandon, but rather an invitation to harmonize with the pulsating rhythm of the cosmos, attuning yourself to the symphony of life unfolding in perfect harmony. The parallels to *Do what thou wilt* are obvious.

Ultimately, the essence of tantra transcends elaborate rituals or esoteric knowledge. It resides in the direct experience of our inherent divinity. Traverse this path with courage and conviction, honoring the sacred trust bestowed upon us—to discern and enact our True Will in perfect harmony with the cosmic dance of existence.

The Little Song "Do as You Please"

"The ineffable way of being of the Prajñāpāramitā and the experience of direct understanding, I have joined together within myself. To the intellectual path of study, I don't aspire. You who claim to be great scholars, do as you please.

In the natural condition, the space which does not fall into limits of measurement or even the concept of direction, whatever presents itself there, I enjoy as an ornament. I don't make any effort to create or reject anything. You who take up preferences, do as you please.

As for the natural state beyond the contamination of thought, I maintain its vivid presence, without any effort. Why analyse it with the limitations of reason? You who are keen on logic, do as you please.

Directly in the space of the dimension of original Purity, I meet all meditative experiences, manifestations of energy and visions in a state of equanimity. With no need to desire an artificial religious practice, I am happy. You who dwell upon mental constructions, do as you please.

In the pure expanse of space, free of any circumstances, shines the dimension of light of the five colours of self-perfected gdangs energy. The Primordial Wisdom of one's own rtsal energy is spontaneously perfected. You who follow some kind of conceptual confirmation, do as you please.

In the uncorrected condition, the space of the natural Dharmatā, State of Knowledge without distraction, clear and vivid, I live joyously, remaining beyond the limits of mental conception. You who have fallen into limits, do as you please.

The indefinable state, natural since the beginning, is that space beyond all definitions of being and non-being. Among all the modes of existence of saṃsāra and nirvāṇa, there is not one that is not perfected. You who are immersed in conflicting thoughts, do as you please.

Through this unique Knowledge, in the state of recognition of the Primordial Base, understanding that all appearances and that which animates them are rtsal and rol pa energy, I am beyond accomplishing anything through effortful strain. You who try to obtain everything by effort, do as you please.

Whatever arises liberates itself for me, a practitioner of Dzogchen, as the narrow path of hope and fear that is linked to effort doesn't exist for me. I'm happy to adopt a free way of being. You who follow rules, do as you please.

For me, a yogin of universal knowledge, free from illusion, primordial purity (kadag) and self-perfection (lhundrub) are not two. In this condition, whatever one does, it is the total accomplishment of self-perfection. You who follow the gradual path, do as you please.

You who are bound by the chains of hope and fear, calmly leave behind this senseless pain, observe your way of being a little, and the opportunity of the Great Perfection may arise for you, too."

— Chögyal Namkhai Norbu

HISTORICAL INFLUENCES & FURTHER READING

"On mature consideration, therefore, I confidently and deliberately take my refuge in the Triple Gem. Namo Tasso Bhagavato Arahato Samma-sambuddhasa!"
— Aleister Crowley, *Berashith: An Essay in Ontology*

Bodhidharma brought Mahayana Buddhism to China around 526 CE at the instruction of his Master, Prajnatara (the twenty-seventh patriarch), to bring the *Dharma* to China. The School of the Great Vehicle found a fertile ground in the established Taoism of China, resulting in the tradition of Buddhism known as *Ch'an* (from the Sanskrit *dhyana*, "mind"). Bodhidharma became the first patriarch of Buddhism for the Ch'an and Zen schools.

Ch'an Buddhism saw the evolution of the teachings of Nagarjuna's "Middle Way" as the central expression of the greater *Prajnaparamita* tradition, whose radiant doctrine of the Void is exemplified in the *Heart Sutra* and the *Diamond Sutra*. The simplicity and central core of Ch'an and Zen, with its Taoist influences, are identical in essence to the deep heart of Thelema, and lend greater understanding to our Thelemic tradition. The doctrine of the *Prajnaparamita* has evolved into the glorious message of the New Dispensation, the Crowned and Conquering Child that is shown in such received documents as *Liber AL vel Legis, Liber VII,* and *Liber Cordis Cincti Serpente,* among others.

In one sense, Thelema may be seen as the "Vajrayana of the New Aeon." It has its rituals, doctrines, magick and mysticism. Thelema itself is very much a Tantrik Magick of the West, an advanced synthesis and evolution of what came before it, stripped of all non-essentials and cultural trappings. The doctrine of the Void is very much alive in the body of Nuit.

Essential Reading List[137]

Advaita Vedanta

Ramana Maharshi. *The Spiritual Teaching of Ramana Maharshi.* Forward by C.G. Jung. Shambhala, 1972.

Ramana Maharshi. *The Collected Works of Ramana Maharshi.* Compiled by Arthur Osborne. Red Wheel/Weiser, 1997.

Swami Vivekananda. *The Yogas and Other Works.* Chosen and with a Biography by Swami Nikhilananda. Ramakrishna-Vivekananda Center, 1984.

Buddhism

Conze, Edward, Trans. *Buddhist Wisdom: The Diamond Sutra & the Heart Sutra.* Vintage Books, 1958.

Coutinho, Steve. *An Introduction to Daoist Philosophies.* New York: Columbia University Press, 2013.

Crowley, Aleister, Trans. Tao Te Ching: *A New Translation with Commentary by Ko Hsuan.* York Beach: ME: Weiser, 1993. Aleister Crowley's translation of the Daodejing.

---

[137] Compiled in collaboration with Charlotte Moore, to whom I am indebted.

DeCaroli, Robert. *Haunting the Buddha: Indian Popular Religions and the Formation of Buddhism.* Oxford University Press, 2004.

Eaton, John and Calthorpe Blofeld, Trans. *The Zen Teaching of Huang Po: On the Transmission of Mind.* Grove Press, 1959. Huang Po was a Ch'an master of 9th Century China.

Garfield, Jay. *The Fundamental Wisdom of the Middle Way, Nagarjuna's Mulamadhyamakakarika.* Oxford University Press, 1995.

Gyatrul Rinpoche. *The Generation Stage in Buddhist Tantra.* Ithaca, NY: Snow Lion, 2005.

Hendricks, Robert G., Trans. *Te-Tao Ching: A New Translation Based on the Recently Discovered Manuscript Wang-Tui Texts.* Modern Library, 1993.

Kalu Rinpoche. *Luminous Mind: The Way of the Buddha.* Boston: Wisdom Publications, 1997.
Provides an excellent introduction to Indo-Tibetan Buddhist tantra.

Khenchen Thrangu Rinpoche. *Pointing Out the Dharmakaya.* Ithaca, NY: Snow Lion, 2003.
Teachings on Shamatha (Calm-Abiding), Vipassana (Insight), and Mahamudra.

Khenchen Thrangu Rinpoche. *The Practice of Tranquility and Insight: A Guide to Tibetan Buddhist* Meditation. Boulder, CO: Snow Lion, 1993.

Price, A.F. & Mou-Lam Wong, Trans. *The Diamond Sutra and the Sutra of Hui-Neng.* Boulder: Shambhala, 1990.

Red Pine, Trans. *Zen Teaching of Bodhidharma.* North Point Press, 1989.

Red Pine, Trans. *The Lankavatara Sutra.* Berkeley, CA: Counterpoint, 2012.

Saso, Michael R. *Taoist Master Chuang.* Sacred Mountain Press, 2000.

Wei Wu Wei. *Ask the Awakened, The Negative Way.* Sentient Publications, CO. 2002.

Wei Wu Wei. *All Else is Bondage.* Sunstar Publications. 2002.

Wei Wu Wei. *Open Secret.* Hong Kong University Press, Hong Kong. 2001.

Watson, Burton, Trans. *The Complete Works of Chuang Tzu.* Columbia University Press, 1968.

Dzogchen

Norbu, Namkhai. *The Crystal and the Way of Light.* Ithaca, NY: Snow Lion, 2000.

Norbu, Namkhai. *Dzogchen: The Self-Perfected State.* Ithaca, NY: Snow Lion, 1996.

Norbu, Namkhai. *The Mirror: Advice on Presence and Awareness.* Shang Shung Foundation, 2017.

Reynolds, John Myrdhin, Trans. *The Golden Letters.* Ithaca, NY: Snow Lion, 1996.

Tenzin Wangyal Rinpoche. *The Tibetan Yogas of Dream and Sleep: Practices for Awakening.* Shambhala, 2022.

Hindu Tantra

Chinnaiyan, Kavitha. *Fractals of Reality: Living the Sricakra.* Michigan: Sfaim Press, 2022.

Dupuis, Stella and Satkari Mukhopadhyaya, Trans. *The Kaulajnananirnaya.* New Delhi: India: Aditya Prakashan, 2018.

Hine, Phil. *Yoginis: Sex, Death & Possession.* Falcon Press, 2025.

Kali, Devadatta. *In Praise of the Goddess: The Devimahatmya and Its Meaning.* Nicolas-Hays, 2003.

Keul, Istvan. *'Yogini' in South Asia: Interdisciplinary Approaches.* New York: Routledge, 2013.

Magee, Michael. *Kali Magic.* Twisted Trunk Publishers, 2022.

Magee, Michael. *Yaksini Magic.* Twisted Trunk Publishers, 2019.

Mallinson, James, Trans. *The Shiva Samhita: A Critical Edition and English Translation.* Yogavidya, 2007.

McDaniel, June. *Offering Flowers, Feeding Skulls: Popular Goddess Worship in West Bengal.* New York: Oxford University Press, 2004.

Padoux, Andre, Trans. *The Heart of the Yogini.* New York: Oxford University Press, 2013.

Peters, Gregory. *Yogini Magic: The Sorcery, Enchantment & Witchcraft of the Divine Feminine.* Falcon Press, 2022.

Saraswathi, Swami Sri Ramananda, Trans. *Tripura Rahasya: The Secret of the Supreme Goddess.* Bloomington, IN: World Wisdom, 2002.

Singh, Jaideva. *Siva Sutras: The Yoga of Supreme Identity.* Delhi, India: Motilal Banarsidass, 2000.

Singh, Jaideva. *Vijnanabhairava or Divine Consciousness.* Delhi, India: Motilal Banarsidass, 2001.

Subramanian, V.K., Trans. *Saundaryalahari of Shankaracarya.* Delhi, India: Motilal Banarsidass, 1977.

Wallis, Christopher D. *Tantra Illuminated: The Philosophy, History, and Practice of a Timeless Tradition.* Boulder, CO: Mattamayura Press, 2012.

Woodroffe, Sir John. *The Garland of Letters: Studies of the Mantra-Sastra.* Madras, India: Ganesh & Co., 1998.

Woodroffe, Sir John. *Kularnava Tantra.* Delhi, India: Motilal Banarsidass, 1965.

Woodroffe, Sir John. *Sakti and Sakta.* Madras, India: Ganesh & Co., 1987.

Woodroffe, Sir John. *The Serpent Power: Being the Sat-Cakra-Nirupana and Paduka Pancaka.* New York: Dover, 1974.

Thelema

Bertiaux, Michael. *Cosmic Meditation.* London: Fulgur Ltd, 2007.

Crowley, Aleister. *Eight Lectures on Yoga.* Falcon Press, 1991.

Crowley, Aleister. *Gems from the Equinox: Instructions by Aleister Crowley for his Magical Order.* San Francisco, CA: Weiser Books, 2007.

Crowley, Aleister. *The Holy Books of Thelema.* York Beach, ME: Weiser, 1989.

Crowley, Aleister. *Liber AL vel Legis: The Book of the Law.* Multiple editions available.

Crowley, Aleister. *Magical & Philosophical Commentaries on the Book of the Law.* Edited by Kenneth Grant. 93 Publishing, 1974.

Crowley, Aleister. *Book 4, Liber ABA.* York Beach, ME: Weiser, 1998.

Grant, Kenneth. *At the Feet of the Guru: Twenty-Five Essays.* London: Starfire Publications, 2006.

Kenneth Grant's *Typhonian Trilogies* are all essential for understanding the deeper aspects of Thelema and the tantra of the Book of the Law. The material is being kept in print with lovingly detailed editions by Starfire Publishing (starfirepublishing.co.uk), London. The volumes in the *Typhonian Trilogies* (in order) are:

Grant, Kenneth. *The Magical Revival.* Starfire Ltd. Publishing, 2010.

Grant, Kenneth. *Aleister Crowley and the Hidden God.* Starfire Publishing Ltd, 2013.

Grant, Kenneth. *Nightside of Eden.* Starfire Publishing Ltd, 2014.

Grant, Kenneth. *Cults of the Shadow.* Starfire Publishing Ltd, 2013.

Grant, Kenneth. *Outside the Circles of Time.* Starfire Publishing Ltd, 2008.

Grant, Kenneth. *Hecate's Fountain.* Starfire Publishing Ltd, 2014.

Grant, Kenneth. *Outer Gateways.* Starfire Publishing Ltd, 2015.

Grant, Kenneth. *Beyond the Mauve Zone.* Starfire Publishing Ltd, 2016.

Grant, Kenneth. *The Ninth Arch.* Starfire Publishing Ltd, 2016.

GLOSSARY

Abiegnus—The Mystical Mountain of Initiation in the Rosicrucian manifestos. Within Abiegnus is the Vault of the Adepts, where the founder of the Rosicrucian tradition was discovered.

abisheka—(Sanskrit). Anointing, lustration. A ritual of initiation.

Abramelin oil—A sacred oil described in S.L. MacGregor Mathers's *The Book of the Sacred Magic of Abramelin the Mage*. Several recipes have been adapted by various groups over time. In Chapter 11 of his book, Mathers translated the recipe as follows:

> *"You shall prepare the sacred oil in this manner: Take of myrrh in tears, one part; of fine cinnamon, two parts; of galangal half a part; and the half of the total weight of these drugs of the best oil olive. The which aromatics you shall mix together according unto the art of the apothecary, and shall make thereof a balsam, the which you shall keep in a glass vial which you shall put within the cupboard (formed by the interior) of the altar."*

Adytum—(Greek) inner sanctuary

aeon—A period of time on a cosmic scale. Crowley thought that aeons lasted approximately two thousand years. Other authorities have advanced the notion that the aeons may permeate one another, and that they may reflect trends in consciousness on a global or cosmic scale. The *New Aeon* reflects our current epoch in time, and the advance of consciousness away from superstition and dogma toward direct realization—gnostic realization—of non-dual consciousness.

agape—(Greek) Love. The universal, cosmic principle of love or *bhakti*. The expression of infinity. See *sunyata*.

amrita—(Sanskrit) Nectar. This is the nectar of immortality that is said to come from *sahasrara*, the *chakra* above the crown of the head.

apanga—(Sanskrit) Gaze. Refers to the intoxicated glances of the *Devi* as seen in many paintings or in traditional *Bharatanatyam* dance. Her eyes are half-closed, and rolled in the intoxication of bliss, or to direct the Will with adamantine clarity. Where the *apanga* is directed indicates the focus of attention or application of certain *marmas* (pressure points) as mapped out on the *Sri Yantra*.

Atu—The Trumps or keys of the Major Arcana of the Tarot, *The Book of Thoth*.

Atziluth—The World of Emanation on the glyph of the *Tree of Life*.

Augoeides—(Greek). The Higher Self or Holy Guardian Angel. A symbol of cosmic consciousness.

Babalon—A manifestation of *Shakti*, the divine feminine principle. Babalon may be seen as the Western equivalent of the great goddess Kali.

Banda—(Sanskrit) locks. These are specifically yogic locks that involve the tightening of certain muscles.

banishing ritual—A ceremonial ritual used to cleanse a space on both an internal and external level.

bhakti—(Sanskrit) Devotional love, usually toward a deity. In a deeper sense, this is the universal unconditional love that is the expression of infinity. See *agape*.

Bija—(Sanskrit) seed. In *mantra,* the *bija* is the root of the deity, a core seed sound from which the full *mantra* grows.

Binah—The World of Creation on the glyph of the *Tree of Life.*

bindu—(Sanskrit) Seed. The point of creation, the individual point event. See *Hadit.*

Bodhicitta—(Sanskrit). The Mind of Enlightenment. This is the mind that strives for awakening for all sentient beings.

Bodhisattva—(Sanskrit) A wisdom-being that has chosen to willingly reincarnate across time to assist all sentient beings in attaining enlightenment.

Cakes of Light—The eucharistic host of *The Book of the Law.* The cakes are made of flour, honey, Abramelin Oil, olive oil, beeswing, and bodily fluids such as menstrual blood and semen. Described in *The Book of the Law,* III:23-25: *"For perfume, mix meal & honey & thick leavings of red wine; then oil of Abramelin and olive oil, and afterward soften & smooth down with rich fresh blood. The best blood is of the moon, monthly; then the fresh blood of a child, or dropping from the host of heaven; then of enemies; then of the priest or of the worshippers; last of some beast, no matter what. This burn; of this make cakes & eat unto me. This hath also another use; let it be laid before me, and kept thick with perfumes of your orison: it shall become full of beetles as it were and creeping things sacred unto me."* Kenneth Grant, in *Hecate's Fountain,* elaborates on the ingredients: *"The verse gives a recipe for making the cakes of light which can be cooked only by a priestess in her scarlet phase [...] These ingredients are particularized in verse 24 as: 1) the blood of the full moon, 2) the first flowering of the pubescent female, or kalas of the stars, 3) "enemies" = thoughts; which implies the need for control of the mind and the direction of thoughts to magical ends, 4) semen produced by IX°+,*

5) semen produced by XI°+. The resulting hell-broth is to be burnt (cooked) and made into cakes of light." The ingredients are reminiscent of the earlier Tantrik sacred nectars, which also include menstrual blood, vaginal fluids, semen and other ingredients. For more on the traditional tantrik ambrosia, see my *Yogini Magic* (Falcon Press). For the Western sexual gnosis, see the glossary entry, *Sanctuary of the Gnosis*.

chakra—(Sanskrit) "Wheel." The *chakras* are the subtle-energy vortices that roughly correspond to anatomical regions in the human body, as well as to certain constellations in space.

chela—(Sanskrit) Student.

cult—A group dedicated to a certain set of practices or beliefs associated with a particular deity.

Dakini—(Sanskrit) Witch. See **Yogini**.

Deva—(Sanskrit) God.

Devi—(Sanskrit) Goddess.

dharma—(Sanskrit) Duty. Law or natural order. The *dharma* of one's life is the expression of the True Will, or *svecchacara*.

diksa—(Sanskrit). Initiation.

dukkha—(Sanskrit) Sorrow, unsatisfactoriness. The First of the Four Noble Truths of Buddhism. The remaining Four Noble Truths detail the origin, cessation and path to the cessation of sorrow.

Dzogchen—"Great Perfection." A Tibetan Buddhist system of practices that emphasizes the innate purity and perfection of the mind, and the direct realization of one's true nature. Practitioners are taught to recognize the primordial state of consciousness, which is said to be free from all conceptual elaboration and limitations.

egregore—Group mind.

Enochian—The name commonly associated with a language of the Angels, first brought to light by Dr. John Dee and Edward Kelley in the late sixteenth century.

Gayatri—(Sanskrit). Song or hymn having a Vedic meter of 8 lines of syllables. *Gayatri* is both a *mantra* and a prayer.

gnosis—(Greek) Direct knowledge of Truth. Direct experience of the ultimate nature of reality.

Grail of Wine—The liquid sacramental eucharist. On one level, this is a cup, grail or chalice filled with wine or another alcoholic beverage. In the *Tantras,* alcohol is considered liquid *shakti,* the Goddess in material form. The grail can also be interpreted as the vagina of the priestess, and the alcohol is the nectar of vaginal fluids or menstrual blood.

gunas—(Sanskrit) The three primary elements or building blocks of manifestation in Hindu symbology. The *gunas* are *rajas* (activity), *tamas* (inertia), and *sattva* (lucidity). These are the elements used in the play of universal existence.

Hadit—The Egyptian solar disk. Represents the primordial point. The seed of creation, the *bindu*.

Heru-ra-ha—A form of the Egyptian god Horus. Represents the True Self, the Holy Guardian Angel. Composed of the twin gods RaHoor-Khuit (active) and Hoor-Paar-Kraat (passive).

Holy Guardian Angel—The Higher Self. The Greek *Augoeides*.

Homa—(Sanskrit) (Also **Yajna** or **Homam**) A sacred Vedic fire ritual performed as a form of worship and offering to various deities. It dates back thousands of years and involves the ritualistic kindling and consecration of a fire, accompanied by the recitation of specific *mantras* or chants.

Hoor-Paar-Kraat—Egyptian god of silence and protection.

Hriliu—Hriliu is the "shrill scream of orgasm." The word comes from the vision of the 2nd Aethyr in *The Vision and the Voice*. It is also identified as the voice of the Dove in *The Heart of the Master*.

iccha—(Sanskrit) "Will."

Ishtadevi/Ishtadeva—(Sanskrit) "Chosen Goddess/God."

Jivanmukta—(Sanskrit) "Liberated while still living." The Adept.

jnana—(Sanskrit) "Knowledge."

kala(s)—(Sanskrit) "Emanation." There are said to be various *kalas* that emanate from the female body, in particular the lunar emanations from the female physiology. These are used in alchemical operations.

Kaula—(Sanskrit) "Clan" or "family."

kavacha—(Sanskrit) "Armor." A spell or ritual act that produces a magical armor.

Kecharimudra—(Sanskrit) "space seal." A yogic practice that is performed by expanding the inner opening of the throat, and rolling the tongue back toward the soft palate as far as possible.

klesha(s)—(Sanskrit) "Block" or "obstruction." These are the ego-blocks and complexes that prevent the free flow of energy.

knock—A ritual act that consists of a solid rap with the hand or other instrument (such as the butt end of a mallet or wand) upon wood or other hard surface to make a "knock" sound. It signifies the beginning or end of an action, a movement, or a section of the ritual.

koan—A paradox or riddle, used in Japanese Buddhism to assist the meditator in crossing over the boundaries of the rational and logical thought process.

kriya—(Sanskrit) "Action." Connotes moving, dynamic energy. Also refers to ritual actions or movements.

lila—(Sanskrit) "Play." The very existence of the universe is one type of play of the Goddess. See *Maya*.

Mahabandha—(Sanskrit). The combination of the three yogic energy locks—*jalandhara banda, uddiyana banda*, and *mula banda*—is the great lock, *maha bandha*.

Mahayana—(Sanskrit) The Greater Vehicle of Buddhism, which saw the introduction of *Bodhicitta* (the Mind of Enlightenment).

mala—(Sanskrit) "Rosary." The traditional device used to count *mantra* recitations. The *mala* is composed of various substances, each having an affinity to different aspects of divinity.

marma(s)—(Sanskrit) Acupressure points. These are mapped out on the human body with the *Sri Yantra*. Through activation of the *marmas*, various *kalas* may be released.

maya—(Sanskrit) "Illusion" or "dream." The universe is said to be the *lila* (play) of the goddess Maya.

Meru—(Sanskrit) The sacred cosmic mountain of Buddhist, Hindu and Jain mythology. It is 84,000 units high and contains the sun, moon and all the planets.

mudra—(Sanskrit) Ritual gestures with the body.

Mudra of Union—A ritual gesture performed with the hands. Identical to the *Yoni Mudra*.

nirvana—(Sanskrit) The state beyond suffering, illusion and attachment. The condition of experiencing gnosis or Truth.

Nuit—The Thelemic-Egyptian Goddess of Infinite Space and Infinite Stars. The iconographic representation of the Void.

Prajnaparamita—(Sanskrit). The perfection of wisdom. This is a central concept of Mahayana Buddhism. Also, the name of the goddess of transcendent wisdom.

prana—(Sanskrit) Life force, which flows in a continuous stream from the sun.

pranava—(Sanskrit) The primal *mantra*, OM (AOM), which contains the three cosmic phases of creation, preservation and destruction.

pranayama—(Sanskrit). The regulation of the breath and *prana* through yogic disciplines.

Prayoga—(Sanskrit) "spells". It has a wide range of related meanings that can be interpreted as "applications," "practices" or "implementations."

Puja—(Sanskrit) Exoteric Hindu ritual (as opposed to esoteric ritual, *sadhana*).

Ra-Hoor-Khuit—The Thelemic-Egyptian god of force and fire.

ruach—In the Hermetic Kabbalah, the *ruach* is the part of consciousness that is associated with the rational mind, the intellect.

sadhaka—(Sanskrit). The initiate of a *sadhana*; one who practices *sadhana*.

sadhana—(Sanskrit). Tantrik, esoteric ritual or spiritual practice.

samadhi—(Sanskrit). The state of union in consciousness where subject and object cease to have any meaning.

Samaya—(Sanskrit). A tantrik vow, oath or promise.

samsara—(Sanskrit) The condition of impermanence, suffering. The material world and temporal existence.

Sanctuary of the Gnosis—(also "Sovereign Sanctuary of the Gnosis") consists of the Hermit Triad, the highest degrees of the O.T.O. under Crowley, which were based on sexual magick. They consisted of the 8th degree (VIII°, masturbatory), 9th degree (IX°, heterosexual) and 11th degree (XI°, homosexual) Kenneth Grant extended this structure and incorporated older tantrik elements into the degrees, resulting in a detailed and precise set of practices. The VIII° has subsections for solitary Priestess, solitary Priest, of Priestess by Priest, and of Priest by Priestess. These are further broken down by method; for example, by tongue for inducing trance states, by hand for bringing oracles. The IX° has subsections for creation and intuition, as well as dream control and other occult techniques. In this expanded recension, the XI° becomes heterosexual coitus during menstruation for works of reification and materialization. The system of the Typhonian Order utilizes these techniques in combination with the energies of the Tunnels of Set and the *kalas* which emanate from the vagina of the Priestess. See *Nightside of Eden*, Kenneth Grant.

Sandhyabhasha—(Sanskrit) "Twilight language." The symbolic, often veiled language of the *Tantras*. Historically thought of as a way to protect the written word from non-initiates, more recent interpretations are that twilight language is itself a type of dream communication that transmits messages through non-rational means.

Sankalpa—(Sanskrit) Intention, will, resolve.

satori—(Japanese) Sudden enlightenment.

Saundaryalahari—(Sanskrit) "Waves of beauty." A tantrik text attributed to Adi Shankara. The first 41 verses are called the *Ananda*

Lahari and are thought to have been written on Mount Meru by Lord Ganesh.

Shakti—(Sanskrit) Female principle of spiritual energy, personified as the Goddess. *Shakti* is dynamic energy, and *Shiva* (male) is awareness. Together they form reality—the universe. There is a plenitude of *shaktis* that manifest as the senses and bodily functions.

Shivalingam—(Sanskrit) A symbol of Shiva in his creative role, or of the union and *Shiva* and *Shakti*. A circular base or *peetham* (Brahma-Pitha) with an elongated bowl. Within the bowl rises a tall cylindrical shape with a rounded head (Shiva-Pitha).

Siddhis—(Sanskrit). Magick powers that are produced from intense yogic practices.

Sign of Baphomet—The Chalice. Stand erect, then spread the legs apart and raise the hands above the head in a gentle curve or arc such that they form a cup. This passive sign allows for an influx of energy to descend into the operator from above.

Sign of Osiris Risen—Stand erect, then cross the arms over the chest, right over left, so that the open hands rest on the shoulders.

Sign of Silence—Stand erect, hands at sides. Extend left forefinger to the lips as though you are telling someone "shhh." This *kriya* (action) has the effect of sealing the aura and collecting energy.

Sign of Typhon-Apophis—The Trident. Stand erect. Raise hands over head to form a V shape. This active sign produces an upward, forceful current of energy.

Stele of Revealing—Egyptian funerary stele of the priest Ankh-af-na-Khonsu from Thebes, 26th dynasty. The Stele plays a prominent role in the Thelemic revelation of *The Book of the Law*.

sunyata—(Sanskrit) The Void, the entirety of all potential creation, the womb matrix of reality. The bulk of this book is devoted to the direct realization of *sunyata*, which expresses itself as *agape*.

svecchacara—(Sanskrit) "Live life according to thy Will." The natural state of being for the Adept, or one who has integrated the three *shaktis* of *iccha* (will), *jnana* (knowledge), and *kriya* (action). See *Thelema*.

Tantrika—(Sanskrit) A Tantrik practitioner.

Thelema—(Greek) "Will". This is the True Will of gnostic illumination, the *dharma* of one's life; the point event or Hadit; the Secret Self; the Star. Thelema also refers to the spiritual philosophy of the Western tantra revealed in *Liber AL vel Legis (The Book of the Law)*. See *svecchacara*.

Vajra—(Sanskrit) Diamond or Thunderbolt.

Vajrayana—(Sanskrit) The Diamond Path. Tibetan tantrik Buddhism.

vamamarga—(Sanskrit) (Also **vamachara***)* Left-hand path, the path of tantra.

Yogini—(Sanskrit) Witch-like tantrik goddesses that reign over magic, sorcery, enchantments and yoga. Also, female adepts of yoga, embodiments of *Shakti*, each an emissary of the Great Goddess. Also called *Dakini* ("witch").

ABOUT THE AUTHOR

Figure 31
Gregory Peters
(Photo by the Author)

Gregory Peters is an explorer of consciousness who has written about tantra, non-duality, and the intersection of East-West spiritual practice. He is an initiate of several tantrik lineages, Dzogchen, and Western esoteric traditions. Gregory was born in Stanford, California and lives in Northern California with his wife and family. Hiking, trekking and travel are some of his favorite activities. A devotee of the Goddess Kali, he enjoys traveling to sacred sites around the world, and exploring spiritual practices from many cultures and traditions. Nature is his primal worship, with the crisp air of the Himalayas or the deep forests favored over temples built by hand.

> *"Nature and the night sky hold a deep wisdom for us, if only we are willing to open up and experience."*

You can learn more about the author at his website:

gregorypetersauthor.com

MORE TANTRA TITLES FROM FALCON

NAGA MAGICK
The Wisdom of the Serpent Lords
by Denny Sargent

What are the Naga? They are the Serpent Lords of Hindu, Tantric and Buddhist traditions. Whether you wish to learn the history and mythos of the Serpent Spirits, or if you wish to work directly with these luminous beings, *Naga Magick* provides unique access to the power and wisdom of the Naga Lords.

YOGINI MAGIC
The Sorcery, Enchantment & Witchcraft of the Divine Feminine
by Gregory Peters
Foreword by Phil Hine

What are the Yoginis? Some say they are witch-like Tantrik goddesses that reign over magic, sorcery, enchantments and yoga. Are they human? Supernatural? Divine? For the sincere practitioner, they can provide great boons of wealth and pleasure... But it will not go well for the fool—the Yoginis will tear off his head and drink his blood.

MORE TANTRA TITLES FROM FALCON

SEX MAGICK, TANTRA & TAROT
The Way of the Secret Lover
by Christopher S. Hyatt, Ph.D.
With Lon Milo DuQuette
Illustrated by David P. Wilson

A wealth of practical and passionate Tantric techniques utilizing the Archetypal images of the Tarot. Nothing is held back. All methods are explicit and clearly described.

TANTRA WITHOUT TEARS
by Christopher S. Hyatt, Ph.D.
With S. Jason Black

For the Westerner, this is the only book on Tantra you will ever need. A bold statement? Perhaps. However, the idea behind this book is simple. It is power. It is Kundalini, dressed in Western clothes. It describes experiences and techniques which allow you to glimpse beyond ordinary day-to-day reality, into the world of marvels — and horrors — of the Hindu and Tibetan Tantric traditions.

www.ingramcontent.com/pod-product-compliance
Lightning Source LLC
Chambersburg PA
CBHW070045080526
44586CB00013B/918